Latina and Latino Voices in Literature

Latina and Latino Voices in Literature

Lives and Works, Updated and Expanded

Frances Ann Day

GREENWOOD PRESS
Westport, Connecticut • London

Library of Congress Cataloging-in-Publication Data

Day, Frances Ann.
Latina and Latino voices in literature : lives and works / Frances Ann Day.—Updated and expanded.
p. cm.
Includes bibliographical references (p.) and index.
ISBN 0-313-32394-1 (alk. paper)
1. American literature—Hispanic American authors—Bibliography. 2. Hispanic American literature (Spanish)—Bibliography. 3. Hispanic American authors—Biography—Bibliography. 4. American literature—20th century—Bibliography. 5. Hispanic Americans in literature—Bibliography. I. Title.
Z1229.H57D3 2003
[PS153.H56]
016.8109'868—dc21 2002028439

British Library Cataloguing in Publication Data is available.

Library of Congress Catalog Card Number: 2002028439
ISBN: 0-313-32394-1

First published in 2003

Greenwood Press, 88 Post Road West, Westport, CT 06881
An imprint of Greenwood Publishing Group, Inc.
www.greenwood.com

Printed in the United States of America

The paper used in this book complies with the Permanent Paper Standard issued by the National Information Standards Organization (Z39.48–1984).

10 9 8 7 6 5 4 3 2 1

Copyright Acknowledgments

Every reasonable effort has been made to trace the owners of copyright materials in this book, but in some instances this has proven impossible. The author and publisher will be glad to receive information leading to more complete acknowledgments in subsequent printings of the book and in the meantime extend their apologies for any omissions.

Dedicated to
Amelia, Isis, Artemisia, and Persephone

And to the memories of
Pura Belpré (1899–1982)
Omar Castañeda (1954–1997)
Lyll Becerra de Jenkins (1925–1997)
and
Jan Romero Stevens (1953–2000)

Contents

Acknowledgments

A warm thank you to all my wonderful friends for checking in with me frequently to offer support, encouragement, and advice during the writing of the second edition of this book, as well as your ongoing support for all my writing projects. And as always, thank you, Roxanna.

I am genuinely thankful to the marvelous authors featured in this book. Your inspiring life stories and affirming books provide important cultural, emotional, and intellectual nourishment for readers of all ages and backgrounds. I acknowledge the valuable contributions that you are making to the fields of children's and young adult literature. I was filled with admiration for each of you as I read about your individual odysseys and the obstacles that you have encountered and overcome. You have so much to teach us about the power of words to heal, strengthen, inform, empower, and validate.

Gracias to Virginia Márquez and all my students at Sonoma State University. I greatly appreciate your thoughtful messages, heartening words, strong ideals, and warm encouragement. Each semester I come away with renewed energy and commitment to continue the important work of creating a world that truly offers freedom and justice for all.

Heartfelt thanks to my editor, Lynn Malloy, and to everyone at Greenwood and Heinemann. Special gratitude is also due to many helpful people who work at the Sonoma County Libraries, especially Nikki Barsky, Kirsten Cutler, Julia Haggar, Patti Lewis, Grete Rivano, and Ann Stroberger.

My gratitude to all the educators, librarians, parents, and others who have responded so enthusiastically to my books. To everyone who has attended one of my workshops, thank you for valuable feedback, support, and advice.

I am grateful to everyone at Children's Book Press, Arte Público Press, Del Sol Books, and the other publishers who generously responded to requests for photographs, review materials, and other information.

Finally, thank you to Margaret Barber, Susan Bergholz, Frida Briggs, Ana Solar Byerly, Isabel Campoy, Anita Cano, Roberto Cano, Ray Castro, Carolina Clare, Ray Coutu, Delia A. Culberson, Michele Delattre, Karyne de Souza, Lesley Farmer, Yvonne S. Freeman, Lee Galda, Marianne Halpin, Zoe Harris, Beverly Vaughn Hock, Deborah Hollis and the Denali Award Committee of the American Library Association, Rosemary Hurtado, Sally Hurtado, Monica Irwin, Edith King, Lyn Miller Lachman, Nancy Lemberger, Lorayne Martinez, Loyola Martinez, Vicky Martinez, Mary Milton, Pam Nerdlinger, Nancy O'Connor, Linda Pavonetti, Lynn Prime, Arthur Ramirez, Nancy Ryan, Perce Smith, Arun Toké, Yoko Kawashima Watkins, Jane West, Yolanda Garfias Woo, Sherry York, and Alphonso Zubizarreta.

Introduction

Latina and Latino Voices in Literature: Live and Works, Updated and Expanded celebrates the lives and works of thirty-five inspiring authors. Readers of all ages are invited to explore the joys of reading authors as well as books. When was it that we each discovered that books were created by real people? As we fell in love with reading, we were intrigued by that special person behind the words in the book. Who are they? Why are they writers? Why do they choose to write picture books, poetry, fiction, personal narrative, folktales, drama, fantasy, or biography? What experiences shaped their lives and thinking and led them to share their joys, struggles, defeats, and triumphs with their readers?

Come along for a passionate journey where reading is not just reading. It is also developing a meaningful connection with the authors who wrote the books that we are enjoying. When we identify with an author, we become much more excited about reading. We develop a unique dialogue with the writer that engages us in an exchange of ideas and perspectives, linking our experiences with those in the book. As our imaginations are expanded, we gain insights into worlds that we have not understood or imagined. When the experience is similar to ours, we feel validated, often finding that our awareness of ourselves has been strengthened and extended. We search for the author's next book and the next, learning to read each one within the context of the complete body of work. We become attuned to nuances in style, subtleties in language, and changes in tone, genre, and perspective. We learn to read as writers, watching for the many exciting ways in which words and sentences and paragraphs can be patterned, collaged, and quilted into magical pieces that transport us far beyond our own time, place, culture, and worldview. As we establish stronger connections with the printed word, we find that we are negotiating more sophisticated meaning from our reading and that our writing is becoming richer and more imaginative.

As we look back on the special bonds that we have established with books and those unique people who created them, we search for ways to share the joys of these experiences with the young people around us. As educators, librarians, and/or parents, we understand the importance of empowering all youngsters with a sense of positive self-identity and self-esteem. We know that they need literature that reflects their cultural experiences and the history of their people. We recognize all persons' need to see themselves in the books that they read and to be validated by the images in the literature available to them. We are aware that omission of these images combined with other destructive forms of racism can lead to alienation, loss of cultural identity, self-doubts, and even self-hatred. As we examine the body of children's and young adult literature, we search for good books that celebrate the lives of all the young people whom we know and cherish. We discover that the field has a history of excluding or distorting the experiences and contributions of Latina/os, African Americans, Native Americans, Asian Americans, and people from other parallel cultures. Although recently there have been significant improvements in publishing the works of diverse authors, the appalling omissions documented by researchers in the field still exist in varying degrees in many schools, libraries, and homes across our country. Knowing that literature has the power to affect the hearts and minds of readers of all ages, we resolve to search for authentic voices from these disenfranchised groups. We are pleased to find many gifted writers from diverse groups who are creating eloquent books for young readers. Wanting all youngsters to feel affirmed, confident, resilient, and capable, we seek ways to spread the word about the vital works of these marvelous authors.

In an earlier book, *Multicultural Voices in Contemporary Literature*, I celebrated the lives and works of forty authors and illustrators from twenty different cultures. In this book, I turn to one of the most dynamic, diverse, fast-growing cultural groups in the United States. In *Latino Voices* (Millbrook Press, 1994), Frances R. Aparicio writes that Latinos are not a race but a mixture of Indian, African, and European peoples, making them one of the most racially diverse people in the world. As *mestizos*, they are as diverse in their language as they are in their race, appearance, socioeconomic class, and location in which they live. Many Latinas and Latinos speak Spanish, but very different oral versions of it, with a wide variety of dialects and differing accents and vocabularies. Latinas and Latinos have come to the United States from Mexico, Central America, South America, and the Caribbean. The largest groups of Latinas and Latinos are Mexican Americans, Puerto Ricans, and Cuban Americans.

Each group of Latinas and Latinos in the United States has a distinct culture due to its separate histories and diverse backgrounds and experiences. Yet there are significant commonalities. *Within* each group, as within every culture, there are differences as well as commonalities. These differences and similarities have resulted in a vibrant mosaic of rich traditions, experiences, and perspectives. As we examine the writings of Latinas and Latinos, we are struck by the beauty, depth, and power expressed therein. The myth of a singular U.S.–Latina/o experience is shattered by the multiplicity of exciting literary works that are being created. The often patronizing, pastoral, and assimilative images of Latina and Latino characters that pervaded literature for young readers in the past are being replaced by eloquent, authentic, beautifully written and illustrated books. Created by Latinas and Latinos about their experiences and perceptions, these fully dimensional books offer youngsters literary mirrors in which they can see themselves and their people and take pride in their heritage. As they learn about their history and culture, their sense of who they are is clarified and affirmed.

This emergent body of literature is crucial not only to the identities of Latina/o youngsters but also for young people from other cultures. It is important that all people become aware of, and learn to value, the myriad ways in which humans explain the world. Without a complete vision of all that it means to be human, we would live impoverished and isolated lives. Fortunately, the world of literature for children and teenagers is gradually being transformed to embrace the wondrous complexity, diversity, and depth of the human experience.

In spite of recent changes in the field of literature for young people, however, many educators, librarians, and parents report that these materials are not yet available to them. Many of the books are being published by small presses and are sometimes difficult to find. Phyllis Tashlik reported in her book *Hispanic, Female and Young* that her students had gone through nine years of education in the New York City Public Schools, and even though the student population is more than a third Latino/a, they had never been introduced to a single novel written by a Latina or Latino author. In an interview in the *Albuquerque Journal*, author Pat Mora pointed out that even though 60 percent of the children in the Santa Fe schools are Latina/o, she has yet to come across a children's book with a main character who is Latina or Latino. Similar appalling findings are being reported from Colorado, California, and around the country.

Adults who select and share books with young people are invited to make a commitment to finding the books that speak to each youngster who touches their lives. *Latina and Latino Voices in Literature: Lives and Works, Updated and Expanded* was written to help educators, librarians, and parents in this important endeavor.

Scope and Organization of This Book

The first edition of this book celebrated the lives and works of twenty-three Latina/o authors. This second edition has been expanded to include twelve new authors, as well as updated information on most of the others from the original publication, and more than 135 new titles have been added. The authors selected for inclusion in this book have roots in the Americas and have created a significant body of work. Some of them are well known and have gained a reputation for their fine work in the field of literature for young readers. Others are being introduced here as promising writers who have something very important to share. Both established and emerging voices are celebrated in the pages that follow. The organization of this book follows the same format as the original. Each chapter features one of these marvelous word-spinners, providing biographical information, a personal quotation, and a photograph so that adults and youngsters alike can get to know them as real people. The information for the biographical profiles was lovingly gathered through personal and telephone interviews, written communication, and/or research of secondary sources. A list of the books written by each author is included along with publication information that will aid in locating them. For most of the books identified, annotations are given along with information about major themes, awards won, and recommended grade levels. The annotations include an analysis of the strengths and weaknesses of each book, often accompanied by a summary of the praise and/or criticism that the book received from other reviewers.

A noteworthy section of this book addresses the issues involved in evaluating and selecting books from a pluralistic perspective. "Evaluating Books for Bias" provides helpful guidelines for examining books for racist, sexist, classist, ageist, ableist, and homophobic attitudes. These attitudes—expressed repeatedly in books and other media—gradually distort youngsters' perceptions until stereotypes and myths are accepted as reality. As we search for ways to create a better world, we are learning to challenge the many forms that bias takes. By teaching young people how to detect bias in books, we are helping them break down barriers, both internal and external.

The appendixes

- Provide information about awards that honor books written by Latinos and Latinas
- Supply a calendar of holidays and special days often celebrated by Latinas and Latinos
- Offer suggestions for activities that teachers, parents, and librarians might use with the books to extend the literary experience
- Provide information about resources such as catalogs, centers, and organizations

In addition, two indexes are provided. In addition to the Title Index, an extensive Topic Index is available to use in planning story sessions and units of study. Themes, curricular areas, genres, and topics are included in this comprehensive index.

As we contemplate the challenges of the twenty-first century, let us honor the legacy of those trailblazing writers, publishers, educators, and librarians who have demonstrated their commitment to all the diverse people of the world. As we continue the important work of bringing together youngsters and good books, we renew our commitment to "keeping hope alive." We are inspired to instill in young people a love of reading as well as a deeper understanding and appreciation of their own and others' cultures. It is with this empowering spirit that *Latina and Latino Voices in Literature: Lives and Works, Updated and Expanded* was created.

Evaluating Books for Bias

(The following guidelines were adapted from *Guidelines for Selecting Bias-Free Textbooks and Storybooks* by the Council on Interracial Books for Children, 1841 Broadway, New York, NY 10023.)

Children are often exposed to racist, anti-Semitic, sexist, classist, ageist, ableist, looksist, homophobic, and size-oppressive attitudes. These attitudes—expressed repeatedly in books and in other media—gradually distort their perceptions until stereotypes and myths are accepted as reality. It is often difficult for a librarian, educator, or parent to persuade young people to question society's attitudes. *But if youngsters can be shown how to detect bias in a book*, they may incorporate this awareness into their worldview. Although the complexities involved in appraising the intangibles present in the literary arts cannot be encompassed in a checklist, the following guidelines are offered as a starting point in the evaluation of books from a pluralistic perspective.

OMISSION

In spite of the fact that many excellent multicultural books are finally being published, omission continues to be one of the biggest problems in literature for young readers today. Exclusion is one of the most insidious and painful forms of bias; a group may be excluded from an entire collection or from the books selected for use in a particular library, school district, school, or classroom. The implicit message is that the group does not exist, is insignificant, or has made no contributions to society. Erasure is destructive not only to the group(s) involved but to the larger society.

ILLUSTRATIONS

Stereotypes. A stereotype is an oversimplified generalization about a particular group that usually carries derogatory implications. Stereotypes may be blatant or subtle. Check for depictions that demean or ridicule characters because of their race, gender, age, ability, appearance, religion, sexual orientation, socioeconomic class, or native language.

Tokenism. Is one person from the group presented as having admirable qualities while all the others of the group are stereotyped? In illustrations, do people of color look just like whites except for being tinted or colored in? Do all "minority" faces look stereotypically alike, or are they depicted as genuine individuals with distinctive features?

Who is doing what? Do the illustrations depict people of color in subservient and passive roles or in leadership and action roles? Are males the active doers and females the inactive observers?

STORY LINE

Bias may be expressed in blatant and subtle ways. Check for the following forms of subtle, covert bias:

Standards for Success. Does it take white male behavior standards for a person of color or a female to "get ahead"? Is "making it" in the dominant white society projected as the only ideal? To gain acceptance and approval, do people of color and females have to exhibit extraordinary qualities?

Resolution of Problems. How are problems conceived, presented, and resolved in the story? Are minority people considered to be "the problem"? Are the conditions facing oppressed groups represented as related to an unjust society? Does the story line encourage passive acceptance or active resistance? Are problems faced by the minority person resolved through the benevolent intervention of a white, able-bodied, middle-class male?

Roles of Females. Are the achievements of girls and women based on their own initiative and work, or are they due to their appearance or to their relationships with males? Are females presented as problem solvers with a life of their own, or is their role in the story only as support to male characters? Is it assumed that female characters will marry and that this is their only or major interest in life? Is there an emphasis on describing the physical appearance of female characters? Are positive female characters portrayed as "beautiful" and negative female characters portrayed as "unattractive"? Are older females portrayed in a negative manner? Are older, unmarried females ridiculed and assumed to be bitter and unfulfilled? Are the images of females of all ages prettified? Are they afraid of snakes, spiders, or mice? Do they have to be rescued by a male character?

LIFESTYLES

Are people of color and their setting depicted in such a way that they contrast unfavorably with the unstated norm of white, middle-class suburbia? Check for inaccuracy and inappropriateness in the depiction of cultures and lifestyles. Are they oversimplified, or do they offer genuine insight into the character? Check for "quaint," "cutesy," or exotic depictions. Check to see if the portrayal of a group is authentic; for example, are all Latinas and Latinos lumped together without acknowledgment of the separate histories and diverse experiences of their groups? Are recent immigrants and people from the same group who were born in the United States portrayed in the same manner?

RELATIONSHIPS BETWEEN PEOPLE

Do the males or white characters possess the power, take the leadership and make the important decisions? Do females, people of color, lesbians, gays, elderly, or disabled people function in essentially supporting, subservient roles?

HEROINES/HEROES

For many years, books showed only "safe" heroes—those who avoided serious conflict with the white, male, able-bodied, heterosexual establishment. Heroines and heroes should be defined according to the concepts and struggles for justice appropriate to their group. When "minority" heroes/heroines do appear, are they admired for the same qualities that have made establishment heroes famous or because what they have done has benefited the establishment? Whose interest is the hero/heroine serving?

EFFECTS ON A YOUNG PERSON'S SELF-IMAGE

Are norms established that limit any youngster's aspirations and self-concepts? Consider the effect of the use of the color white as the ultimate in beauty, cleanliness, virtue (*angel* food) and the color black or use of "dark" as evil, dirty, menacing (*devil's* food).

AUTHOR'S OR ILLUSTRATOR'S BACKGROUND

Analyze the biographical data available about the author and illustrator. What qualifies the author or illustrator to deal with the subject? If they are not members of the group that they are depicting, is there anything in their background that would specifically recommend them as creators of the book? There has been considerable debate recently regarding what has been termed cultural borrowing. Is it ethical for mainstream writers to appropriate the literature of other cultures? Indeed, some people believe that it is impossible to write authentically from a perspective that one has never experienced personally. In addition, people who have been silenced in the past do not take kindly to someone else trying to tell their stories now that those stories are finally being recognized as significant. The publishing industry is still a world filled with scarcity; if an established Euro-American author submits a manuscript for a story representing another culture, will there be room for the emerging writer from that culture to compete? These important issues and related questions are addressed in a special edition on multicultural literature in the March/April 1995 issue of *Horn Book* as well as in other journals and books.

AUTHOR'S OR ILLUSTRATOR'S PERSPECTIVE

Children's books in the past have often been written by authors who were white, members of the middle class, heterosexual, able-bodied, and Christian, with one result being that a narrow Eurocentric perspective has dominated children's literature in the United States. For example, distorted images frequently portray Latinas and Latinos in assimilative and patronizing ways, often putting such characters in pastoral settings. It is important to include books that present multiple perspectives. Does the total collection present many worldviews? Are readers encouraged to look at a situation from several viewpoints?

LOADED WORDS

Examples of loaded adjectives are *savage, primitive, conniving, lazy, superstitious, treacherous, wily, crafty, inscrutable, docile, backward, bitter*, and *barren*. Check for sexist language that excludes or in any way demeans females. The generic use of the words *man* and *he* was accepted in the past but is outmoded today. The following examples show how sexist language can be avoided: *ancestors* instead of *forefathers, humankind* instead of *mankind, firefighters* instead of *firemen, synthetic* instead of *man-made, chair* or *chairperson* instead of *chairman*, and *she or he* instead of *he*.

COPYRIGHT DATE

Books on minority themes—often hastily conceived—suddenly began appearing in the mid- and late 1960s. Most of these books were written by white authors, edited by white editors, and published by white publishers. They often reflected a white, middle-class, mainstream point of view. Not until the early 1970s did the children's book world begin to even remotely reflect the realities of a pluralistic society. The copyright date may be *one* clue as to how likely the book is to be overtly biased, although a recent copyright date, of course, is no guarantee of the book's sensitivity. Conversely, *do not throw out all the books with old copyright dates!* Use these guidelines to examine each one and then use the biased books as teaching tools with children, students, and colleagues.

Lives and Works

Alma Flor Ada

Latina of Cuban Roots (1938–)
Birthday: January 3
Address: School of Education
University of San Francisco
San Francisco, CA 94117

My vocation as a writer started as a young child. I couldn't accept the fact that we had to read such boring textbooks while my wonderful storybooks waited at home. I made a firm commitment while in the fourth grade to devote my life to producing schoolbooks that would be fun—and since then I am having a lot of fun doing just that.

(*Something About the Author,* 4)

Books by Alma Flor Ada

For Children

Abecedario de los animales (Animal Alphabet). Illustrated by Vivi Escrivá. Mariuccia Iaconi, 1990. Audiocassette available.
After the Storm. Spanish edition: *Despues de la tormenta*. Translated from the Spanish by Rosa Zubizarreta. Illustrated by Vivi Escrivá. Santillana, 1993.
A la sombra de un ala (In the Shadow of Wings). Illustrated by Ulises Wensel. Mariuccia Iaconi, 1988.
Barquitos de papel (Paper Boats). Illustraciones de Pablo Torrecilla. Laredo, 1993.
Barreletes (Kites). Illustraciones de Pablo Torrecilla. Laredo, 1995.
Bear's Walk. Hampton-Brown, 1993. Audiocassette Available.
Choices and Other Stories from the Caribbean. With Janet Thorne and Philip Wingeier-Rayo. Illustrated by Maria Antonia Ordonez. Friendship Press, 1993.
The Christmas Tree / El arbol de Navidad: A Christmas Rhyme in English and Spanish. Illustrated by Terry Ybañez. Hyperion, 1997.
Daniel's Mystery Egg. Harcourt, 2001.
Daniel's Pet. Harcourt, 2002.
Dear Peter Rabbit. Spanish edition: *Querido Pedrín*. Translated into Spanish by Rosalma Zubizarreta. Illustrated by Leslie Tryon. Atheneum, 1994.
Días de circo (Circus Time). Illustraciones de Pablo Torrecilla, Laredo, 1995.
The Empty Piñata. Spanish edition: *La piñata vacía*. Translated from the Spanish by Rosalma Zubizarreta. Illustrated by Vivi Escrivá. Santillana, 1993.
Encaje de piedra (Stone Lace). Illustrated by Kitty Lorefice de Passalia. Laredo, n.d.
Friend Frog. Harcourt, 2000.
Friends. Spanish edition: *Amigos*. Illustrated by Barry Koch. Santillana, 1989.
Gathering the Sun: An Alphabet in Spanish and English. Illustrated by Simón Silva. Translated by Rosa Zubizarreta. Lothrop, Lee, & Shepard, 1997.
Giraffe's Sad Tale. Hampton Brown, 1993. Audiocassette available.
The Gold Coin. Spanish edition: *La moneda de oro*. Translated from the Spanish by Bernice Randall. Illustrated by Neil Waldman. Atheneum, 1991, 1994.
The Golden Cage. Spanish edition: *La jaula dorada*. Translated by Rosalma Zubizarreta. Illustrated by Vivi Escrivá. Santillana, 1993.
How Happy I Would Be. Spanish edition: *Me gustaría tener*. Illustrated by Vivi Escrivá. Santillana, 1989.
How the Rainbow Came to Be. Spanish edition: *Cómo nació el arco iris*. Translated from the Spanish by Bernice Randall. Illustrated by Vivi Escrivá. Santillana, 1991.
I Don't Want to Melt. Spanish edition: *¡No quiero derretirme!* Translated by Rosalma Zubizarreta. Illustrated by Vivi Escrivá. Santillana, 1993.
I Love Saturdays y domingos. Illustrated by Elivia Savadier. Atheneum, 2002.
In the Barrio. Spanish edition: *En el barrio*. Illustrated by Liliana Wilson Grez. Scholastic, 1994.
In the Cow's Backyard. Spanish edition: *La hamaca de la vaca*. Translated by Rosalma Zubizarreta. Illustrated by Vivi Escrivá. Santillana, 1991.
It Wasn't Me. Spanish edition: *No fui yo*. Translated from the Spanish by Rosalma Zubizarreta. Illustrated by Vivi Escrivá. Santillana, 1992.
Jordi's Star. Illustrated by Susan Gaber. G. P. Putnam's Sons, 1996.
The Kite. Spanish edition: *El papalote*. Translated from the Spanish by Rosalma Zubizarreta. Illustrated by Vivi Escrivá. Santillana, 1992.

The Lizard and the Sun/La lagartija y el sol. Illustrated by Felipe Dávalos. Translated by Rosalma Zubizarreta. Doubleday, 1997.

The Malachite Palace. Illustrated by Leonid Gore. Atheneum, 1998.

Mediopollito/Half-Chicken: A New Version of a Traditional Story. (Bilingual) Translated by Rosalma Zubizarreta. Illustrated by Kim Howard. Doubleday, 1995.

My Name Is María Isabel. Spanish edition: *Me llamo María Isabel*. Translated by Ana M. Cerro. Illustrated by K. Dyble Thompson. Atheneum, 1993; Aladdin, 1995.

Olmo and the Blue Butterfly. Spanish edition: *Olmo y la mariposa azul*. Illustrated by Vivi Escrivá. Laredo, 1992; SRA Macmillan/McGraw-Hill, 1995.

El pañuelo de seda (The Silk Scarf). Illustraciones de Viví Escrivá. Laredo, 1993.

Paths: José Martí, Frida Kahlo, César Chávez. Spanish edition: *Caminos*. Written with F. Isabel Campoy. Illustrated by Waldo Saavedra and César de la Mora. Santillana, 2000.

Pín, pín sarabín (Pin, Pin, Sarabin). Illustraciones de Pablo Torrecilla, Laredo, 1993.

Pregones (Vendors' Calls). Illustraciones de Pablo Torrecilla. Laredo, 1993.

El reino de la geometría (The Kingdom of Geometry). Illustrated by José Ramón Sánchez. Laredo, n.d.

The Rooster Who Went to His Uncle's Wedding: A Latin American Folktale. Illustrated by Kathleen Kuchera. Putnam, 1993.

A Rose with Wings. Spanish edition: *Rosa alada*. Translated from the Spanish by Rosa Zubizarreta. Illustrated by Vivi Escrivá. Santillana, 1993.

Serafina's Birthday. Translated from the Spanish by Ana M. Cerro. Illustrated by Louise Bates Satterfield. Atheneum, 1992.

Smiles: Pablo Picasso, Gabriela Mistral, Benito Juárez. Spanish edition: *Sonrisas*. Written with F. Isabel Campoy. Illustrated by Rosario Valderrama and Francisco González. Santillana, 2000.

The Song of the Teeny Tiny Mosquito. Spanish edition: *La cancíon del mosquito*. Illustrated by Vivi Escrivá. Santillana, 1989.

Strange Visitors. Spanish edition: *Una extrana visita*. Translated by Rosalma Zubizarreta. Illustrated by Vivi Escrivá. Santillana, 1989.

Steps: Rita Moreno, Fernando Botero, Evelyn Cisneros. Spanish edition: *Pasos*. Written with F. Isabel Campoy. Illustrated by Isaac Hernández, Ricardo Radosh, and Waldo Saavedra. Santillana, 2000.

A Surprise for Mother Rabbit. Translated from the Spanish by Rosalma Zubizarreta. Illustrated by Vivi Escrivá. Santillana, 1992.

La tataranieta de Cucarachita Martina (Martina's Great-grandaughter). Illustrated by Ana López Escrivá. Laredo, n.d.

The Three Golden Oranges. Illustrated by Reg Cartwright. Atheneum Books, 1999.

Turkey for Thanksgiving Dinner? No, Thanks! Spanish edition: *¿Pavo para la cena de gracias? ¡No gracias!* Translated from the Spanish by Rosa Zubizarreta. Illustrated by Vivi Escrivá. Santillana, 1993.

Under the Royal Palms: A Childhood in Cuba. Spanish edition: *Bajo las palmas reales*. Atheneum, 1998.

The Unicorn of the West. Spanish edition: *El unicornio del oeste*. Translated by Rosalma Zubizarreta. Illustrated by Abigail Pizer. Atheneum, 1993.

Voices: Luis Valdez, Judith Francisca Baca, Carlos Juan Finlay. Spanish edition: *Voces*. Written with F. Isabel Campoy. Illustrated by Pablo Rulfo, Isaac Hernández, and Beatriz Rodríguez. Santillana, 2000.

El vuelo de los colibríes (The Flight of the Hummingbirds). Illustrated by Judith Jacobson. Laredo, 1995.
What Are Ghosts Afraid Of? Spanish edition: *El susto de los fantasmas*. Translated from the Spanish by Rosalma Zubizarreta. Illustrated by Vivi Escrivá. Santillana, 1992.
Where the Flame Trees Bloom. Spanish edition: *Donde florecen los flamboyanes*. Illustrated by Antonio Martorell. Atheneum, 1994.
Who's Hatching Here? Spanish edition: *¿Quién nacerá aquí?* Illustrated by Vivi Escrivá. Santillana, 1989.
With Love, Little Red Hen. Illustrated by Leslie Tryon. Atheneum, 2001.
Yours Truly, Goldilocks. Illustrated by Leslie Tryon. Atheneum, 1998.

Additional sets of Small Books, Big Books, Early Learning Packs, Chart Sets, and Comprehensive Collections by Alma Flor Ada (many cowritten with F. Isabel Campoy) are available from Del Sol Books, (888) 335-7651. Many of Alma Flor Ada's books, cassettes, videos, and so on are also available through Del Sol.

Books for Teachers, Librarians, and Parents

A Chorus of Cultures: Developing Literacy through Multicultural Poetry. Written with Violet J. Harris and Lee B. Hopkins. Hampton-Brown, 1993. 1-800-333-3510.
Culture through Literature and Music: Cassette Guide (Spanish Elementary Series) Illustrated by Jan Mayer. Addison-Wesley, 1989.
DLM Pre-Kindergarten and Kindergarten Early Childhood Programs. Written with Pam Schiller. McGraw-Hill, 1995.
The Magical Encounter: Spanish Language Children's Literature in the Classroom. Laredo, 1990.
The Power of Two Languages: Literacy and Biliteracy for Spanish-Speaking Students. Coeditor with Josefina Villamil Tinajero. Macmillan/MacGraw-Hill, 1993.
Mariposa Literature Kits: Teacher's guides for approximately sixty books. Available through Mariuccia Iaconi 1-800-955-9577.
Whole Language and Literature: A Practical Guide. Addison-Wesley, 1989.

Alma Flor Ada is a renowned author, translator, scholar, educator, storyteller, and advocate for bilingual and multicultural education. She has written many distinguished books for children in Mexico, Argentina, Peru, Spain, and the United States in both English and Spanish. She has also written and edited numerous textbooks, educational materials, and magazine articles and served as editor in chief of the *Journal of the National Association of Bilingual Education*. A professor of multicultural education at the University of San Francisco, she travels throughout the United States facilitating workshops for educators. She has been the recipient of many awards and grants, including the University of San Francisco Outstanding Teacher Award, the California Parent Teacher Association Yearly Award, and Latina Writers' Award. Among her most substantive contributions to the field of children's literature are the programs that she has developed in collaboration with F. Isabel Campoy, which include Música Amiga, a program for learning through songs, and Puertas al Sol, a comprehensive collection of poetry, art, theater, and biographies.

Ada was born in Camagüey, Cuba, in a hacienda on the outskirts of town. She lived there with her parents, Alma Lafuente Ada, a teacher, and Modesto A. Ada, a surveyor and professor, and their extended family. In *Where the Flame Trees Bloom* (*WFTB*), Ada describes her childhood and provides insight into the experiences that shaped her development. Her grandmother taught her to read before she was three years old by writing the names of plants on the ground with a stick. In this way, reading and nature became closely intertwined for her. Her grandmother was a gifted storyteller, and her father invented stories to explain to her all that he knew about the history of the world. As Ada writes about her impressions of the people, events, animals, and plants that surrounded her for the first eight years of her life, a picture emerges of a beautifully sensitive and loving person. For the first seven years of her life, she was the only child living in the very large, very old house. Ada writes about her special connection with the large trees that surrounded their home. "Though I grew up surrounded by loving people and fascinated by all the life around me, it was to the trees that I told all my sorrows and my joys, and especially my dreams" (*WFTB*, 6). Ada writes about her childhood feelings and questions concerning issues of justice, freedom, and respect for all living beings. Even as a child, she questioned discrimination, poverty, and slavery. "How could anyone dare to think that he could own or control anyone else?" (*WFTB*, 3). Growing up during World War II, she wondered, "How could it be . . . that people could hate one another so much that they would want to fight and kill each other?" (*WFTB*, 65).

When Ada was eight years old, her family moved into the city. She had loved the countryside and open air, and the move was difficult for her. "Like a plant transplanted into too small a pot, lacking sunshine and rain, I withered" (*WFTB*, 74). But with the indomitable spirit characteristic of her ancestors, she gradually adjusted to the change. An avid reader, Ada enjoyed the wonderful storybooks that she had at home but was dismayed by the lack of imagination in her textbooks. When she was in the fourth grade, she decided to devote her life to remedying this situation by creating schoolbooks that would be fun to read.

After earning her undergraduate degree from Universidad Central de Madrid in Spain in 1959, Ada moved to Peru, where she completed her master's degree and doctorate at Pontificia Universidad Catolica del Peru. She was an instructor and head of the Spanish department at Colegio Alexander von Humboldt in Lima, Peru, before moving to the United States, where she has worked as an associate professor of Romance languages at Emory University in Atlanta, Georgia, and a professor of language and codirector of the Institute for Bilingual Bicultural Services at Mercy College of Detroit, Michigan. In 1976, Ada moved to California to accept a position with the University of San Francisco, where she is currently a professor of education and director of doctoral studies. She has traveled to a variety of locations as a visiting professor, including Texas, Guam, and Spain. In addition, Ada has been a Fulbright scholar, has served as a board member for *Sesame Street* in Spanish, and has worked as a publishing house consultant as well as chairing numerous seminars and policy conferences on bilingual education. She has been involved with many other projects, activities, and groups including being a founding member and president of the International Association for Children's Literature in Spanish and Portuguese.

As an author and translator, Ada has worked tirelessly to make stimulating textbooks and storybooks available to Spanish-speaking children and speakers of English who are learning Spanish. Her efforts to promote bilingualism have resulted in children's books that are printed in both Spanish and English, enabling youngsters to learn from and appreciate both languages. Drawing upon the inspiration of the great storytellers from her childhood and her own unique gift for writing, Ada has written many memorable books for young readers. She often explores themes of identity and self-discovery in her books. Ada also skillfully employs elements from folklore, sometimes retelling traditional Latin American tales. She has a unique way of writing about the wonders hidden within each of her fascinating characters, enabling listeners and readers to connect with their struggles and joys.

Ada's writing has been greatly influenced by her passion for multicultural and bilingual education and her work as a scholar of Romance languages. She has also been inspired by her own children, who helped her remember what it was like to be a child. Once when she was writing a scholarly book, her three-year-old daughter complained that she was writing ugly books. This comment instantly took Ada back to her childhood resolution of creating books that were fun to read. Ada notes, "One of my greatest joys is that my daughter collaborates with me" (*Something about the Author*, 84, 5) Her daughter, Rosalma Zubizarreta, has translated many of her books into both Spanish and English.

In her videotape *Writing from the Heart*, Ada talks about her life and writing. As she reads from some of her books, her genuine love for literature and her young readers is apparent. She tells the viewer that writing helps her understand her feelings and gives her great joy. She enthusiastically encourages children to write, saying, "Everyone can be an author. Everyone is special!" This renowned expert in bilingual and multicultural education is making a significant contribution to the field of children's literature, not only by creating so many fine books but also by inspiring potential writers of all ages to write and by encouraging educators to reform the curriculum to meet the needs of children from diverse populations.

More Information about Alma Flor Ada

www.almaflorada.net
Contemporary Authors, Volume 123, 2–3.
Contemporary Authors Online. The Gale Group, 2000.
Something about the Author, Volume 43, 25–26.
Something about the Author, Volume 84, 1–6.
Under the Royal Palms: A Childhood in Cuba by Alma Flor Ada. Atheneum, 1998.
Where the Flame Trees Bloom by Alma Flor Ada. Atheneum, 1994.

Videotapes

Meeting an Author. Available through Del Sol (888) 335-7651.
Writing from the Heart. Available through Del Sol (888) 335-7651.

Selected Works by Alma Flor Ada

Abecedario de los animales

Preschool–2

- Alphabet
- Poetry
- Music
- Sounds

Two delightful poems for each letter of the alphabet and exquisite color illustrations have made this charming book a favorite of children and teachers. The poems about the letters playfully explore sounds, shapes, and words associated with each letter. This large-format book is available with a cassette on which Suni Paz sings the songs for each letter.

Dear Peter Rabbit

Parents' Choice Honor Award
Grades K–Adult

- Goldilocks
- The Three Bears
- The Three Little Pigs
- Little Red Riding Hood
- Peter Rabbit
- Communication
- Letter-writing

When Peter Rabbit is invited to a housewarming party by one of the three little pigs, an intriguing adventure begins to unfold. The correspondence among well-known storybook characters is cleverly woven together, providing an engaging tale with a touch of mystery. The enchanting drama culminates in a birthday party that brings these literary favorites together face-to-face. As a child, Alma Flor Ada had many imaginary conversations with characters from her storybooks. Many years later, drawing upon her interest in children's literature, she ingeniously combined familiar elements of popular fairy tales to create an enchanting extension of that make-believe world. Each character writes in a unique voice, and the letters are printed in individual styles. Leslie Tryon's captivating illustrations, rendered in pen and ink with watercolors, invite the reader back again and again to enjoy the delightful details. Spanish edition: *Querido Pedrín*. Companion volumes: *Yours Truly, Goldilocks* and *With Love, Little Red Hen.*

The Empty Piñata

Preschool–2

- Cinco de mayo
- Piñatas
- Sharing

When Elena's uncle gives her a beautiful piñata, she empties her piggybank and sets off to buy candy to fill it before she takes it to school. But on the way to the store, she decides to buy some seeds to feed a hungry little bird. Next she finds a lost kitten, then a puppy, and before long she has spent all her money. Alas, she cannot buy the candy to fill the piñata. But her generosity is rewarded, and she happily shares her piñata with her classmates at the Cinco de Mayo party at school. Cinco de Mayo, the fifth of May, is the celebration of the day that Benito Juarez and the Mexican army were victorious over the French army in the Battle of Puebla in 1862. An expert in the field of children's literature, author Alma Flor Ada was aware of the paucity of books for young children on Cinco de Mayo. She dedicated her appealing book to "Eréndira and Marcos Guerrero, and all Mexican American children, in hopes that they will take full pride in their cultural heritage." Young listeners and readers will be charmed by Elena's generosity, the rhymes and repetitions of the predictable text, and the attractive illustrations by Vivi Escrivá. Spanish edition: *La piñata vacía.*

Encaje de piedra (Stone Lace)

Marta Salotti Award (Argentina)
Grades 1–6

- Mystery

This intriguing mystery story is set in the Middle Ages in Spain. It invites young readers to explore issues of friendship, trust, biculturalism, bilingualism, discrimination, and the value of learning a second language.

Friends

Grades K–5

- Geometry
- Math
- Friendship
- Overcoming Differences

This clever book features geometrical figures who are segregated until two circles discover the joy of getting to know others. This is an excellent antibias book for introducing the beauty of diversity. Prejudice and tolerance are treated in a sensitive and easy-to-understand manner. It is sure to prompt lively discussions and help promote a feeling of goodwill toward differences. Indeed, friends can come in many different shapes and colors. Spanish edition: *Amigos*.

Gathering the Sun: An Alphabet in Spanish and English

NCSS/CBC Notable Book in the Field of Social Studies
NCTE Notable Book in Language Arts
Once Upon a World Book Award, Simon Weisenthal Center
Pura Belpré Honor Award
All Ages

- Bilingual
- Farmworkers
- Poetry

Dedicated "to the living memory of César Chávez," this magnificent book combines heartwarming poems with beautiful, sun-drenched paintings. From árboles (trees) to zanahoria (carrot), Ada and Silva celebrate history and heritage, family and friends, honor and pride, and the bounty of the harvest. This important book pays tribute to the unsung farmworkers who bring food to our tables. Cassette and CD available (Spanish only).

The Gold Coin

Christopher Award
National Council of Social Studies Notable Children's Trade Book
Grades K–12

- Self-Discovery
- Healers

Determined to steal an old woman's gold, a thief follows her all around the countryside and, in the process, learns a very important lesson. As this award-winning book opens, Juan overhears Doña Josefa say to herself, "I must be the richest person in the world," as she holds a gold coin in her hand. He decides to wait until she leaves her hut to steal the coin. Later, he ransacks her house but fails to find the coin. He tracks her from place to place, each time missing her. As he travels, he discovers that Doña Josefa not only heals people but gives them gold coins. How he finds himself digging potatoes, picking corn, squash, and beans, and helping with the coffee harvest is part of the magic of this special book. When he finally catches up with Doña Josefa, he realizes that he, too, has been touched by her goodness. The satisfying ending will touch the hearts of readers of all ages.

Set in an unnamed South American country, this original tale invites readers to consider the nature of true wealth. As Juan rediscovers the joys of a home-cooked meal, the pleasure that comes from sharing it with others, and the beauty of a sunrise, he gradually changes. Neil Walman's lovely watercolors and Ada's inspiring text capture the subtle transformation of a man who had been a thief for many years. The author dedicated this unique fable to her daughter, "To Rosalma, who believed this story should reach all children." Spanish edition: *La moneda de oro.*

I Love Saturdays y domingos

Grades K–3

- Bilingual
- Biracial Children
- Grandparents

A little girl recounts the joys of her weekends when she visits her Grandma and Grandpa on Saturdays and her *abuelita y abuelito* on *los domingos. BookList* wrote, "[This] picture book gracefully embraces and celebrates a young child's involvement in her dual heritages."

In the Barrio

Preschool–2

- Neighborhoods
- Sense of Community

Through simple text and engaging illustrations, this groundbreaking little book lovingly brings the barrio alive. A young Latino boy proudly takes the reader on a tour of his neighborhood, pointing out some of his favorite things. We see colorful murals, listen to lively mariachis playing at a birthday party, and touch the red chiles hanging at the vegetable market. We can almost taste the sweet pan dulce, the delicious enchiladas, and the tangy fruit ices. The narrator's grandmother gives him a warm hug and helps him with his schoolwork. The backgrounds of Liliana Wilson Grez's detailed pictures are filled with images of Latino culture such as a star piñata, a calendar featuring a rooster, and curtains and tile decorated with Mexican motifs. The images presented are very positive for the most part, but the fumes from cars and the loud sirens of fire engines are included as well. *In the Barrio* provides a welcome contrast to the negative images that many people have of barrios. Spanish edition: *En el barrio.*

The Lizard and the Sun/La lagartija y el sol

National Association of Parenting Publications Gold Medal
Grades K–5

- Bilingual
- Folklore
- Mexico

This traditional Mexican folktale features a tenacious little lizard who bravely searches until she finds the sun, bringing light, warmth, and energy back to the earth. Striking illustrations include historically accurate renditions of the city of Tenochtitlán, capital of the Aztec empire. In the author's note, Ada writes that she based this tale on a paragraph that she read "a very long time ago in an old reading textbook."

Mediopollito/Half-Chicken: A New Version of a Traditional Story

American Folklore Society Aesop's Accolade
Preschool–2

- Bilingual
- Chickens
- Folklore
- Weather Vanes

Mediopollito/Half-Chicken is a traditional folktale that explains the origin of rooster weather vanes. As a child in Cuba, author Alma Flor Ada heard it told by her grandmother. Since then, she has encountered the story many times in two distinct versions. In this book, she has chosen to retell her grandmother's version, in which a helpful chicken is rewarded for his good deeds. The story begins on a ranch in Mexico where Half-Chicken is hatched with only one wing, one leg, one eye, and half as many feathers as other chicks. Later, on his way to visit the court of the viceroy in Mexico City, he stops to help first water, then fire, and last, wind. But he is not prepared for the trouble that awaits him in the city. Will someone rescue Half-Chicken? Accompanied by Kim Howard's dynamic illustrations, the predictable and repetitive nature of the tale makes it an appealing read-aloud choice. This story is unique because it celebrates Half-Chicken's differences instead of using them as a reason to reject him. As a result, his confidence and self-esteem enable him to take risks and achieve an important role.

My Name Is María Isabel

NCSS/CBC Notable Book in the Field of Social Studies
Grades 2–5

- Newcomers
- Schools
- Identity

Third grader María Isabel, born in Puerto Rico and now living in the United States, faces a challenge at her new school. There are two other Marías in the class so her teacher decides to call her Mary. María Isabel's name is very special to her because she was named after her beloved grandmothers. When the teacher calls on her, she doesn't answer because she doesn't realize that the teacher is talking to her. As the teacher becomes increasingly irritated with her, María Isabel finds herself exclud-ed from the school's Winter Pageant. How can she reclaim her name? How can she explain to her parents why she isn't singing her favorite holiday song? And how can she find the courage to explain her dilemma to an impatient teacher?

This poignant story beautifully elucidates the integral connection between an individual's name and her sense of self. As a newcomer to the school and to the mainland, María Isabel faces a number of uncertainties and challenges. The issue with her name adds to her discomfort. Alma Flor Ada's gentle story utilizes understatement: María Isabel finds friends, does well in math, and feels comfortable at home. Yet, the name change and the resulting problems overshadow everything else. Ada does a beautiful job of juxtaposing María Isabel's thoughts about her predicament with the insights that she gains from reading a book. As she ponders the issues in *Charlotte's Web,* she is able to make connections with events in her own life. As the story ends, María Isabel has learned some important lessons about herself and those around her. Another important aspect of the book is the way in which Ada portrays María Isabel's teacher. She is able to admit to herself that she made a mistake and proceeds to make amends. Her character, as well as the others in the book, is carefully drawn and avoid stereotypes.

My Name Is María Isabel is an engaging story that combines the efforts of a Puerto Rican family to adjust to a new life with a shared sense of pride in their heritage. Augmented by K. Dyble Thompson's realistic black-and-white drawings, the story reads aloud well and provides an excellent introduction to the issues faced by many newcomers. Spanish edition: *Me llamo María Isabel.*

Paths: José Martí, Frida Kahlo, and César Chávez

Grades 2–5

- Biography

Part of the *Puertas al sol/Gateways to the Sun* Collection, this fascinating volume lovingly chronicles the lives of three notable Latino/a people through easy-to-read text, photographs, and paintings. About writer José Martí (1853–1895), the authors write, "Martí [devoted] his life to the fight for freedom, against tyranny, against injustice, and against those who harmed the poor" (11). The section honoring the extraordinary Mexican painter Frida Kahlo (1907–1954) includes several of her self-portraits. César Chávez (1927–1993) is recognized for devoting his life to improving working conditions for farmworkers in the United States. The collection also includes poetry, art, theater, and language. Other biographies in the series are *Smiles: Pablo Picasso, Gabriela Mistral, and Benito Juárez; Steps: Rita Moreno, Fernando Botero, and Evelyn Cisneros;* and *Voices: Luis Valdez, Judith Francisca Baca, and Carlos Juan Finlay.* Spanish editions: *Caminos, Sonrisas, Pasos,* and *Voces.*

El reino de la geometría

Grades 3–6

- Geometry
- Hierarchies
- Math

In the Kingdom of Geometry, all the geometrical figures live in harmony until King Square decides that squares are superior. This clever book is an effective tool for discussing discrimination, injustice, and oppression.

The Rooster Who Went to His Uncle's Wedding: A Latin American Folktale

Grades Preschool–3

- Chickens
- Cumulative Tales
- Folklore

This cumulative folktale from Latin America features the rooster, a universal folk character humanized in many cultures. In this tale, a vain rooster sets out early one morning for his uncle's wedding. But before long he encounters unexpected problems. He asks for help first from grass, then lamb, next dog—the list of recalcitrant characters grows with each brightly colored page. Will anyone help poor rooster? Alma Flor Ada's first memories of this story are of hearing it as a little girl in Cuba from her grandmother. Her lively adaptation, using harmonious repetition and economical language, will delight young listeners and readers. Spanish edition: *El gallo que fue a la boda de su tío.*

Under the Royal Palms: A Childhood in Cuba

Pura Belpré Award
Grades 3–8

- Authorship
- Autobiographical Short Stories
- Cuba

In this inspiring companion volume to *Where the Flame Trees Bloom*, the author offers another heartwarming collection of reminiscences drawn from her childhood in Cuba in the 1940s. Fascinating, poignant, and often humorous, these autobiographical short stories paint a loving portrait of Ada's vibrant extended family and provide insight into the experiences that shaped her life and writing. Black-and-white family photographs add to the richness of this eloquently written book. Spanish edition: *Bajo las palmas reales.*

The Unicorn of the West

Grades 1–5

- Identity
- Unicorns

In this gentle tale, a mysterious animal searches for his identity. He has never before met anyone like himself or, for that matter, any other creatures at all. Now, each season brings a new friend: a spring robin, a summer butterfly, and an autumn squirrel. Each promises to try to "find someone just like you, so I can tell you who you are." With winter comes a new sound, an enchanting melody that beckons the beautiful white animal to a meeting with three others like himself. They introduce themselves as the Unicorns of the North, East, and South and explain that he is the Unicorn of the West. Every seven years on the first full moon after the winter solstice, the unicorns gather to ensure that beautiful dreams live on and that there is enough love for all in the world. Reassured, the Unicorn of the West returns to his home in the forest. There he is reunited with the robin, butterfly, and squirrel who have traveled to the other three corners of the world and brought back news of the other unicorns. This satisfying story ends with the promise of enduring friendship as well as universal well-being.

Abigail Pizer's lovely watercolors perfectly capture the magical mood of this original fable. It will appeal not only to young children who will enjoy listening as it is read aloud but to many fourth and fifth graders who are also often captivated by the allure of unicorns. Spanish edition: *El unicornio del oeste.*

Where the Flame Trees Bloom

Grades 3–8

- Authorship
- Autobiographical Short Stories
- Cuba

This warm collection of eleven short stories provides insight into the childhood of renowned author Alma Flor Ada. As she reminisces about her first eight years growing up in rural Cuba, Ada paints a loving portrait of family and home. Beginning with an introduction to her homeland, Ada writes about the people, events, and experiences that greatly shaped her development. Throughout the collection, Ada's reverence for all living beings is apparent. She writes lovingly of her strong connections with the ancient flame trees, fruit trees, and bamboo trees that surrounded the family hacienda. She recognized the racism in the comic books distributed to the students at her school. Provided as propaganda during World War II, the books portrayed the Japanese people in an extremely negative way. After she arrived at her house, the young student, feeling great sadness and shame, tore the books into pieces.

In *Where the Flame Trees Bloom*, Ada offers readers precious gems from her childhood. Her writing is elegant and yet straightforward and easy to read. Each story stands well on its own. Spanish edition: *Allá donde florecen los framboyanes.* Companion volume: *Under the Royal Palms: A Childhood in Cuba.*

Francisco X. Alarcón

Photo: Courtesy of
Children's Book Press

Mexican American (1954–)
Birthday: February 21
Contact: Children's Book Press
2211 Mission Street
San Francisco, CA 94110

For me, poetry is about life, family, community. I also believe that poems are really incomplete until someone reads them. Then they come alive and start dancing in the imagination.

(*Laughing Tomatoes*, 31)

Books by Francisco X. Alarcón

For Children

Angels Ride Bikes and Other Fall Poems/Los Ángeles andan en bicicleta y otros poemas de otoño. Illustrated by Maya Christina Gonzales. Children's Book Press, 2000.
From the Bellybutton of the Moon and Other Summer Poems/Del ombligo de la luna y otros poemas de verano. Illustrated by Maya Christina Gonzales. Children's Book Press, 1998.
Iguanas in the Snow and Other Winter Poems/Iguanas en la nieve y otros poemas de invierno. Illustrated by Maya Christina Gonzales. Children's Book Press, 2001.
Laughing Tomatoes and Other Spring Poems/Jitomates risueños y otros poemas de primavera. Illustrated by Maya Christina Gonzales. Children's Book Press, 1997.

For Adults

Body in Flames/Cuerpo en llamas. Translated by Francisco Aragon. Chronicle Books, 1990.
De amor oscuro/Of Dark Love. Moving Parts, 1991.
From the Other Side of Night/Del otro lado de la noche: New and Selected Poems. University of Arizona Press, 2002.
Loma Prieta. We Press, 1990.
Mundo 21. D. C. Heath, 1995.
Quake Poems. We Press, 1989.
Snake Poems: An Aztec Invocation. Chronicle Books, 1992.
Sonnets to Madness and Other Misfortunes: Poems. Creative Arts, 2001.
Tattoos. Nomad, 1985.

Francisco X(avier) Alarcón, a renowned poet, educator, scholar, and activist, is considered a leader in the Chicano literary movement. He did his undergraduate studies at California State University in Long Beach and his graduate studes at Stanford University. Currently, he lives in Davis, where he directs the Spanish for Native Speakers Program at the University of California.

Born in Wilmington, California, Alarcón was raised in both Mexico and the United States. As a child, he was mesmerized by his grandfather's tales of ancient Mexico. He notes, "I started writing poems by jotting down the songs my grandmother used to sing to us. I would write at the kitchen table, surrounded by our pets, smelling my grandma's delicious cooking" (*Laughing Tomatoes*, 31).

The recipient of many awards, fellowships, and awards, including the 2002 Fred Cody Award, Alarcón hopes to nurture future generations of Latino/a writers through his many appearances as a guest poet in the school. "The thing that makes me the most happy is to go to classrooms and to experience my book with the children, to laugh at the same time as the children are laughing" (Children's Book Press Catalog). Alarcón is committed to helping fill the void in Spanish and bilingual books for children.

His collections of bilingual poetry for young readers have been celebrated by reviewers as "brilliant," "beautiful in two languages," and "a model for children."

More Information about Francisco X. Alarcón

Contemporary Authors. Volume 147, 7–10.
Contemporary Authors Online. The Gale Group, 2001.
Dictionary of Literary Biography. Volume 122, 3–7.
UC Davis Magazine. Summer 2000, 20–23.
Something about the Author. Volume 104, 1–4.
"The Poet Behind the Series: An Interview with Francisco X. Alarcón," by Imelda Basurto. *The New Advocate* (Winter 2002) 1–8.

Selected Works by Francisco X. Alarcón

Angels Ride Bikes and Other Fall Poems/Los Ángeles andan en bicicleta y otros poemas de otoño

National Parenting Publications Gold Award
Américas Commended List
Cooperative Children's Book Center Choice
Grades K–Up

- Bilingual
- Fall
- Los Angeles
- Poetry
- Seasons

This vividly illustrated collection of twenty playful bilingual poems invites readers to experience fall in Los Angeles, "where people from all over the world can make their dreams come true." The poet remembers his abuela escorting him to his first day of school as a non-English speaker, his mother's words, "¡sí se puede!—yes, you can do it!" and Day of the Dead celebrations where his family dedicated an altar to their loved ones.

From the Bellybutton of the Moon and Other Summer Poems/ Del ombligo de la luna y otros poemas de verano

Pura Belpré Honor Award
Américas Commended List
Cooperative Children's Book Center Choice
Skipping Stones Honor Award
Grades K–Up

- Bilingual
- Mexico
- Poetry
- Seasons
- Summer

With a poet's magical vision, Francisco Alarcón reminisces about childhood trips with his family to Mexico to visit his *abuela* and other relatives. In the afterword, he writes, "For me, Mexico was and still is an enchanted land where all senses come alive: colors are more colorful, tastes are tastier, and even time seems to slow down." The title of the book refers to Mexico-Tenochtitlan, a city on a small island in the middle of Lake Texcoco. Alarcón envisions "this ancient city gleaming as if it were the bellybutton of the moon reflected in the lake." Lighthearted illustrations perfectly capture the spirit of summers in Mexico.

Iguanas in the Snow and Other Winter Poems/Iguanas en la nieve y otros poemas de invierno

Américas Commended List
Pura Belpré Author Honor Award
Grades K–Up

- Bilingual
- Poetry
- Seasons
- Winter

Whimsical paintings accompany nineteen buoyant poems, inviting readers to celebrate winter by the seashore, in the magical city of San Francisco, and in the ancient redwood forests of the Sierra Mountains. In the title poem, a family frolic in the snow reminds the poet's mother of the iguanas playing near the family home in Mexico. The poet dedicated this exuberant collection "To all the children who by writing their own poetry have inspired me to continue writing poetry."

Laughing Tomatoes and Other Spring Poems/Jitomates risueños y otros poemas de primavera

Pura Belpré Honor Award
National Parenting Publications Gold Medal Award

Riverbank Review Children's Books of Distinction Finalist
Grades K–Up

- Bilingual
- Poetry
- Seasons
- Spring

Exuberant paintings accompany twenty delightful poems bursting with the energy of spring. In the title poem, laughing tomatoes are "the happiest of all vegetables" (12). Alarcón's lively poems honor the wonders of life and nature, welcome the morning sun, and pay tribute to children working in the fields. In "My Grandma's Songs," one of the most moving poems, Alarcón pays tribute to his abuela's delightful songs, which continue to inspire him to this day.

Isabel Allende

Chilean (1942–)
Birthday: August 2

I believe that one writes because one cannot avoid doing so. The need to do it is an overwhelming passion. If I don't write, words accumulate in my chest, grow and multiply like carnivorous flowers, threatening to choke me if they don't find a way out.

(*World Authors,* 19)

I have had a tormented and long life, and many things are hidden in the secret compartments of my heart and my mind. Sometimes, I don't even know that they are there, but I have the pain—I can feel the pain; I can feel this load of stories that I am carrying around. And then one day I write a story, and I realize that I have delivered something, that a demon has come out and has been exorcised.

(*Conversations with Isabel Allende,* 355–356)

Books by Isabel Allende

Aphrodite: A Memoir of the Senses. Translated from Spanish by Margaret Sayers Peden. HarperFlamingo, 1998. Spanish edition: *Afrodita: Recetas, cuentos y otros afrodisiacos*.
City of Beasts. Harper Collins, 2002.
Daughter of Fortune: A Novel. Translated from Spanish by Margaret Sayers Peden. HarperCollins, 1999. Spanish edition: *Hija de la fortuna*.
Eva Luna. Translated from Spanish by Margaret Sayers Peden. Knopf, 1988; Bantam, 1989; HarperCollins, 1995.
The House of the Spirits. Translated from Spanish by Magda Bogin. Knopf, 1985; Bantam, 1986. Spanish edition: *La casa de los espíritus*.
The Infinite Plan. Translated from Spanish by Margaret Sayers Peden. HarperCollins, 1993. Spanish edition: *El plan infinito*.
Of Love and Shadows. Translated from Spanish by Margaret Sayers Peden. Knopf, 1987; Bantam, 1988. Spanish edition: *De amor y de sombra*.
Paula. Translated from Spanish by Margaret Sayers Peden. HarperCollins, 1994.
Portrait in Sepia. Translated from Spanish by Margaret Sayers Peden. HarperCollins, 2001. Spanish edition: *Retrato en sepia*.
The Stories of Eva Luna. Translated from Spanish by Margaret Sayers Peden. Macmillan, 1991.

Isabel Allende is one of the best known and most widely read women writers from Latin America. She has mesmerized readers throughout the world with her blend of magical realism, political and social issues, and fascinating characters. Highly praised for her powerful writing, her books have been translated into numerous languages, and many of have become best-sellers.

Allende was born in Lima, Peru, the eldest child of Francisca Llona Barros and Chilean diplomat Tomás Allende. Her father was a first cousin of Salvador Allende, president of Chile, with whom the family maintained a close relationship. Her parents separated when she was three years old, and she returned with her mother and two younger brothers to Santiago, Chile. She grew up in the home of her maternal grandparents, Isabela and Augustine Llona, who exerted a strong influence on her imagination and development. Her grandmother was an extraordinary woman with a wonderful sense of humor and compassion. A magical storyteller, she left a deep imprint on her granddaughter. Allende writes that the character that she loves most in all her books is Clara from *The House of the Spirits*, who was inspired by her beloved grandmother.

Allende's mother, who was the most important person in her childhood, also told her stories. She created an imaginary world where they were all happy, where the ruthless laws of nature and human vices did not exist. "That was where my passion for stories was born, and I call upon those memories when I sit down to write" (*Paula*, 33). She notes that nobody thought her storytelling inclinations could be useful. "I was a girl and therefore my education was not directed toward creativity" (*World Authors*, 19). Nevertheless, her interest in storytelling did not vanish with menstruation, as her Nani predicted it would, but instead expanded. She loved books, often reading under the covers at night with a flashlight. She discovered a trunk of books in the cellar of the house and spent long hours voraciously gobbling them down. When she was nine, she dove into the complete works of Shakespeare and later developed a devotion to science fiction. Allende writes that she was a lonely and angry child. "I always believed I was different; as long as I can remember I have felt like an outcast, as if I didn't really belong to my family, or to my surroundings, or to any group" (*Paula*, 50).

When her mother remarried, again to a diplomat, the family left Santiago to follow him on his assignments. Allende's mother gave her a notebook, saying, "Here, write what's in your heart" (*Paula*, 56). The ten-year-old girl left the complex mural that she had painted on her bedroom wall, "in which were registered my desires, fears, rages, childhood doubts, and growing pains" (*Paula*, 55), and moved to Bolivia, where she lived with her family for several years. Because she was Chilean, she was the victim of offensive schoolyard pranks in the new country. She sought refuge in the family garden, where she found private places to read and secret places to hide her notebook with the story of her life. From Bolivia the family moved to Lebanon, where Allende learned French. When she was fifteen, they returned to Chile, where she finished high school and began working as a secretary for the Food and Agricultural Organization of the United Nations. She was interested in writing and soon entered the field of journalism and communications. She wrote a column for a women's magazine and edited a leading magazine for children titled *Mampato*. She also wrote short stories for children and wrote and produced plays.

On September 13, 1973, a military coup in Chile led to the assassination of President Salvador Allende. This event and its aftermath of repression and violence have had a profound impact on Isabel Allende and her writing. Risking her life, she stayed in Chile for fifteen months, helping her compatriots escape military persecution and providing food and aid to the families of the victims of the regime. "Because of my work as a journalist I knew exactly what was happening in my country, I lived through it, and the dead, the tortured, the widows and orphans, left an unforgettable impression on my memory" (*Dictionary of Literary Biography, DLB*, 34). Allende was forced to flee her beloved homeland in 1975. She settled with her family in Caracas, Venezuela, where she worked as a teacher and school administrator and later wrote satirical articles for one of the leading newspapers in the country.

Suffering from the pain of exile and concerned about her grandfather, who was dying in Chile, Allende sat down on January 8, 1981, to write him one last letter. That momentous letter turned into the manuscript for her first book, *The House of the Spirits*. Allende describes the experience: "From the first lines I wrote, other wills took control of my letter, leading me far away from the uncertain story of the family to explore the more secure world of fiction. . . . I wrote without effort, without thinking, because my clairvoyant grandmother was dictating to me" (*Paula*, 275). Allende had spent more than twenty years on the periphery of literature—journalism, television scripts, theater, short stories—but it took three books before she wrote "writer" as her profession when she filled out a form. *The House of the Spirits* was translated into fifteen languages and became an overnight best-seller wherever it appeared. Since then Allende has written five additional books and has joined the ranks of the most distinguished writers in contemporary literature.

The enormous appeal of Allende's writing is often attributed to the nature of her style: a dynamic combination of characters and events structured around a fast-paced narrative. Her work has been described as "enthralling," "richly imaginative," "a genuine rarity," "moving and compelling," and "a unique achievement." Allende writes to improve the world, bearing witness to social and political injustices. She believes, "All of us who write and are fortunate enough to be published ought to assume the responsibility of serving the cause of freedom and justice" (*DLB*, 40). Throughout her work, women's issues are central, and often the protagonist is endowed with a gift for writing. Even her minor characters have a defined personality, a complete biography, and an individual voice.

In 1988 Allende moved to Marin County, north of San Francisco. She has taught literature at several institutions, including the University of California at Berkeley, and has won numerous awards and honors from around the world, among them doctorates of letters from Bates College, Dominican College, and New York State University. She was selected to the Women's Hall of Fame in Marin, California, and won the Feminist of the Year Award presented by the Feminist Majority Foundation in 1994. Her books have been translated into approximately twenty-seven languages, and several of them have been made into movies.

More Information about Isabel Allende

www.isabelallende.com

Authors and Artists for Young Adults, Volume 18, 1–7.

Contemporary Authors, Volume 130, 7–9.

Contemporary Literary Criticism, Volume 39, 27–36.

Conversations with Isabel Allende, edited by John Rodden. Translated from Spanish by Virginia Invernizzi. University of Texas Press, 1999.

Critical Approaches to Isabel Allende's Novels, edited by Sonia Riquelme Rojas and Edna Aquirre Rehbein. Lang, 1991.

Dictionary of Literary Biography, Volume 145, 33–41.

Isabel Allende: Life and Spirits by Celia Correas Zapata. Arte Pública Press, 2002.
¡Latina! Women of Achievement, edited by Diane Telgen and Jim Kamp. Visible Ink Press, 1996.
Latin American Writers by Lynn Shirey. Facts on File, 1997.
Narrative Magic in the Fiction of Isabel Allende by Patricia Hart. Fairleigh Dickinson University Press, 1989.
World Authors. H. W. Wilson Company, 1991, 8–22.

Selected Works by Isabel Allende

Daughter of Fortune

Willa Literary Award for Historical Fiction
Grades 12–Adult

- Chile
- China
- Gold Rush
- Historical Fiction
- San Francisco
- Socioeconomic Class

Abandoned at birth, Eliza Sommers is raised in the British colony of Valparaíso, Chile, by wealthy British importers Rose Sommers and her rigid brother, Jeremy. Soon after Eliza falls in love with Joaquín Andieta, a clerk who works for Jeremy, gold is discovered in California. When Joaquín leaves to seek his fortune, Eliza, pregnant and desperate, decides to follow him. Enlisting the help of Tao Chi'en, a healer, she stows away on a ship bound for San Francisco. After the harrowing voyage, during which Tao nurses her through a miscarriage, Eliza, disguised as a boy, searches for the elusive Joaquín. Her journey gradually transforms her as she reinvents herself; she discovers personal freedom, independence, and a future, not with Joaquín but with Tao Chi'en. (Late in the book it is revealed that Eliza is the daughter of Rose's brother, John Sommers. The identity of her mother is unknown.) *Daughter of Fortune*, a sweeping, engrossing historical novel, draws upon cultures from four countries: Chile, China, England, and the United States. This fast-paced adventure story has been praised for its unconventional, independent-minded protagonist; well-developed gallery of intriguing secondary characters; passionate storytelling; and beautiful narrative of admirable force. Allende explores many compelling issues (including interracial relationships and the sexual enslavement of young girls) and revisits her favorite themes: love, independence, freedom, women's role, and exile. Spanish edition: *Hija de la fortuna*.

Eva Luna

American Book Award
Grades 12–Adult

- Storytelling
- Authorship

Isabel Allende's third novel is basically a bildungsroman about a twentieth-century Scheherazade who learned early to "barter words for goods" and to use her imagination to survive as a female from the poverty class in an unnamed politically unstable Latin American country. Eva's mother dies when she is six years old but remains with her in spirit throughout her life. The young orphan is buffeted from one servant position to another, at times living on the street, all the while buoyed by her rebellious nature and her inventiveness in turning carrots into princesses and paintings into voyages. When she learns to read and write, she is euphoric and discovers that writing is the best thing that had ever happened to her. The passages describing her feelings when she first sits down to write are breathtaking. "I believed that that page had been waiting for me for more than twenty years, that I had lived only for that instant" (251). With no fortune but her stories, she becomes a successful writer of a unique new kind of soap opera for television.

Woven into Eva's "autobiography" is the life story of her future lover, Rolf Carlé, starting with his childhood in Nazi Austria to his immigration to South America and his eventual work as a filmmaker. Set in a country that closely resembles Venezuela, the story spans four decades of the twentieth century, with a focus on two dictatorships and the guerrilla movement around 1959 to 1969. The epic tale is filled with fantasy, foreshadowing, and ironic humor. Eva denounces the abuses and cruelty of dictatorships, the corruption that permeates all aspects of government, and the violence of military repression. As with her other books, Allende's canvas is large, including topics such as child abuse, suicide, mummies, concentration camps, murder, class issues, a stillborn birth of a two-headed baby, disappearances of political prisoners, prostitution, infidelities, and sadism. Unlike Allende's first two books, which featured protagonists from upper-class families, Eva Luna's only fortune is her imagination. All three books speak to women's issues and celebrate writing.

The House of the Spirits

Grand Roman d'Evasion Prize
Grades 12–Adult

- Historical Fiction
- Magic Realism

Isabel Allende's first novel traces the experiences of four generations of the del Valle-Trueba family, through the first seventy-five years of the twentieth century. Set in an unnamed South American country (similar to Chile), the epic story focuses on the lives of three remarkable women who successively serve as the central characters: Clara, Blanca, and Alba. Interwoven into the 368-page book is the story of Esteban Trueba, who is, respectively, the husband, father, and grandfather of the female protagonists. The book begins at the turn of the century, in the childhood home of Clara del Valle, who will be the mother and grandmother as well as the spiritual leader of the clan. Endowed with a gift for clairvoyance, Clara can predict the future, communicate with the spirits, read fortunes, and recognize people's intentions. As the story unfolds against the backdrop of the tragic political history of the country, Allende explores the complex relationships between individual and family, family and country, past and present, and spiritual and political. She makes a significant contribution to our understanding of class and gender issues as well as the history of Chile.

Dedicated "To my mother, my grandmother, and all the other extraordinary women of this story," the book is not strictly autobiographical but is based loosely on Allende's memories and her family's experiences in Chile. Her maternal grandparents provided inspiration for two of the book's central characters: Clara, the warmhearted, mystical matriarch who, while taking gifts to the poor, advises her daughter, "This is to assuage our conscience, darling. But it doesn't help the poor. They don't need charity; they need justice" (117); and her violent, landowner-politician husband, Esteban.

The House of Spirits pays tribute to the women of Latin America and everywhere. Their strength and creativity in combatting the patriarchal system are inspiring. Clara's mother, one of the first feminists in the country, works for women's right to vote; Clara, ignoring her husband, fills her house with her spiritualist friends, conducts consciousness-raising sessions at the country estate, and concentrates on her visionary tasks; Blanca defies her father and her class by choosing a lifelong relationship with a revolutionary peasant leader who opposes everything that her father believes in; Esteban's sister, Férula, becomes his rival for Clara's attentions; and Alba joins the student movement, steals her grandfather's weapons and hides them for the opposition, and falls in love with a guerrilla leader. The peasant women do not fare as well. Esteban, with his characteristic cruelty, rapes all the young women on his country estate, as well as many from neighboring haciendas, and ignores all his children who are born as a result of these violations. In the only passage in the book that bears criticism, Pancha, Esteban's first victim, is portrayed as enjoying sex with him the day after he brutally rapes her. Esteban's violence is extended to animals, his employees, his wife, and his daughter. "In the end, Esteban's brutal, violent behavior leads to the torture, mutilation, and rape of his beloved granddaughter, Alba, when the military, which he supports, takes over the country" (*DLB*, 35).

In the epilogue, it is revealed that Alba is the major narrator of the book. She uses her grandmother Clara's journals and her own memories to reconstruct the history of her family. Her grandfather, Esteban, is the secondary narrator. By juxtaposing the two voices, Allende contrasts the two perspectives, lending insight into differences in gender and generational interpretation of events. It was her grandmother Clara's spirit who came to Alba during the horrific days of her imprisonment, to suggest that she write in her mind a testimony that not only would call attention to the terrible treatment that she was enduring but would occupy her attention and thus save her life. Later, near the end of the book, Alba writes that the days of the perpetrators are numbered because they are unable to destroy the spirits of the women. She resolves to overcome her own terrors, reclaim the past, and break the terrible chain of unending blood and sorrow.

Allende wrote that *The House of Spirits* was the result of nostalgia. She started a letter to her dying grandfather, and it metamorphosed into a book. She writes, "I intended to save the past, to gather again the loved ones, to bring the dead back to life. I wanted to recover all that I had lost, my land, my family, the objects that had been with me during all my life, my memories and the memories of those who were no longer with me" (*World Authors*, 19).

Allende is a remarkable storyteller. That this is her first novel makes it all the more extraordinary. The manuscript for *The House of the Spirits* was rejected at first because of the length of the text and because the author was a woman and unknown. Once published, it became an instant success. A best-seller in Europe, it was soon translated into fifteen languages. The book was initially censored in Chile, but people found a way to smuggle it into the country, and it has become a best-seller there also. Hailed for its passion and imagination, the novel is an original and important work. It was awarded the Quality Paperback Book Club New Voice Award Nomination in 1986. The author, in a number of interviews, credits the spirit of her clairvoyant grandmother with protecting the fortune of the book. Spanish edition: *La casa de los espíritus*.

Of Love and Shadows

Grades 12–Adult

- Dictatorships
- Historical Fiction
- Journalism

Isabel Allende's second novel tells the story of the disappearance of fifteen people in an unnamed South American country that has fallen under the rule of a military dictatorship. At the center of the novel are Irene Beltrán, a journalist from an upper-class family, and her lover, Francisco Leal, a photographer, the son of political exiles from Spain. When the two set out to research the story of Evangelina Ranquileo, a young woman who appears to have supernatural powers, they find themselves caught up in a series of events that change their lives irretrievably. The story traces Irene's political awakening and self-discovery. As part of the upper class, "she had been educated to deny any unpleasantness, discounting it as a distortion of the facts" (111). As she works on the case, she develops a social consciousness that compels her to risk her life to uncover the evidence of atrocities committed by military personnel. After she and Francisco discover the body not only of Evangelina but of many others in an abandoned mine, their determination to expose these crimes leads to a machine-gun attack on Irene. As soon as she is able to travel, the two flee into exile across the border, pledging to return to their beloved homeland someday.

As she did in her first book, *The House of the Spirits*, Allende bears witness to historical events in Chile. Although the country is unnamed, the fictionalized story is based on a highly publicized incident that occurred in 1978 when the bodies of fifteen people were discovered in an abandoned mine near the village of Lonquén, outside Santiago. In the epigraph, Allende explains that the story was confided to her and that she carried it in her memory until she could write it down so it would not be "erased by the wind."

Allende's analysis of class issues is reason enough to read this book. She writes that "two countries were functioning within the same national boundaries: one for the golden and powerful elite, the other for the excluded and silent masses" (168). She also touches on a number of other significant issues and topics including prostitution, suicide, family rape, religion, marital discord and harmony, resistance movements, hunger strikes, street demonstrations, homosexuality, and the neglect of elderly people.

Most of the minor characters in the book are well drawn and interesting. Rosa, the Beltrán family maid, is a strong person who is aware of the world around her. She is much more supportive than Irene's mother; unfortunately, there is a fat oppressive description of her early in the book. Readers should also be prepared for the gratuitous gory description of the killing of a hog. But the major flaw in the book is the misleading way in which incest is portrayed. The interactions between Evangelina and her older brother are described only through his voice. Research shows that incest between a young girl and her older brother is the result of an unequal power relationship and that it results in debilitating trauma to the young girl. This is a significant error in the book that should not be overlooked during discussions. By discussing this and other issues introduced in the book, readers will become better informed and more equipped to live in a complex and often confusing world.

Paula

Grades 12–Adult

- Authorship
- Autobiography
- Dying and Death

Isabel Allende's sixth book is a soul-baring memoir, which began as a letter to her comatose daughter, Paula. As Allende sat at her cherished daughter's bedside, she wrote this vivid account of her grandparents' and parents' lives and her remembrance of her own childhood, adolescence, and womanhood. Woven into her life story are poignant passages on her daughter's illness and her unsuccessful efforts to save her life.

"Listen, Paula, I'm going to tell you a story, so that when you wake up you will not feel so lost." With these loving words, Allende begins her memoir, dedicated to her daughter. Twenty-eight-year-old Paula Frias Allende has fallen into a coma caused by porphyria, a rare metabolic disorder. As her mother keeps a desperate vigil in the corridors of the hospital in Madrid and later in her home in California, Paula edges closer to death. Allende enlists the help of every kind of remedy and therapy, including the services of an acupuncturist, a psychic, a hypnotist, and a number of other healers, but she must finally confront the painful truth: nothing will bring Paula back to the world of the living. Devastated, Allende cries, "I will never again be the person I was" (207). The death of her daughter at such a young age and the military coup in her beloved homeland, Chile, are the two major tragedies of her life. "I plunge into these pages in an irrational attempt to overcome my terror" (9). Allende points out that until the twentieth century—and even now in all but the most privileged families—losing a child is a common experience. As she unburdens her heart, she provides insight into what it takes to bear that loss and gives a rare gift to her readers.

Until this book Allende had never shared her past. Describing her life as a "multilayered and ever-changing fresco" that only she can decipher, she recalls both positive and bitter memories. She writes that her life has been "filled with intense emotion. I have lived the extremes; few things have been easy or smooth for me" (112). "For nearly fifty years I have been a toreador taunting violence and pain with a red cape, secure in the protection of the good luck birthmark on my back—even though in my heart I suspected that one day I would feel the claws of misfortune raking my shoulder" (206–207). Allende traces the lives of her ancestors, reveals personal and family secrets, and recounts the turbulent history of Chile. She records the years of her exile in Venezuela and her recent move to the United States. She investigates her development as a writer after spending "more than twenty years on the periphery of literature—journalism, short stories, theater, television scripts, hundreds of letters" (275).

Paula is a deeply affecting book, written in the magical prose typical of Allende's novels. The author examines the decisions that she made as a woman, as a Chilean, and as a writer; reaffirms her reality; and says good-bye to her beloved daughter. This book has been a best-seller in the United States, Latin America, and Europe and has brought a new audience to Allende's writing. Both new readers and longtime admirers will embrace this fine autobiography, one of her best works to date.

Portrait in Sepia

Grades 12–Up

- Chile
- Historical Fiction
- Photography

"Through photography . . . I try desperately to conquer the transitory nature of my existence, to trap moments before they evanesce, to untangle the confusion of my past" (303), declares Aurora del Valle, the protagonist of this complex, intriguing saga set in Chile and California. Beginning in 1862, eighteen years before Aurora's birth, and ending in 1910, when she is thirty years old, this compelling historical novel continues the story begun in *Daughter of Fortune*. Aurora, the granddaughter of Eliza Sommers and Tao Chi'en, suffers a brutal trauma when she is five years old and spends the next twenty-five years searching for her history. Photography awakens her artistic spirit, offers her a way to cope with her nightmares, and sustains her during a loveless marriage. Finally, the pieces of her heritage fall into place, and she discovers the source of her grief and finds the courage to liberate herself. *Portrait in Sepia*, an ambitious novel about memory, family secrets, war, loss, and much more has been praised for its vast gallery of memorable characters, supreme storytelling, and artful evocation of the nineteenth century. Spanish edition: *Retrato en sepia*. (Note: In 1985, *The House of the Spirits*, the third book in this trilogy, was published. Years later, Isabel Allende wrote the first two books: *Daughter of Fortune* and *Portrait in Sepia*.)

The Stories of Eva Luna

Grades 12–Adult

- Short Stories
- Storytelling

The Stories of Eva Luna is a collection of twenty-three tales that cover an array of themes and present an abundance of fascinating characters, some of whom appeared in *Eva Luna*. The book opens with a request from her lover for a story that has never been told. And so Eva and her much-celebrated creator begin a series of entertaining tales that combine magic, fantasy, psychological insight, and sharp social satire. The stories nestle into a variety of settings—deserts, convents, jungles, boarding-houses, brothels, taverns, tropical mountain villages, mansions, and palaces. Readers familiar with *Eva Luna* will recognize Agua Santa, Calle República, and La Colonia as well as Rolf Carlé, Riad Halabí, and Ines, a schoolteacher. Allende weaves a tapestry of themes and topics—euthanasia, revolution, prostitution, greed, revenge, love, exile, illegal organ plunder, murder, calamity, betrayal, and "layers of blood, sweat, and sorrow"—all in a vibrant tribute to storytelling.

One of the most memorable stories, "Two Words," celebrates the power of language. Belisa Crepusculario makes her living selling words—verses, dreams, letters, and "invented insults." Born into a poor family and without a source of income, she discovers that "words make their way in the world without a master" (11). When she writes a political speech for a Colonel, he captures the nation's heart and sets out to right the wrongs of history.

When asked about the inspiration that led to her stories, Allende responded that most of them came from things that had really happened. "If You Touched My Heart" is the heartrending story of Hortensia, who was held prisoner in a pit for forty-seven years by an abominable and abject man. Allende based the story on a television news report in which she watched a woman being removed from a cellar, wrapped in a blanket. Since she was never in the news again, Allende set out to answer questions about how such an atrocity could have happened. The last story in the book and the most elaborate is "And of Clay Are We Created." Allende and many other viewers saw a report on television in 1985 about a volcanic eruption in Colombia that killed thousands of people and trapped Omaira Sánchez, a young girl, in a mudslide. Allende's heartbreaking story features Rolf Carlé as the newscaster who tries to rescue the young victim. As he keeps her company for several days until she dies, he finally grieves the sorrows of his own tormented past. Eva tells the story as she watches the horrifying drama unfold on television. Allende refers to this event again in a later book, *Paula*, writing that she tried to exorcise Omaira's story from her mind by telling her story, but "she is a dogged angel who will not let me forget her" (*Paula*, 309). When Allende's daughter fell into a coma, the writer remembered Omaira's face. Both Paula and Omaira were trapped. Allende was finally able to decipher the message in Omaira's eyes: "patience, courage, resignation, dignity in the face of death" (*Paula*, 310). Spanish edition: *Cuentos de Eva Luna*.

Julia Alvarez

Photo: © Bill Eichner

Dominican American (1950–)
Birthday: March 27
Contact: Susan Bergholz Literary Services
17 West 10th Street, #5
New York, NY 10011

I think fiction is truth. It uses strategies of storytelling to get you involved, to weave you into the narrative web, in order to tell you some truth of the human heart.

(*Champaign-Urbana News-Gazette*, December 30, 1994, 3)

Books by Julia Alvarez

Before We Were Free. Knopf, 2002.
A Cafecito Story. Chelsea Green, 2002.
How the García Girls Lost Their Accents. Algonquin Books, 1991; NAL Dutton, 1992. Spanish edition: *De cómo las chicas García perdieron su acento*.
Homecoming. Grove Press, 1984, 1986; Dutton, 1995.
The Housekeeping Book. Burlington, 1984.
How Tía Lola Came to (Visit) Stay. Knopf, 2001.
In the Time of the Butterflies: A Novel. Algonquin Books, 1994; NAL Plume, 1995. Spanish edition: *En el tiempo de las mariposas*.
In the Name of Salomé: A Novel. Algonquin Books, 2000.
Old Age Ain't for Sissies. Crane Creek Press, 1979.
The Other Side/El Otro Lado. NAL Plume, 1995.
The Secret Footprints. Illustrated by Fabían Negrin. Knopf, 2000.
Something to Declare. Alqonquin Books, 1998.
¡Yo! Alqonquin Books, 1997. Spanish edition: *¡Yo!*

Julia Alvarez has won acclaim for her fiction, which includes *How the García Girls Lost Their Accents*, *In the Time of the Butterflies*, and *In the Name of Salomé*. Long before she discovered her novelist's voice, she was writing engaging poetry. In poetry and prose, her eloquent voice speaks about the experience of being an immigrant to the United States. The recipient of numerous awards and honors, her work has been widely anthologized. She has taught English at several universities and is currently professor of English at Middlebury College in Vermont.

Alvarez was born in New York City and spent her early years in the Dominican Republic, where she lived with her parents and sisters on her mother's family property. Surrounded by her extended family, Alvarez and her sisters were brought up along with their cousins by her mother, aunts, and maids. She was ten years old when her family fled the repressive regime of Rafael Leonidas Trujillo. Her father had been part of an underground resistance movement that was planning the revolutionary overthrow of the tyrannical dictator. The family narrowly escaped from Santo Domingo, then known as Ciudad Trujillo, to New York City, similar to the fictional García family in Alvarez's first novel. In "Exile," one of her poems, she writes about "the night we fled the country" and the "loss much larger than I understood."

The young immigrant soon experienced homesickness, alienation, and prejudice. She missed her homeland and her large, close-knit family. She responded to the loss by turning inward. The introverted young girl became an avid reader, immersing herself in books.

During her high school years in Catholic schools and Abbot Academy, she encountered teachers who encouraged her in her writing, so that early on in her new language, she wanted to become a writer. For this reason, she chose Middlebury College as a school reputed for its writing program. There she majored in literature and worked at the Bread Loaf Writers' Conference, where she met other young writers and mentors.

Graduating summa cum laude from Middlebury College, the young scholar went on to earn her master's degree in creative writing at Syracuse University. In addition to teaching in a number of locations, including Delaware, Kentucky, North Carolina, California, Massachusetts, Vermont, and Illinois, she was selected as a Jenny McKean Moore Visiting Writer at George Washington University in Washington, D.C. Now, as a professor in the English Department at Middlebury College, her responsibilities include teaching beginning and advanced creative writing workshops as well as a variety of literature courses including a Hispanic American literature course, a Chaucer, Milton, and Shakespeare course, and other courses in interdisciplinary subjects.

In addition to teaching, Alvarez has served as a judge, consultant, panelist, and assistant editor in a variety of capacities. She often gives readings, lectures, and presentations at conferences, bookstores, classes, book fairs, and other locations and has been interviewed on numerous radio and television programs. Alvarez has won many prestigious awards and honors, including a National Endowment for the Arts grant for poetry in 1987–1988, a PEN Syndicated Fiction Prize in 1987, and an Ingram Merrill Foundation Grant awarded for fiction manuscripts in 1990. In 1988, she was one of five artists selected from an international competition to live and work in an artist colony at Altos de Chavon in the Dominican Republic. Her responsibilities included conducting workshops and giving readings of her own work.

Alvarez's work has been praised for its significance to Latino culture, women's issues, and the immigrant experience. *Library Journal* commented, "Alvarez is a gifted, evocative storyteller of promise." Her prose, poetry, and children's books are innovative and unforgettable.

More Information about Julia Alvarez

Contemporary Authors Online. The Gale Group, 2001.
Contemporary Literary Criticism, Volume 93.
Dictionary of Hispanic Biography, Gale, 1996.
The Hispanic Literary Companion, edited by Nicolás Kanellos. Visible Ink, 1997.
Julia Alvarez: A Critical Companion by Silvio Sirias. Greenwood Press, 2001.
Latina Self-Portraits: Interviews with Contemporary Women Writers, edited by Bridget Kevane and Juanita Heredia. University of New Mexico Press, 2000.
¡Latinas! Women of Achievement, edited by Diane Tegen and Jim Kamp. Visible Ink, 1996.
Notable Hispanic American Women. Gale Research, 1993.
Something to Declare by Julia Alvarez. Alqonquin Books, 1998.

Selected Works by Julia Alvarez

Before We Were Free

Grades 6–Up

- Dominican Republic
- Revolutions

Protagonist Anita de la Torre never questioned her freedom living in the Dominican Republic. But by her twelfth birthday in 1960, most of her relatives have emigrated to the United States, her Tío Toni has disappeared without a trace, and the government's secret police terrorize her remaining family because of their suspected opposition to Trujillo's dictatorship. Drawing upon the courage and strength of her family, Anita must overcome her fears and fly to freedom, leaving all that she once knew behind.

How the García Girls Lost Their Accents

PEN Oakland/Josephine Miles Book Award

American Library Association Notable Book

Grades 11–Adult

- Dominican Republic
- Immigrants
- Language

"They will be haunted by what they do and don't remember. But they have spirit in them. They will invent what they need to survive" (223). With these words, Chuchu, one of the maids, bids farewell to the Garcia sisters, who, with their parents, must flee the repressive regime of Rafael Leónidas Trujillo. The lively story of their adjustment to life in the United States is told through a series of interconnected vignettes beginning in adulthood and moving backward to their childhood as wealthy members of the upper class in the Dominican Republic. Although fictional, Alvarez's celebrated first novel about the four García sisters growing up in New York City sprang from the themes of rootlessness and assimilation that she and her sisters experienced. In this engaging chronicle of a family in exile, each person struggles to regain her equilibrium in her own unique way. For the daughters, the changes are terrifying and exhilarating, liberating and excruciating. Trying to live up to their parent's version of honor while accommodating the expectations of a new culture is confusing and frustrating. The new identities that they forge in the land of wild and loose Americans are at odds with the proper island life that they remember. As members of the privileged class, they miss the special pampering from the chauffeurs, gardeners, maids, and nursemaids of their earlier years.

Experiences at school are among the most notable. Yolanda, who has never been interested in school before, develops an interest in writing poetry. "[I]n New York . . . since the natives were unfriendly, and the country inhospitable, she took root in the language" (141). By the time she enters college, she thinks she is quite Americanized but soon finds herself feeling profoundly out of place. "For the hundredth time, I cursed my immigrant origins" (94).

Readers interested in exploring language issues will find plenty to discuss as the García sisters attend expensive schools to smooth the accent out of their English (hence the title of the book). Other topics include anorexia, mental illness, pedophilia, marijuana, illegitimate children, and, of course, class privilege.

Years later, Yolanda returns to the island hoping to establish the roots that she could never find in the States. She reflects on the twenty-nine years since her family was uprooted from their homeland. "She and her sisters have led such turbulent lives—so many husbands, homes, jobs, wrong turns among them" (11). Alvarez's first book of fiction, written with humor and insight, tells the irrepressible stories of how four immigrants came to be at home—and not at home—in the United States.

How Tía Lola Came to (Visit) Stay

Grades 4–7

- Aunts
- Divorce
- Dominican Americans
- Language

When Tía Lola arrives from the Dominican Republic, Miguel and Juanita Guzmán have just moved from New York City to rural Vermont with their recently divorced mother. Tía Lola quickly charms everyone but Miguel with her lively music, vivid storytelling, and surprise parties. However, ten-year-old Miguel, who is concerned about being accepted by his Vermont classmates, gradually learns to love his vivacious aunt. This warm, humorous story concludes with a trip to the Dominican Republic, where the children meet their mother's relatives for the first time. *How Tía Lola Came to (Visit) Stay* has been praised for its vivid characterization, evocative imagery, and the musicality of the narrative. This excellent book is especially important because of the scarcity of Latino/a literature for this age group.

In the Name of Salomé

Grades 12–Up

- Dominican Republic
- Historical Fiction
- Mothers and Daughters
- Poets
- Revolutionaries

This powerful novel weaves together the stories of two fascinating women—mother and daughter, one a poet, the other a teacher—and explores how they each, in very different ways, dedicated their lives to revolutionary causes. Set in the politically chaotic Dominican Republic of the late nineteenth century, on the campuses of three universities in the United States, and in the idealistic Communist Cuba of the 1960s, this ambitious book spans a century, alternating between Salomé's first-person recollections and Camila's third-person, reverse chronological narratives. Based on the lives of Salomé Urena (1850–1897), whose fervent patriotic poems turned her—at seventeen—into a Dominican Republic national icon and her daughter, Profesora Camila Henríquez Ureña (1894–1973), the novel was hailed by *Publishers Weekly* as "one of the most politically moving novels of the past half century." This immensely interesting, carefully researched book has also been praised for its dense and deeply layered narrative, stirring prose, and original and illuminating perspective. Alvarez writes, "As different as their lives were, both women eventually came together in their mutual love of [their homeland] and in their faith in the ability of women to forge a conscience for Our Americas" (*Hispanic*, June 2000, 76).

In the Time of the Butterflies: A Novel

National Book Critics Circle Award Finalist in Fiction

American Library Association Notable Book

American Library Association Best Books for Young Adults

Grades 12–Adult

- Dictatorships
- Dominican Republic
- Historical Fiction
- Women Revolutionaries

On November 25, 1960, the bodies of three young women were found at the bottom of a cliff on the north coast of the Dominican Republic.

Among the leading opponents of the dictatorship of General Rafael Leónidas Trujillo, these women had been instrumental in the formation of an underground resistance movement and had actively worked for the revolutionary overthrow of the oppressive regime. Martyred, the Mirabal sisters have become legendary figures in their country, where they are known as *Las Mariposas*, the Butterflies, from their underground code names.

Now, three decades later, Julia Alvarez has fictionalized their story in a powerful novel that pays tribute to the spirit of the real Mirabals. (Alvarez's family narrowly escaped to the United States four months before the ambush and murder of Minerva, Patria, and María Teresa Mirabal.) Against the historical backdrop of the brutal, thirty-one-year Trujillo regime, Alvarez chronicles the personal lives, political awakenings, and revolutionary strategies of each of the sisters. In alternating chapters, each Butterfly speaks in her own voice, beginning with her childhood in the 1940s. The surviving sister, Dede, speaks across the decades, framing the narrative with her own poignant story of loss and dedication to her sisters' memories. The stories of the convent-educated women, members of a wealthy, conservative Catholic family, slowly unfold as each acquires revolutionary fervor, building to a gripping intensity. Alvarez artfully captures the atmosphere of the police state, in which interminable atrocities terrify and silence the populace. As the sisters endure the arrests of their compatriots, their own imprisonment, and the threatened disintegration of their movement, they respond in individual, complex ways. Yet they continue to risk their lives to save their beloved country. As Alvarez notes in her postscript, they did what "few men—and only a handful of women—had been willing to do" (323).

Few books have been written about *Las Mariposas* or the Trujillo dictatorship. Alvarez explains that the situation is similar to what happened in the United States after the Vietnam War, when the novels took some time to come out. "There's a way in which a culture has to sit on something for a while and then begin to understand it, and then redeem that time by telling the story."

The author achieves a beautifully balanced sense of personal as well as historical drama. She writes, "I hope that through this fictionalized story I will bring acquaintance of these famous sisters to English-speaking readers. November 25, the day of their murders, is observed in many Latin American countries as the International Day against Violence toward Women. Obviously, these sisters, who fought one tyrant, have served as models for women fighting against injustices of all kinds" (324). As Dede contemplates the sacrifice of the Butterflies, she muses, "People keeping their mouths shut when a little peep from everyone would have been a chorus the world couldn't have ignored" (317). Alvarez has written an important book, for as the saying goes, if people are not aware of history, they are bound to repeat it.

The Other Side/El otro lado

Grades 12–Adult

- Poetry

The poems in *The Other Side/El otro lado* reveal Julia Alvarez's engaging voice and the full range of her poetic talents. In the opening poem, "Bilingual Sestina," Alvarez reflects on her immigrant experience of leaving the Dominican Republic for a strange country and a new language. The "Making Up the Past" poems examine the life of exile as experienced by the young Alvarez. It was a "loss much larger than I understood" at the time, as a part of her was set adrift. Alvarez's poems move from childhood memories of "melting into the USA," through college inspirations to write poetry, to adult issues. Alvarez speaks of letting go of the losses and trying hard to feel luckier than she felt. The book closes with the long, multipart title narrative, set at an artist's colony not far from her childhood home where Alvarez worked on her writing residency. She suffered a writing block, and the first few weeks were torture. Finally, the cruelty and struggles experienced in the States "melt away," and she begins "writing in earnest." She eloquently expresses self-doubts, fears, and homesickness as she searches for a way to make up her "divided Dominican American mind." Alvarez's lyrical collection is an innovative examination of internal conflict, rootlessness and self-evolution.

The Secret Footprints

Grades 1–4

- Dominican Republic
- Folklore
- Taino Indians

"On an island not too far away . . . lived a secret tribe called the ciguapas," a group of beautiful creatures whose feet were attached backwards, so no human could follow their footsteps. But their secret was almost discovered once when a bold young ciguapa named Guapa ventured into the land of the humans. How her curiosity nearly costs the tribe their freedom makes for a captivating tale. Radiant paintings accompany this lyrically told, magical story. Appended is a fascinating note about the origins of the tale.

Something to Declare

Grades 11–Up

- Authorship
- Essays

In her first book of nonfiction, Julia Alvarez offers twenty-four engaging essays about the two major (and interlocking) issues of her life—growing up with one foot in each of two cultures and writing. This accessible book provides an excellent introduction to Alvarez's life and work. For example, "Chasing the Butterflies" is a fascinating essay about her research for her powerful novel *In the Time of the Butterflies. Something to Declare* has been praised for its open and lively tone, gentle touches of humor, and thoughtful, universal moments.

¡Yo!

Grades 11–Adult

- Authorship
- Dominican Americans
- Writing

In her third novel, Julia Alvarez returns to one of the characters from *How the García Girls Lost Their Accents*. Yolanda (Yo) Garcîa, like Alvarez herself, has become a successful writer who bases much of her work on her own family, friends, and lovers. Ironically, Yo is not allowed to tell her own story. Instead, each of the sixteen chapters in the novel presents the voice of someone who knows her well, including her mother, her father, her three sisters, a teacher, a student, a landlady, and her third husband. These and other narrators provide a composite portrait of Yo's journey, from her childhood to her college years and beyond as she searches for her identity as an immigrant from the Dominican Republic and as she struggles to find her path as a storyteller. *¡Yo!* has been highly praised as a brilliant work of art; a charming, hilarious book; and a complex, exhilarating adventure. Spanish edition: *¡Yo!*

Rudolfo Anaya

Photo: Mimi

Mexican American (1937–)
Birthday: October 30
Contact: Susan Bergholz Literary Services
17 West 10th Street, #5
New York City, NY 10011-8746

Our challenge is to incorporate into the curriculum all the voices of our country. . . . You shortchange your students and you misrepresent the true nature of their country if you don't introduce them to all the communities who have comprised the history of this country. To deny your students a view into these different worlds is to deny them tools for the future.

("The Censorship of Neglect," in *The Anaya Reader,* 412)

Books by Rudolfo Anaya

The Adventures of Juan Chicaspatas. Arte Público Press, 1985.
Alburquerque. University of New Mexico Press, 1992; Warner Books, 1992.
The Anaya Reader. Warner Books, 1995.
Aztlán: Essays on the Chicano Homeland. Coedited with Francisco Lomeli. Bilingual Press, 1984; University of New Mexico Press, 1991.
Bless Me, Ultima. Warner Books, 1993.
Cuentos Chicanos: A Short Story Anthology. Coedited with Antonio Marquez. University of New Mexico Press, 1984.
Cuentos: Tales from the Hispanic Southwest. Illustrated by Jamie Valdez. Museum of New Mexico Press, 1980.
Elegy on the Death of César Chávez. Illustrated by Gaspar Enriquez. Cinco Puntos Press, 2000.
Farolitos for Abuelo. Illustrated by Edward Gonzales. Hyperion, 1999.
Farolitos of Christmas. Illustrated by Edward Gonzales. Hyperion, 1995, 1998.
First Tortilla. Hyperion, forthcoming.
Heart of Aztlán. University of New Mexico Press, 1988.
Jalamanta: A Message from the Desert. Warner Books, 1996.
The Legend of la Llorona. Tonatiuh-Quinto Sol, 1984.
Maya's Children: The Story of La Llorona. Hyperion, 1997.
My Land Sings: Stories from the Rio Grande. Illustrated by Amy Córdova. Morrow, 1999.
Rio Grande Fall. Warner Books, 1996.
Roadrunner's Dance. Illustrated by David Diaz. Hyperion, 2000.
Shaman Winter. Warner Books, 2000.
The Silence of the Llano. Tonatiuh-Quinto Sol, 1982.
Tierra: Contemporary Fiction of New Mexico. Editor. Cinco Puntos Press, 1989.
Tortuga. University of New Mexico Press, 1988.
Voces: Anthology of New Mexican Writers. Editor. University of New Mexico Press, 1987.
Zia Summer. Warner Books, 1995.

Rudolfo Anaya, the highly acclaimed author of *Bless Me, Ultima*, was born October 30, 1937, in Pastura, a village lying south of Santa Rosa in eastern New Mexico. When he was a baby, his parents sat him on a rug on the floor. They placed a variety of items around him—saddle, pencil, paper, and so on. He crawled to the pencil and paper. He has continued to follow this interest in writing to this day.

Anaya was a very curious child; his mother noticed that he always asked a lot of questions, and she knew that he was destined to follow an unfamiliar path. He grew up speaking Spanish at home so when he started school, the transition from a Spanish-speaking world to an English-speaking one resulted in a period of adjustment. Although schoolwork was not difficult for Anaya, he soon realized that he was different and that he had a unique way of perceiving the world.

Anaya's family moved to Santa Rosa when he was a small child and to Albuquerque when he was fifteen. Subsequently, he suffered a spinal injury when he dove into an irrigation ditch and endured an extended stay in a hospital. When he returned home, he was walking with a cane. (He later wrote *Tortuga*, based loosely on this experience.) During his convalescence, he learned to hide his pain, to live within; he learned the true meaning of loneliness. Later, he eloquently expressed this pain and loneliness in his writing.

Anaya attended high school in Albuquerque, where discrimination made life difficult for his people. There were no Mexican American teachers, and the literature and history of his people were not a part of the curriculum. This widespread omission of information about his heritage understandably resulted in feelings of alienation in the young student as it did in many of his peers. Even during his undergraduate days at the University of New Mexico, there was no mention of Mexican history or art. Indeed, he was still corrected for allowing his Spanish accent to show.

Anaya wrote poetry and prose to assuage the pain, loneliness, and alienation. He struggled for seven years to write his first novel, *Bless Me, Ultima*, which became one the first Chicano best-sellers. The book was awarded the prestigious Premio Quinto Sol Award for the best novel written by a Chicano in 1972. Since then, he has written many other books, poems, plays, articles, and screenplays. Today, Rudolfo Anaya is considered one of the leading Latino writers in the United States.

After teaching junior and senior high school, Anaya taught creative writing at the University of New Mexico. Later, as a full professor of English, he specialized in Chicano literature. He recently retired after many years of teaching to devote his energies to writing, lecturing, editing, and traveling.

More Information about Rudolfo Anaya

The Anaya Reader by Rudolfo Anaya. Warner Books, 1995.
Authors and Artists for Young Adults. Volume 20, 13–20.
Contemporary Authors: Autobiography Series. Volume 4, 15–28.
Contemporary Authors New Revision Series. Volume 32, 9–10.
Contemporary Authors Online. The Gale Groups, 2001.
Contemporary Literary Criticism. Volume 23, 22–27.
"A Conversation with Rudolfo Anaya," by Jennifer Battle. *The New Advocate*, Spring 2001, 103–109.
Dictionary of Literary Biography. Volume 82, 24–34.
Dictionary of Literary Biography. Volume 206, 11–19.
The Hispanic Literary Companion, edited by Nicolás Kanellos. Visible Ink, 1997.
Multicultural Voices in Contemporary Literature by Frances Ann Day. Heinemann, 1999.
Rudolfo A. Anaya: Focus on Criticism, edited by Cesar A. Gonzalez. Bilingual Press, Arizona State University, n.d. (602) 965-3867.

A Sense of Place—Rudolfo A. Anaya: An Annotated Bio-Bibliography by Cesar A. Gonzalez T. and Phyllis S. Morgan. Ethnic Studies Library, 2000.

Selected Works by Rudolfo Anaya

Alburquerque

PEN Center West Award for Fiction

Grades 12–Adult

- Adoption
- Alburquerque
- Authorship

Against the backdrop of a historic city coming to grips with the complexities of urban growth, a young man searches for his biological father. Abrán González, a former Golden Gloves champion, is unaware that he was adopted until he learns this secret from his birth mother on her deathbed. This revelation sparks a quest that finds him rubbing shoulders with Alburquerque politicians, draws him back into the dreaded boxing ring, and threatens to shake his identity. Meanwhile, a writer struggles to find himself in his stories, a Vietnam War veteran searches for a way to return to his pueblo, and two mayoral candidates develop competing plans for the future of the city.

This far-reaching story introduces a number of interesting characters and provides fascinating information about the history of Alburquerque. Rudolfo Anaya, who has lived in the Alburquerque area all his life, writes, "Legend says the Anglo stationmaster couldn't pronounce the first "r" in "Albur," so he dropped it as he painted the station sign for the city. This novel restores the original spelling, Alburquerque." As he writes about his beloved city, Anaya helps readers understand the deep roots and traditions of New Mexico's people. He bares the soul of the city, writing about the conquest of the native territories by the Spanish and Anglos and the appropriation of land, water, and culture by the invaders. He takes a piercing look at racism, anti-Semitism, and class oppression, writing that "they suffered the punishment of the old prejudices, prejudices that still existed. The city was still split. The Anglos lived in the Heights, the Chicanos along the valley. . . . One didn't have to go to El Paso and cross to Juarez to understand the idea of border" (38). Several of the characters are of mixed heritages and, finding themselves living in a hypocritical society that worships racial purity, are struggling to find their identities. The book handles these important issues with insight and sensitivity with one exception: the use of the offensive term "Japs." When disparaging remarks are made by racist characters, it is clear that they are wrong. But in this case, the word was uttered by the mayor, an otherwise admirable character.

Followers of Anaya's work will recognize Juan Chicaspatas from *The Adventures of Juan Chicaspatas* and Ben Chávez as Benjie, the son of Adelita and Clemente Chávez in *Heart of Aztlán*, both earlier books. The character of Ben Chávez, a writer, bears some interesting similarities to Rudolfo Anaya himself. Hoping to create a consciousness for the people, Chávez is writing an epic that explores the Mesoamerican mythic elements that Chicanos had incorporated into their heritage. By writing about him, the author is able to explore some of the issues faced by writers. As Chávez struggles to find himself in his stories, he wonders, "Had he wasted his life writing books?" (267). Several other characters in this book, including Sonny Baca, Gloria Dominic, Frank Dominic, and Marisa Martínez, continue their journeys in Anaya's next novel, *Zia Summer*.

Anaya draws on his trademark magic realism but adds a touch of madcap adventure and political satire in *Alburquerque*. Reviewers praised the novel for its intense spirituality, describing it as rich and tempestuous, gentle and fierce, embodying a deep caring for the land and culture of the Southwest. Both readers who are unfamiliar with Alburquerque and those for whom it is an old friend will enjoy this tale of political intrigue and genealogical mystery set in the historic city.

The Anaya Reader

Grades 12–Adult

- Collection of short stories, essays, plays, and excerpts from novels

This anthology of mixed-genre pieces contains four outstanding essays analyzing the omission of Chicano/a literature, history, and culture in the curriculum: "An American Chicano in King Arthur's Court," "Take the Tortillas Out of Your Poetry," "On the Education of Hispanic Children," and "The Censorship of Neglect." It also includes excerpts from old favorites such as *Bless Me, Ultima* and *Tortuga* as well as many pieces previously unpublished or available only in small press editions. This important collection pays tribute to Anaya's versatility as a writer, featuring fiction, short stories, essays, plays, and even a poem. Anaya dedicated this comprehensive, 562-page book to his wife, "Patricia, my constant companion and confidante during the long years of birthing these collected pieces, and to a new generation of readers." Note: "The Silence of the Llano" is a disturbing piece about death, grieving, child neglect, and rape. It ends with a foreboding hint of impending family rape, described in the foreword as "a re-creation of a traditional tale of incest."

Bless Me, Ultima

Premio Quinto Sol Literary Award
Grades 9–Adult

- Career Aspirations
- *Curanderas*
- Death
- Dreams

Bless Me, Ultima, Anaya's first novel, has become a classic of contemporary literature, with well over 1 million copies in print. It depicts the maturation of Antonio Marez, a boy growing up in Guadalupe, a small New Mexico farm village. Seven-year-old Antonio narrates (in flashback form) this story of his relationship with his spiritual guide, Ultima, a *curandera* (healer). He struggles with spirituality, confused about the teachings of the Catholic Church, and with his discovery of a genuine spirituality and legitimate morality outside the church, in nature. The book deals with a wide variety of subjects drawn together with intense force. Antonio struggles to understand good and evil, to establish his identity, to conquer childhood fears, and to find his way in his family, school, and community. Throughout the novel, Antonio's trials are balanced with his association with Ultima. She allows him to participate in her life-affirming practices of healing and stabilizing negative forces. Although the novel details only two years in Antonio's life, he changes and grows in profound ways. The skillful cross-weaving of social, cultural, and psychological levels of action results in a very powerful book. Spanish edition: *Bendiceme, Ultima*.

Cuentos Chicanos: A Short Story Anthology

Grades 10–Adult

- Short Stories

The twenty-one short stories in this collection offer highly personalized visions of the world presented in styles that range from oral narratives to experimentation with stream-of-consciousness. From tragic to lighthearted, cynical to exuberant, these stories are distinguished by their diversity and vitality. The collection beautifully captures the dimensions, subtleties, nuances, and paradoxes of Chicano life and culture.

Cuentos: Tales from the Hispanic Southwest

Grades 4–10

- Bilingual
- Folktales
- Southwest

Twenty-three tales of magic, myth, legend, and the events of everyday life in the Latino/a villages of New Mexico and southern Colorado were selected and adapted in Spanish and then retold in English. Rich traditions, values, customs, and wisdom flow through this collection of *cuentos*. A glossary of regional, archaic, and idiomatic words is included.

Elegy on the Death of César Chávez

Skipping Stones Honor Award
Grades 4–Adult

- Biography
- César Chávez
- Migrant Farmworkers
- Poetry

Powerful mixed-media collages beautifully complement this heartfelt expression of grief, loss, and hope. A moving tribute to César Chávez (1927–1993), who devoted his life to improving working conditions for farmworkers, this poignant elegy cries out to people to "rise together and build a new society" (18). Anaya eloquently captures the love and respect that people felt for the legendary labor and civil rights leader and encourages everyone to continue his work. In the Author's Note, Anaya writes, "There is a lot of work to be done if we are to continue César's battle against injustice. We must all come together—from all cultural backgrounds—to fight for equality" (29). This important book includes a detailed chronology of César Chávez's life.

Farolitos for Abuelo

Grades K–5

- Christmas
- Death
- Grandfathers
- Traditions

Luz' beloved Abuelo dies of pneumonia after diving into a frigid river to save a young boy from drowning. Heartbroken, Luz keeps Abuelo's memory alive by planting and harvesting his garden as he taught her. During the first Christmas without him, she places *farolitos* around his grave as a special way of celebrating his life. In the Author's Note, Anaya writes about this tradition, which has grown in his hometown, where "hundreds of people place farolitos at the cemetery. By nightfall thousands of these lanterns glow in the cold night as a celebration of joy and remembrance." This beautifully illustrated, touching story is punctuated with Spanish words for which a glossary is appended. Prequel: *The Farolitos of Christmas.*

The Farolitos of Christmas

Tomás Rivera Mexican American Children's Book Award
Grades K–5

- Christmas
- Grandfathers
- Illness
- Tradition and Change

Luz's *abuelo* (grandfather) is ill and unable to make the traditional *luminarias* (small bonfires) for Christmas Eve, so the *pastores* (shepherds) can see to perform their annual songs and stories. Luz solves the problem by designing *farolitos* (small lanterns) made out of brown paper bags and candles. The family happily makes dozens of them and uses them to line the path to the road. This beautifully illustrated book presents a positive image of a young Mexican American girl who is a risk-taker and who shows ingenuity in solving problems. Glossary included. Sequel: *Farolitos for Abuelo.*

Heart of Aztlán

Grades 9–Adult

- Moving
- Leadership
- Newcomers
- Technology

This is a compelling novel about the adjustments that the Chavez family must make when they move from the rural community of Guadalupe to the barrio of Barelas in Albuquerque. As they set out in search of a new future for their family, they encounter unforeseen changes that challenge their adaptability, threaten their lives, and shake them to their very core. Mythological themes, rich symbolism, and the sense of a shared communal soul combine with an inspiring social message to leave the reader with a feeling of hope. An empathic portrayal of people dispossessed of their heritage and struggling to survive in an alien culture, this philosophical novel draws inspiration from the myth of Aztlán, the mythological place of the Aztecs.

Maya's Children: The Story of La Llorona

Grades K–4

- Immortality
- La Llorona

"La Llorona," the legendary tale from Latin America about the crying woman who searches for her children along rivers, lakes, and lonely roads, is retold by Anaya in a tender, evocative style. Modifying the most frightening aspects of the original story in which La Llorona takes the life of her children, Anaya has created a version appropriate for young children. Señor Tiempo, jealous of Maya's immortality, deceives her and takes her children away. Youngsters of all backgrounds will be interested in this tale that most Latino/a children have heard in at least one of its many versions. In the Author's Note, Anaya provides background information about La Llorona and discusses the reasons for the changes that he made to the tale.

My Land Sings: Stories from the Rio Grande

Tomás Rivera Book Award
Grades 5–Up

- Folklore
- Short Stories

Ten captivating short stories (five traditional and five original) are dedicated "to the cuentistas, those wonderful storytellers from the Río Grande valley who kept our culture alive through our rich oral tradition." In the Preface the author writes, "As a boy, I loved to hear people tell stories. . . . The stories I listened to as a child instilled in me a sense of belonging to a community and a knowledge of its values" (7, 9). Here readers will find tales about La Llorona, Doña Sebastiana, the Fountain of Youth, the Golden Carp, the Dance of the Devil, First Man and First Woman, and much more.

Roadrunner's Dance

Américas Award for Children's Literature
Grades K–3

- Desert Animals
- Rattlesnake
- Roadrunner

Because Rattlesnake has taken over the road and refuses to let anyone use it, Desert Woman enlists the aid of all the animals to create a new creature with the necessary skills to negotiate with the snake. Captivating illustrations complement this fascinating original tale that explains how roadrunners came into being. In the Author's Note, Anaya provides information about roadrunners and explains that this story emerged from his interest in creation stories. He writes, "Every living creature has a special gift. We all need to find our abilities and use them wisely."

Tortuga

Before Columbus Foundation American Book Award
Grades 10–Adult

- Autobiographical Fiction
- Euthanasia

- Hospitals
- Paralysis

Patterned on the mythic journey motif of classical literature, *Tortuga* is the first-person story of a paralyzed sixteen-year-old boy's quest for wellness and understanding. The novel takes place in a hospital for young people and traces Tortuga's recovery from a nearly fatal accident. (The novel is loosely autobiographical.) Tortuga (turtle) is the nickname given the boy by his peers because his body is encased in a shell-like cast. The novel has numerous themes and a great deal of symbolism. One of the most important themes is that physical health is inextricably fused with emotional and spiritual well-being. Tortuga symbolizes the "magic mountain" near the hospital as well as the protagonist's body cast and his psychological shell. Tortuga's literal journey ends with his leaving the hospital on crutches to return home. Note: The male characters in this complex book are developed more fully than the female characters.

Zia Summer

Grades 11–Adult

- Mystery
- Alburquerque
- Environmental Issues

Zia Summer is the first book in Rudolfo Anaya's intriguing mystery series featuring Sonny Baca, a private eye who is the great-grandson of the fabled lawyer/detective Elfego Baca. Sonny always carries his forebear's Colt .45 and is both haunted and inspired by the legendary stories surrounding *el Bisabuelo*'s exploits. Until now, Sonny has settled for trailing cheating spouses and investigating dubious insurance claims. But when his beloved cousin, Gloria, is murdered, he finds himself embroiled in a case that challenges his resources and endangers his life. Pursuing leads in the sensational murder case with a vengeance, Sonny encounters power-hungry politicians, an international computer entrepreneur, police department corruption, a desperate drug dealer, environmental extremists, an enigmatic psychic, ruthless land developers, cantankerous ranchers, two recently fired employees, several mysterious cult members, and insidious family secrets. Is there a connection between Gloria's death and the cases of cattle mutilations plaguing the area? How many other murder cases have been swept under the rug? What is the significance of the Zia sun symbol, which was etched into the body of the murder victim? Is Sonny in over his head in this bizarre case that leads him into a passionate environmental battle over nuclear waste transport and disposal? Mystery lovers will enjoy this exciting new tale by the famed writer of the Southwest and look forward to others in the Sonny Baca mystery series.

But *Zia Summer* is much more than a mystery. Woven into the story are the illuminating rays of Chicano myth, language and tradition, the sacredness of the land, the quest for personal and cultural identity, and spirituality and healing. The 386-page book is filled with the history of the Alburquerque area, written by one who has lived there all of his life. (Anaya reminds us that Alburquerque was the original spelling of the word.) Anaya's far-reaching work provides insight into a number of contemporary social issues, including those surrounding the nuclear weapons industry. In broaching the subject of witchcraft, Anaya clearly distinguishes between the positive work done by many witches and the evil spread by the few engaged in destructive endeavors. In typical Anaya-style, the book incorporates extensive symbolism, ancient and not-so-ancient spirits, and elucidative dreams and nightmares, along with plenty of action and memorable characters. The protagonist, notwithstanding his unacknowledged overindulgence in alcohol and gratuitous lechery, earns the reader's admiration with his emerging awareness of social issues, his openness to new ideas, especially those presented by his elders, his willingness to push against both internal and external barriers, and his dedicated search for his cousin's killer(s). A number of the characters in this novel first appeared in an earlier book, *Alburquerque.*

George Ancona

Photo: Marina Ancona

Mexican American (1929–)
Birthday: December 4
Contact: Lothrop, Lee, and Shepard
1350 Avenue of the Americas
New York, NY 10019

Discovering the world of books was a revelation, because I could work with what was inside of me. I could explore my own feelings, my own curiosities. . . . It was a freedom, a discovery, and a search: the right to search for myself and what I wanted to say with my life and what I wanted to do.

(*The Multicolored Mirror,* 60)

For me, a children's book is like taking a child for a walk, hand in hand, and discovering something about our world.

(*Contemporary Authors,* 21)

Books by George Ancona

Written and Photographed

And What Do You Do? Dutton, 1976.
Aquarium. Clarion, 1991.
Bananas: From Manolo to Margie. Clarion, 1982, paper, 1990.
Barrio: José's Neighborhood. Harcourt, 1998. Spanish edition: *Barrio: El barrio de José.*
Carnaval. Harcourt Brace, 1999.
Charro. Harcourt Brace, 1999. Spanish edition: *Charro.*
Cuban Kids. Marshall Cavendish, 2000.
Cutters, Carvers and the Cathedral. Lothrop, Lee, and Shepard, 1995.
Dancing Is. Dutton, 1981.
Earth Daughter. Simon and Schuster, 1995.
Fiesta Fireworks. Lothrop, 1998.
Fiesta U.S.A. (English and Spanish editions). Lodestar Books, 1995.
Freighters. Crowell, 1985.
The Golden Lion Tamarin Comes Home. Macmillan, 1994.
Growing Older. Dutton, 1978.
Harvest. Marshall Cavendish, 2001.
Helping Out. Clarion, 1985.
I Feel. Dutton, 1978.
It's a Baby. Dutton, 1979.
Man and Mustang. Macmillan, 1992.
Mayeros: A Yucatec Maya Family. Lothrop, 1997.
Monster Movers. Dutton, 1984.
Monster on Wheels. Dutton, 1974.
My Camera. Crown, 1992.
Pablo Remembers: The Fiesta of the Day of the Dead. Lothrop, 1993. Spanish edition: *Pablo recuerda: La fiesta del día de los muertos.*
The Piñata Maker/El Piñatero. Harcourt Brace, 1994.
Powwow. Harcourt Brace Jovanovich, 1993.
Ricardo's Day. Scholastic, 1994.
Riverkeeper. Macmillan, 1989.
Sheepdog. Lothrop, Lee, and Shepard, 1985.
Teamwork. Crowell, 1983.
Turtle Watch. Macmillan, 1987.
Viva Mexico! The Fiestas. Marshall Cavendish, 2002.
Viva Mexico! The Folk Arts. Marshall Cavendish, 2002.
Viva Mexico! The Foods. Marshall Cavendish, 2002.
Viva Mexico! The Past. Marshall Cavendish, 2002.
Viva Mexico! The People. Marshall Cavendish, 2002.

Photographed

The American Family Farm by Joan Anderson. Harcourt Brace Jovanovich, 1989.
Artist of Handcrafted Furniture at Work by Maxine Rosenberg, 1988.
Balance It by Howard Smith. Four Winds, 1982.
Being Adopted by Maxine Rosenberg. Lothrop, Lee, and Shepard, 1984.

Being a Twin, Having a Twin by Maxine Rosenberg. Lothrop, Lee, and Shepard, 1985.
Bodies by Barbara Brenner. Dutton, 1973.
Brothers and Sisters by Maxine Rosenberg. Clarion, 1991.
Caras by Barbara Brenner. Spanish by Alma Flor Ada. Dutton, 1977.
Christmas on the Prairie by Joan Anderson. Clarion, 1985.
City! New York by Shirley Climo. Macmillan, 1990.
City! San Francisco by Shirley Climo. Macmillan, 1990.
City! Washington, D.C. by Shirley Climo. Macmillan, 1991.
Dolphins at Grassy Key by Marcia Seligson. Macmillan, 1989.
Earth Keepers by Joan Anderson. Gulliver Green/Harcourt Brace, 1993.
Faces by Barbara Brenner. Dutton, 1970.
Finding a Way by Maxine Rosenberg. Lothrop, Lee, and Shepard, 1988.
Finding Your First Job by Sue Alexander. Dutton, 1980.
The First Thanksgiving Feast by Joan Anderson, Clarion, 1984.
French Pioneers by Joan Anderson. Lodestar, 1989.
From Map to Museum by Joan Anderson. Morrow Junior Books, 1988.
The Glorious Fourth in Prairietown by Joan Anderson. Morrow, 1986.
Grandpa Had a Windmill, Grandma Had a Churn by Louise Jackson. Parents, 1977.
Handtalk: An ABC of Finger Spelling and Sign Language by Remy Charlip and Mary Beth Miller. Four Winds Press, 1974.
Handtalk Birthday: A Number and Story Book in Sign Language by Remy Charlip and Mary Beth Miller. Four Winds Press, 1987.
Handtalk School with Mary Beth Miller. Four Winds Press, 1991.
Handtalk Zoo with Mary Beth Miller. Four Winds Press, 1989.
Harry's Helicopter by Joan Anderson. Morrow Junior Books, 1990.
Jackpot of the Beagle Brigade by Sam Epstein and Beryl Epstein. Macmillan, 1987.
Joshua's Westward Journal by Joan Anderson. Morrow Junior Books, 1987.
Just beyond Reach by Bonnie Larkin Nims. Scholastic, 1992.
Living in Two Worlds by Maxine Rosenberg. Lothrop, Lee, and Shepard, 1986.
Making a New Home in America by Maxine Rosenberg. Lothrop, Lee, and Shepard, 1986.
Miguel Lost and Found in the Palace. Museum of New Mexico Press, 2002.
Mom Can't See Me by Sally Hobart Alexander. Macmillan, 1990.
Mom's Best Friend by Sally Hobart Alexander. Macmillan, 1992.
My Feet Do by Jean Holzenthaler. Dutton, 1979.
My Friend Leslie by Maxine Rosenberg. Lothrop, Lee, and Shepard, 1983.
My New Baby-Sitter by Christine Loomis. Morrow Junior Books, 1991.
My Special Friend by Floreva G. Cohen. Board of Jewish Education, 1986.
Over Here It's Different: Carolina's Story by Mildred Leinweber Dawson. Macmillan, 1993.
Over on the River by Louise A. Jackson. Parents Press, 1980.
Pioneer Children of Appalachia by Joan Anderson. Clarion, 1986.
Richie's Rocket by Joan Anderson. Morrow Junior Books, 1993.
Sally's Submarine by Joan Anderson. Morrow Junior Books, 1995.
A Snake Lover's Diary by Barbara Brenner. Dutton, 1970.
Spanish Pioneers of the Southwest by Joan Anderson, 1989.
Twins on Toes by Joan Anderson. Lodestar, 1993.
A Williamsburg Household by Joan Anderson. Clarion, 1988.

George Ancona is the highly regarded photographer and/or author of more than seventy books for young readers. His fine work has won numerous awards, which are listed with the following reviews of the individual books. The son of Mexican parents from small villages in the Yucatán, he grew up in Coney Island. He has enjoyed a long and distinguished career in a variety of art-related fields, including filmmaking, embarking on his work in children's literature in 1970. Since then, he has become one of the most respected names in the field. Presently, he lives in Santa Fe, New Mexico, with his family.

Born in New York City in 1929, the year of the stock market crash and the beginning of the depression, Ancona was named Jorge Efraín. But since they lived in the United States, he was called George except by his family, who used the diminutive, Jorgito. Living in Brooklyn, the Ancona family's neighbors were immigrants from Poland, Germany, Italy, Ireland, and other European countries. Ancona's family spoke Spanish at home. His sister, Neri Alicia, was born three years after him and had a heart condition that resulted in her being unable to attend school. Their playpen was the fire escape, where their mother placed blankets and they spent hours sitting and playing. Ancona remembers, "Climbing over the windowsill was like entering a rocket ship to visit another world" (*Something about the Author Autobiography Series, SAAS*, 2). At other times, he sat at the kitchen table drawing or helped his mother hang freshly washed clothes on the clothesline attached to the rear window of the apartment. Now when he hears certain songs, they take him back to those days when his mother sang in Spanish while she worked.

As they were for many people, the depression years were difficult for Ancona's parents. To supplement the income that he earned working sporadically as an accountant, his father tried selling the apple dumplings that his wife made. He also worked on a construction project and as a men's suit salesperson. Ancona's mother made a quilt from sample fabric swatches saved from that job, a blanket that kept him warm during those cold winters of his childhood. He remembers pretending that the squares were acres of farmland for his toy animals when he was sick and had to stay in bed. Ancona wore the outgrown clothes given to him by a cousin. He fondly remembers a leather aviator's helmet, complete with goggles, which inspired many flights of imagination. He also inherited an old Boy Scout uniform. He wryly recalls, "While all the other tenderfoots had spanking new uniforms, mine was older and more experienced" (*SAAS*, 3).

The family moved to Coney Island by the time Ancona was ready to start school. They lived in a cold-water flat that was heated by a wood-burning stove in the kitchen. Ancona wore a wool hat while he slept on a cold, enclosed porch. When he got up to get ready for school, he made a mad dash to dress by the warm stove. He will long remember his first day of school. The building was an imposing sight with its iron gates and heavy wire mesh on the windows. Ancona's family spoke only Spanish at home, and this plus many other new experiences and faces resulted in a very stressful day. "At some point during the day I wet my pants, which only increased my sense of alienation" (*SAAS*, 4).

Ancona's parents became active in the Parent–Teacher Association (PTA). He remembers listening and watching them with a mixture of pride and embarrassment at school meetings. His friends came to his house for tacos and Mexican hot chocolate, which his mother beat in a carved wooden bowl. By sixth grade, Ancona was on the Safety Squad and had the dubious responsibility of enforcing rules, which his friends from the nearby parochial school didn't appreciate. This resulted in threats, fights, and torn shirts, which, of course, upset his parents. His mother supplemented the family income doing sewing piecework at home; his father also brought home wire piecework. Ancona helped out by taking care of his younger sister, trimming lace on fancy garments, and bending small wires that were used in displays. The family worked while sitting around the table, listening to the radio. Ancona's imagination soared as he listened to *Green Hornet*, *Let's Pretend*, and *The Lone Ranger*.

Coney Island was a fascinating place for a young child. Ancona remembers the amusements parks, silent movies, and outings to various parts of the city. He feels that the hours spent exploring the docks of the East River prepared him for his wanderlust years. He was often filled with wonder and awe at the sights and sounds of the ships, and often his imagination took flight. His father usually recorded these outings with his camera. Ancona became very impatient watching him make prints in the makeshift darkroom in the family bathroom and was sure that he would never be a photographer. But he did enjoy making shaded pencil drawings of the pictures in his father's photography books. As a teenager, he sketched and painted the boat wrecks, tugboats, barges, and oil tanks along the Coney Island Creek, which he describes as a foul-smelling, polluted body of water, even then. He recalls being a very quiet child and sitting for hours by the creek, doing woodcuts.

From the age of twelve, Ancona worked after school, on Saturdays, and on school holidays in his neighbor's car service business. Always a resourceful person, he also collected newspapers, rags, and metal and sold them at the junkyard down the street.

In junior high, Ancona's favorite classes were shop classes where he studied metalwork, woodworking, and electrical wiring. The sign-painting class where he learned the pleasures of painting letters and making the backdrop scenery and murals for a school play had a strong influence on his life's work. The beginning of his career as a designer started in high school. As a part of the Art Squad, a group of students interested in art, he helped design the yearbook and made posters for school events and competitions. The chair of the Art Department invited top designers, photographers, and architects to speak to, and display their work for, the students. This early exposure to professional artists inspired Ancona tremendously.

While still in high school, Ancona attended art classes at the Brooklyn Museum. It was there that he met and showed his work to Rufino Tamayo, the celebrated Mexican painter, who invited him to visit him in Mexico. After graduation, Ancona took a bus to Mexico City, where Señor Tamayo arranged for him to attend the Academia de San Carlos, the leading art school in Mexico. He spent his evenings studying lithography at La Escuela de Arte del Libro (School for the Art of the Book). He took his father's camera on this trip and for the first time was serious about his work with it. He sketched, painted, and photographed and learned a great deal. Images of poverty seared themselves into his conscience, and he did several paintings of poor people. While in Mexico, Ancona went to Yucatán to meet his relatives, where his grandmother took him on memorable rounds of visits to various strands of the family.

Back in New York, Ancona entered the Art Students' League on scholarship from the Art Squad. When his scholarship ended, he served as an apprentice in art studios. When his portfolio was professional enough, he got a job in the promotion department of the *New York Times*. Next, he worked as a staff designer at *Esquire* magazine. Subsequent jobs included art director for *Apparel Arts, Seventeen*, and NBC Television and Radio Networks. From television, Ancona moved into the world of fashion, where he learned a great deal about photography and film production.

During his spare time, Ancona collaborated with a friend to make his first film, *The Gift*, about an older successful artist and a young couple on an island in the East River. Next he made a documentary of the South Bronx. He notes, "Having started out as someone who loved to draw and paint I was spending more and more time with film and still cameras" (*SAAS*, 11). When he was thirty years old, he decided to move into the uncertain, but freeing, world of freelancing. He produced films for *Sesame Street* and worked on documentaries and industrial films in Brazil, Pakistan, Hong Kong, and Japan. His work filming a children's series titled *Big Blue Marble* took him to Iceland, Tunisia, and Switzerland.

Ancona's introduction to children's books came when his friend Barbara Brenner invited him to illustrate with photographs a book that she had written. The publication of *Faces* in 1970 was the beginning of a new direction for Ancona, one that has proven to be very satisfying and successful. His next step was to write the text for a book of his photographs. This was an exciting challenge because he had never studied writing. To his delight, he has found that by combining words with his pictures, he can enhance the meaning of his stories. "To me, words seem like the colors that I would use to paint pictures" (*SAAS*, 16).

"In time I've discovered that the world of children's books suits me just fine" (*SAAS*, 14). Fulfilling his childhood dreams of traveling and exploring new places, Ancona's research has taken him to Honduras, Brazil, Mexico, and many other places. He makes strong connections with people while working on these projects. He has many interesting stories to share about each book that he has written and/or photographed. His unique work has been recognized for the wide range of topics explored, the fascinating text, and breathtaking photography. His numerous books reflect his good humor, his infectious energy, and his compassionate eye for the human side of people and events.

More Information about George Ancona

Contemporary Authors, Volume 19, 21.
Contemporary Authors Online. The Gale Group, 2001.
"Going around the Block" by George Ancona. *The Multicolored Mirror: Cultural Substance in Literature for Children and Young Adults*, edited by Merri V. Lindren. Cooperative Children's Book Center, 1991.
Multicultural Voices in Contemporary Literature by Frances Ann Day. Heinemann, 1999.
Something about the Author Autobiography Series (*SAAS*). Volume 18, 1–18.
Something about the Author. Volume 12, 10–12.

Selected Works by George Ancona

Barrio: José's Neighborhood

Grades K–4

- Barrios
- Murals
- San Francisco

This wonderful book features eight-year-old José Luís, who lives in the Mission District of San Francisco. Colorful photographs and lively text describe the school (César Chávez Elementary School), recreation, holidays, and family life as experienced by José. Of special interest are the photographs and descriptions of the magnificent murals on the walls and buildings "that sing out the stories of the people who live there—their backgrounds, heartaches, and hopes for the future." Glossary included. Spanish edition: *Barrio: El barrio de José.*

Carnaval

Grades 3–7

- Brazil
- *Carnaval*
- Festivals

Beautiful photographs and fascinating text capture the festivities of the annual celebration of *Carnaval* as experienced in the small Brazilian town of Olinda. In the author's note, Ancona provides information about the history of *Carnaval*.

Cuban Kids

Grades 3–7

- Cuba
- Traditions

Renowned photojournalist George Ancona first went to Cuba in 1957, when the revolution was already under way. Forty years later he returns to capture on film the ways in which Cuba has changed since his last visit. What results is a timely and remarkable photo-study of the children of Cuba. Colorful pictures show Cuban children at school, in a doctor's office, making music, dancing, and celebrating. Ancona concludes, "Despite the hardships, the shortages, and the embargo, Cuban kids are growing up with a love of their country, traditions, and culture" (39). *BookList* wrote, "A very fine portrait of modern Cuba." Includes a map, author's note, and glossary.

Fiesta U.S.A.

Grades 2–6

- Day of the Dead
- Las Posadas
- Los Matachines
- Three Kings' Day

Welcome to four lively fiestas celebrated by Latino/a people who live in the United States. George Ancona's vibrant photographs and warm text pay tribute to the festivals that celebrate the Day of the Dead, Las Posadas, Los Matachines, and Three Kings' Day. On November 2, we go to San Francisco, where we join the procession that commemorates people who have died. Next we go to Albuquerque, New Mexico, where we join Sandra and her family in the procession of Las Posadas, which takes place during the nine days before Christmas. Our next stop is in the tiny village of El Rancho in northern New Mexico, where we learn about Los Matachines. The Matachines represent the arrival in Mexico of Hernán Cortés, the Spanish conqueror of the Aztecs. On January 6, our last stop is in East Harlem in New York City for Three Kings' Day. Twelve days after Christmas, La Fiesta de los Reyes Magos celebrates the three kings who came bearing gifts for the baby Jesus. In the introduction, Ancona tells us that when Spanish-speaking people leave their homelands for the United States, they bring their customs, fiestas, and foods. The four fiestas featured in the book bring the community together, preserve traditions, and provide an opportunity to have fun. "For the children of immigrants, fiestas offer a chance to experience a bit of what it was like for their parents growing up in the old country." Ancona has created a beautiful book with lively illustrations and interesting text. Spanish edition: *Fiesta U.S.A.*

Harvest

Américas Commended List

Grades 2–7

- César Chávez
- Food
- Migrant Farmworkers

This poignant book tells the story of the unsung workers who endure backbreaking work in the fields to put food on our tables. Vibrant photographs show laborers picking strawberries, lettuce, green peppers, broccoli, celery, raspberries, grapes, pears, and apples. Interspersed throughout the book are first-person accounts from people such as Señor Jesus Suarez, who retired after forty-seven years in the fields. This important book ends with a profile of César Chavez. Glossary included.

Living in Two Worlds

Grades 2–Up

- Biracial Children

A photo-essay about the special world of biracial children, this book presents an introduction to the issues involved, including the advantages of being from two cultures and the problems and conflicts that it entails. Approximately 2 percent of children born in the United States are of mixed racial and ethnic heritage. With warmth and sensitivity, the author and photographer present the stories of several biracial children, often in their own words. The book tells us, "In big and small ways, biracial children are reminded frequently that they look different from other children." They are subjected to teasing and embarrassing questions. Text and photographs show the children interacting with both sets of grandparents, sharing their traditions with their classmates at school, and inviting friends into their homes. The book ends with an afterword by a psychologist in which he states, "Biracial children are potential participants in the experiences, customs, joys, sorrows, accomplishments, and wisdoms of two cultures. If concerned adults care to pass this heritage along to them over time, the children, in turn, will amaze us with the loving and wonderfully creative ways they combine the two."

This book is written for young children and therefore presents a positive view of the issues. A book for older children might go into the complexities of living in a racist society that does not provide support for people of color. Many authors from mixed backgrounds write compellingly about being outcasts of both cultures and about being stigmatized by the larger society. Mature students will find much to discuss as they analyze this book and the comments made in the afterword. Hopefully the following statement is accurate and not just wishful thinking: "My own study of biracial teenagers reveals a psychological profile of children who have a robust self-image and carry on largely satisfying and constructive relationships with family and friends." Ancona goes on to say that his subjects come largely from families where a premium has been placed on family sharing and multiracial living. In my experience as a teacher of biracial students, the families avoid talking with their children about their backgrounds. One third grade student told me that his mother was Korean. When I gently responded that then he was half Korean, he didn't believe me. Denial, erasure, and marginalization are more widespread than many of us want to believe.

What can we do as writers, educators, librarians, and parents to create a society that celebrates differences? It may be appropriate to paint a rosy picture for the very young, but at what age do we start telling young people the truth? Many of us grew up knowing about prejudice. Others remember feeling betrayed when they discovered that things were not as they had been presented to them when they were children. How do we balance a reassuring, positive outlook with the realities of living in an oppressive, hierarchical society? *Living in Two Worlds* provides a starting place for lively discussions and illuminative writing.

Making a New Home in America

Grades 2–6

- Immigration
- Newcomers

Text and photographs present the stories of five children who came to the United States as immigrants from Japan, Cuba, India, Guyana, and

Vietnam. With warmth, sensitivity, and frankness, the author and photographer explore the feelings of these newcomers as they adjust to a new country. Leaving the country of one's birth, and saying good-bye to old friends and familiar customs are not easy. Adjusting to a new language, strange schools, and unfamiliar people is realistically portrayed. The children talk about the confusion, fear, and sadness that they experienced when they first arrived. The difficulty of making new friends is acknowledged as the children talk about the way that they were teased, ignored, and misunderstood. After a period of adjustment, they begin to become aware of the positive aspects of their new home. They still enjoy going back to their homelands to visit but gradually start calling the United States home. The book ends with a reassuring profile of sixteen-year-old Tuan, originally from Vietnam, who has been in the United States for ten years. For immigrants who are having difficulty adjusting, this book, if it is translated into their languages, will provide hope that things will improve. Hopefully, it will help those who were born in the United States to be more sensitive and welcoming toward their newcomer classmates and neighbors.

Over Here It's Different: Carolina's Story

Grades 3–7

- Dominican Republic
- Gender Roles
- Immigration
- Moving
- Newcomers

The experiences of an eleven-year-old girl who emigrated from the Dominican Republic to New York City when she was seven are related in text and photographs. Eleven-year-old Carolina Liranzo reflects on the many changes that she has encountered during the past four years and discusses the two worlds she lives in. She misses aspects of her earlier life and realizes that someday she may want to go back to live in the Dominican Republic. At first the adjustment to the noisy, crowded, cold city and new language were difficult, and Carolina was homesick. But after four years, she is quick to point out all the advantages of her new home. Her school experience has been a positive one, unlike that of many newcomers who are subjected to ridicule and exclusion. Carolina's parents are concerned that she will forget her first language, Spanish. They want to maintain a firm hold on the language and most of the values of the Dominican Republic.

Carolina is an interesting, appealing person, and her story is an upbeat, hopeful one. The author chose a child who has weathered the difficult adjustment period and who loves both of her countries. This book provides a contrast to other volumes that reveal the isolation, heartbreak, and confusion experienced by the newcomer who is greeted with indifference, suspicion, hostility, and even violence. The rosy picture presented in *Over Here It's Different* combined with other immigrant stories will provide a balanced picture for readers.

Pablo Remembers: The Fiesta of the Day of the Dead

Bank Street College Children's Book of the Year

Grades 4–Up

- All Souls' Day
- All Hallows Eve
- All Saints Day

During the three-day celebration of the Day of the Dead, a young Mexican boy and his family make elaborate preparations to honor the spirits of loved ones who have died. For Pablo, Shaula, Cristina, and Angelita, this year's celebration is especially important. Their *abuelita* (grandmother) died two years ago, and they miss her very much. On October 31, All Hallows Eve, the children make a children's altar, to invite the *angelitos* (spirits of dead children) to come back for a visit. November 1 is All Saints Day, and the adult spirits will come to visit. November 2 is All Souls Day, when the families go to the cemetery to decorate the graves and tombs of their relatives. The three-day fiesta is filled with marigolds, the flowers of the dead; *muertos* (the bread of the dead); sugar skulls; cardboard skeletons; tissue paper decorations; fruit and nuts; incense, and other traditional foods and decorations.

Creating *Pablo Remembers* was a very special experience for photojournalist George Ancona. He later wrote, "Recently I have been going back to my roots for subjects to photograph and write about" (*SAAS*, 14). The idea for the book was rejected by thirteen publishers before Lothrop, Lee, and Shepard offered him a contract to write it. The children featured in the book became like nieces and nephews to him while he was taking the pictures and researching the project. His beautiful photographs accompany his fascinating text, resulting in an engaging book that will delight and teach readers of all ages. He includes a note at the end of the book in which he provides more information about the history of the celebration of the Day of the Dead. He notes, "Publicly, the community makes light of death and pokes fun at it. Privately, people honor the memories of their deceased family members." The book ends with a glossary of Spanish words such as *comparsa* (a costumed parade), *estampa* (a die-cut tissue paper design), and *velita* (a small candle). Spanish edition: *Pablo recuerda: La fiesta del día de los muertos.*

The Piñata Maker/El Piñatero

Parents' Choice Award
Grades 2–7

- Bilingual
- Fiestas
- Mexico
- Piñatas

Told in English and Spanish, this colorful book describes how Don Ricardo, a craftsperson from Ejutla de Crespo, Oaxaca, Mexico, makes piñatas for all the village birthday parties and other fiestas. Now seventy-seven years old, Tío Rico, as everyone calls him, has been making piñatas for fifteen years. Before that he made sombreros, but now his rheumatism limits his activities. Well known for his beautiful piñatas, he also makes puppets, masks, decorations for the church, and figures for processions. The many steps involved in creating a piñata from making the paste to cutting and gluing the tissue paper are documented through photographs and text. For this book, Don Ricardo demonstrates how to make a swan, a carrot, and the traditional *piñata de picos*, or star piñata, but he also makes flowers, animals, and fruits. As he works, he stops several times to answer the door to a boy who is selling old newspapers and some children who are picking up puppets for a party. The third knock brings visitors who are selecting a piñata for a birthday party to which Don Ricardo is invited. After the piñata is filled with a wonderful assortment of fruits, nuts, sugarcane, small toys, and sweets, the party begins.

Author and photographer George Ancona has created a beautiful book about a fascinating art, one that is sure to enhance appreciation for the skill and hard work that go into making piñatas. He adds a note on how he and his children made simple piñatas from boxes and balloons. *The Piñata Maker* provides a glimpse of life in a village in southern Mexico and an engaging portrait of a talented craftsperson. Ancona notes that the setting of this book is in the same area as *Pablo Remembers*, which he had researched a year earlier. He enjoyed returning to visit his old friends from the earlier book.

Turtle Watch

American Library Association Notable Book
Children's Science Book Award
New York Academy of Sciences Award
Junior Literary Guild Selection
Grades 1–6

- Endangered Species
- Turtles
- Wildlife Conservation

"After surviving seventy million years of environmental upheaval, sea turtles are on the verge of extinction." So begins this eloquent tribute to the people who are working to save these magnificent animals. In black-and-white photographs and gentle, informative text, George Ancona documents the efforts of oceanographers to protect these endangered animals. Noting that sea turtles are easy prey to humans who kill and use them for food, jewelry, wallets, shoes, and cosmetics, he writes that many nations are now supporting projects to protect turtles and to alert people to their rapid disappearance. Ancona takes us to a beach near the small town of Praia do Forte on the northeast coast of Brazil, where one of many wildlife conservation projects is located. He describes how the oceanographers find the turtle nest and carefully remove the eggs for safekeeping. When the eggs have hatched, they help the baby turtles make their way back to the ocean. The local fisherpeople and their children are now taking the eggs to the scientists, not to market.

Ancona's descriptions and photographs of each step in the painstaking process, including a loggerhead turtle laying her eggs, two children carefully gathering eggs and taking them to the scientists, and the tiny turtles valiantly struggling into the ocean make for rewarding reading. This important book makes a strong case for cherishing and preserving the sea turtle and, by extension, all the precious members of our planet. It shows how a well-planned conservation program can address the economic needs of local residents while preserving the environment.

Viva Mexico! The Fiestas

Viva Mexico! The Folk Arts

Viva Mexico! The Foods

Viva Mexico! The Past

Viva Mexico! The People

Grades 2–6

- Art
- Ethnology
- Fiestas
- Food
- History
- Mexico
- Social Life and Customs

This beautifully photographed series provides an excellent introduction to the diverse people of Mexico. Each carefully researched book includes a bibliography, glossary, and index.

Gloria Anzaldúa

Photo: Margaret Randall

Chicana (1942–)
Birthday: September 26
Contact: Aunt Lute Books
P.O. Box 410687
San Francisco, CA 94141
(415) 826-1300

To write, to be a writer, I have to trust and believe in myself as a speaker, as a voice for the images. I have to believe that I can communicate with images and words and that I can do it well. A lack of belief in my creative self is a lack of belief in my total self and vice versa—I cannot separate my writing from any part of my life. It is all one.

(*Borderlands*, 73)

Books by Gloria Anzaldúa

Borderlands/La frontera: The New Mestiza. Spinsters/Aunt Lute, 1987.

Friends from the Other Side/Amigos del otro lado. Illustrated by Consuelo Méndez. Children's Books Press, 1993.

Making Face, Making Soul/Haciendo caras: Creative and Critical Perspectives by Feminists of Color. Editor. Aunt Lute Foundation, 1990.

Prietita and the Ghost Woman/Prietita y la Llorona. Illustrated by Christina Gonzalez. Children's Book Press, 1995.

This Bridge Called My Back: Writings by Radical Women of Color, coedited with Cherríe Moraga. Persephone Press, 1981, 1983; Third Woman Press, 2002.

This Bridge We Call Home: Radical Visions for Transformation, coedited with AnaLouise Keating. Routledge, 2002.

This Way DayBreak Comes: Women's Values and the Future, written with Annie Cheatham and Mary C. Powell. New Society Publishers, 1986.

Gloria Anzaldúa is a prominent Chicana lesbian feminist, *tejana* patlache poet, and cultural theorist from the Rio Grande Valley of South Texas, now living in Santa Cruz, California. She is one of the most original and powerful voices in feminist literature, known for her groundbreaking work in tackling the difficult and immense task of changing culture and all its oppressive "interlocking machinations." Her prophetic analysis of the intersections of race, gender, class, language, and sexual orientation offers insights into ways that diverse cultures might begin to come together and heal the wounds inflicted by centuries of oppression. Her vision invokes new human possibility, providing hope that profound changes are possible.

Born a seventh-generation American on the ranch settlement named Jesus Maria of the Valley of South Texas, Anzaldúa is the daughter of Amalia García Anzaldúa and Urbano Anzaldúa. When Anzaldúa was eleven, the family moved to the small town of Hargill, Texas. Her father died when she was fifteen, and she helped support her family by working in the fields weekends, vacations, and summers until she earned her B.A. from Pan American University in 1969. The experience of working in the fields instilled in her a deep respect for farm laborers. She learned about the hardships of being a migrant worker during the year that she traveled with her family from the South Texas valley to the fields of Arkansas. In 1972, she earned her M.A. in English and education from the University of Texas in Austin. She worked as a liaison between migrant camps and public school superintendents, principals, and teachers and was subsequently hired to direct the migrant and bilingual programs for the state. During the ensuing years, she has devoted her energies to writing, speaking, teaching, and leading workshops. She has taught creative writing, Chicano studies, feminist studies, and related classes at the University of Texas, the University of California at Santa Cruz, and Vermont College of Norwich University. She has been a writer-in-residence at the Loft in Minneapolis as well as an artist-in-residence in Chicano studies at Pomona College. She is presently in the doctoral program in literature at the University of California at Santa Cruz.

Writing with admirable candor about her rebellion against the confines of her early home life and women's role, she recounts the struggles of her childhood. She writes about the internalized racism within her own family and how it affected her sense of herself. When she was born, her grandmother inspected her dark skin color. Anzaldúa notes that Mamágrande Locha loved her anyway, because "[w]hat I lacked in whiteness, I had in smartness" (*This Bridge Called My Back*, 198). Her struggles with her mother centered around housework—she resisted her mother's orders to scrub and clean and instead spent her time reading, studying, and drawing. From an early age she knew she was different. "I felt alien, I knew I was alien" (*Borderlands*, 43). She turned to reading—"Books saved my sanity, knowledge opened the locked places in me and taught me how to survive and then how to soar" (*Borderlands*, Preface). The strength of her rebellion enabled her to remain true to herself. She is the only one not only of her family but of the region to pursue a higher education.

The act of reading forever changed her life. But in many of the books that she read, her people were portrayed in racist ways, relegated to the roles of villains, servants, or prostitutes. Her teachers were also racist. She remembers being punished with three raps on the knuckles with a sharp ruler for speaking Spanish at recess at school. She writes about being required to take two speech classes to rid her of her accent at Pan American University. In the award-winning book (Before Columbus Foundation American Book Award) *This Bridge Called My Back*, she writes, "The schools we attended or didn't attend did not give us the skills for writing nor the confidence that we were correct in using our class and ethnic languages. I, for one, became adept at, and majored in English to spite, to show up, the arrogant racist teachers who thought all Chicano children were dumb and dirty" (165–166). In the 1960s she read her first Chicano novel, *City of Night*, by John Rechy, a gay Texan. "For days, I walked around in stunned amazement that a Chicano could write and could get published" (*Borderlands*, 59). When she started teaching, she tried to supplement the required reading with works by Chicanos but was reprimanded and forbidden to do so by the principal. Even in graduate school, she was not allowed to make Chicano literature an area of focus, so she left the Ph.D. program at the University of Texas in 1977.

From the time that she was seven years old, Anzaldúa read in bed with a flashlight and told her sister stories to keep her from telling their mother. The stories that she created night after night were the beginning of her life's work. She now thinks of writers as shape-changers, creating new ways of perceiving the world, new possibilities. She describes the agonies and ecstasies of writing in *Borderlands*. "Daily, I battle the silence.

. . . Daily, I take my throat in my hands and squeeze until the cries pour out" (71–72). Ultimately, her writing brings her great joy—it heals her. When she doesn't write for a prolonged period of time, she gets physically sick. She states that being a writer feels very much like being Chicana or being a lesbian, often coming up against barriers and yet being in a state of limbo where nothing is defined or definite.

With her characteristic strong sense of self, she has broken out of the mold not only in her life but also in her writing. The struggle continues, however. Anzaldúa tells about her mother's reaction to her essay "La Prieta" (The Dark One) in *This Bridge Called My Back,* in which she writes about her childhood and her lesbianism. "My mother told me that if I told the people in my little town that I was a lesbian, she would take a gun and shoot herself" (*Dictionary of Literary Biography,* 9). Her mother refused to welcome her lesbian friends into her home, and Anzaldúa vowed never to go home until she could bring whomever she wanted. After three painful years, her mother relented, realizing that they both had lost. Anzaldúa shows how lesbians and gays are not only ostracized, harassed, and brutalized by the societies in which they live but often excluded, demeaned, and disowned by their own families.

Going against the tide at home, in her culture, in education, and in society, Anzaldúa transfers the hard-won, but valuable, lessons to her writing. She has earned a reputation as an innovative writer who utilizes a daring approach, mixing language, modes, and genres. Her work breaks new ground, opening up a fresh space for new inquiry, thought, and vision. A prolific writer, her work appears in myriad journals, anthologies, and alternative presses. Recently, she entered a new writing field—children's literature. Her first book for young readers, *Friends from the Other Side/Amigos del otro lado,* is a bilingual picture book featuring an admirable young Chicana and her new friends who have just crossed the United States/Mexico border in search of a new life. Her second book for children, *Prietita and the Ghost Woman,* tells the story of a young Mexican American girl who becomes lost during her search for an herb to cure her mother and is aided by the legendary *la Llorona.* Anzaldúa is currently working on a short story collection and a book theorizing on the production of writing, knowledge, and identity.

Anzaldúa, who identifies herself as queer or dyke, often reads her work publicly, gives lectures, and participates in workshops and panel discussions. She serves on editorial boards for various publications nationally and has been a contributing editor of the lesbian press journal *Sinister Wisdom* since 1984 and was a coeditor of the SIGNS lesbian issue. In addition to the awards for her books, she received a National Endowment for the Arts Fiction Award, the 1991 Lesbians Rights Award, and the Sappho Award of Distinction in 1992. Although she is involved with many other activities, writing is her first priority. "The Writing is my whole life, my obsession" (*Borderlands,* 75).

More Information about Gloria Anzaldúa

Borderlands/La frontera: The New Mestiza. Spinsters/Aunt Lute, 1987.
Contemporary Authors Online. The Gale Group, 2000.
Dictionary of Literary Biography. Volume 122, 8–17.
The Gay and Lesbian Literary Heritage: A Reader's Companion to the Writers and Their Works, from Antiquity to the Present edited by Claude J. Summers. Henry Holt, 1995.
Gloria E. Anzaldúa: Interviews/Entrevistas, edited by AnaLouise Keating. Routledge, 2000.
Making Face, Making Soul/Haciendo caras: Creative and Critical Perspectives by Feminists of Color. Aunt Lute Foundation, 1990.
The Oxford Companion to Women's Writing in the United States, edited by Cathy N. Davidson and Linda Wagner-Martin. Oxford University Press, 1995.
This Bridge Called My Back: Writings by Radical Women of Color. Persephone Press, 1981; Third Woman Press, 2001.
Women Reading and Writing: Self-Invention in Paula Gunn Allen, Gloria Anzaldúa, and Audre Lorde by AnaLouise Keating. Temple University Press, 1996.

Selected Works by Gloria Anzaldúa

Borderlands/La frontera: The New Mestiza

Literary Journal's One of the 38 Best Books of 1987

Hungry Mind Review's One of the Best Books of the Twentieth Century

College–Adult

- Chicana Studies
- Lesbian Studies
- Women's Studies
- Poetry

This book is included as a resource for educators, librarians, and parents in the hope that its insights into the debilitating nature of racism and other oppressions will provide valuable information to adults as they plan ways to continue the important work of creating a fair and just society.

Gloria Anzaldúa explores in prose and poetry the contradictory existence of those living on the border between cultures and languages. In this powerful, multifaceted work, which defies conventional notions of genre, she interweaves Spanish and English, poetry, memoir, and historical analysis. Breaking out of traditional forms and employing a remarkable combination of imagination, insight, scholarly research, and poignancy, she has created a unique, illuminating document. It makes a significant contribution to our understanding of how deeply cultural differences cut and how important it is that we learn to regard them as strengths instead of problems.

The book's first half, "*Atravesando Fronteras*/Crossing Borders," is composed of essays that mix theory, prose, poetry, history, anthropology, psychology, literature, and personal and collective experience. The second half of the book is made up of eloquent poetry. The book opens at the border, the steel curtain, "the 1,950 mile-long open wound. . . . This is my home/this thin edge of barb wire" (2). Anzaldúa grew up in the Lower Rio Grande Valley of South Texas near the United States/Mexico border. "I grew up between two cultures, the Mexican (with a heavy Indian influence) and the Anglo (as a member of a colonized people in our own territory). I have been straddling that *tejas*-Mexican border, and others, all my life." This is a place of contradictions, where cultures clash and economic systems collide. "*Tejanos* lost their land and, overnight, became the foreigners."

Anzaldúa's painful, ongoing journey toward mestiza self-retrieval takes her through many barriers and obstacles: the psychological borderlands, the spiritual borderlands, language borderlands, and sexual orientation borderlands. In the section titled "Fear of Going Home: Homophobia," she writes, "For the lesbian of color, the ultimate rebellion she can make against her native culture is through her sexual behavior" (19). She notes that homosexuals of color have been at the forefront of all liberation struggles in this country. (Because homophobia forces some of us into the closet, our presence is not always obvious.) Anzaldúa is an inspiring example of a lesbian of color who is working to create new possibilities, striving to pull the human race into a future free from oppression.

On this personal, historical, and mythic odyssey, Anzaldúa writes about patriarchy, La Llorona, Coatlicue, Serpent Skirt, the Aztec War of Flowers, the United Farm Workers, her childhood, her writing process, the sexual victimization of women, the history of Texas, and much more. She juxtaposes personal narrative with historical analysis, naturalism with surrealism, fear with courage. In "How to Tame a Wild Tongue," she speaks of linguistic terrorism, tongues of fire, and overcoming the tradition of silence that is imposed on women in her culture. She remembers being punished with three raps on the knuckles with a sharp ruler for speaking Spanish at recess at school. Now she experiments with language proclaiming, "I will have my voice: Indian, Spanish, white. I will have my serpent's tongue—my woman's voice, my sexual voice, my poet's voice. I will overcome the tradition of silence" (59).

In a poem titled "El sonavabitche," Anzaldúa tells the story of the woman advocate who confronts the man who has been exploiting Mexican immigrant laborers. She exposes the cruel practice of working them and then turning them in before paying them. In "*Cihuatlyotl*, Woman Alone," she writes about her refusal to be taken over, her determination to be true to herself. She says that "my life's work/requires autonomy like oxygen" (173). The book ends with an affirming poem, "Don't Give In, Chicanita," in which Anzaldúa writes, "But they will never take that pride/of being mexicana-Chicana-tejana/nor our Indian woman's spirit" (202).

This innovative work provides a glimpse into the mind of a gifted Chicana lesbian writer who is trying to create a new consciousness and find a way to heal the divisions in our world. Hers is a poetically prophetic voice speaking to our hearts and minds about the crucial work of the twenty-first century, which is about the coming together of diverse cultures.

Friends from the Other Side/Amigos del otro lado

Grades 3–Up

- Bilingual
- *Curandera*
- Immigration
- Newcomers
- Poverty

An admirable young Mexican American girl befriends a boy who has crossed the Rio Grande from Mexico with his mother to begin a new life in the United States. This bilingual story opens as Prietita meets Joaquín when he comes to her house to sell firewood. As he leaves, some of the neighborhood kids start calling him names and yelling at him to go back where he belongs. Prietita intervenes when one of the boys picks up a rock to throw at Joaquín. As the story unfolds, the friendship between Prietita and Joaquín grows. But what can she do to help him heal the sores on his arms? And how can she protect Joaquín and his mother from the Border Patrol as it cruises up the street?

In her first book for children, Gloria Anzaldúa has tackled what may be considered by some a controversial topic, one that many would rather ignore. Poverty is a painful subject, but omitting it from the field of children's literature will not make it go away. Anzaldúa, known for her groundbreaking work, is to be commended for her honesty and courage in portraying a neglected group in literature for young readers. By introducing the reader to Joaqúin and his mother, she has enabled us to see them as real people. By Prietita's example, the reader learns how to resist peer pressure and take a stand against prejudice and cruelty. How can we overcome the tendency to bully newcomers and those who are perceived to be weaker? Can children's literature impact these deplorable attitudes? Anzaldúa has taken an important step in addressing these issues.

She has also provided us with an exemplary young Latina protagonist. We need more characters like Prietita who demonstrate that Latinas are courageous, assertive, adventurous, divergent thinkers and good problem solvers and leaders. As the book ends, Prietita takes an important step toward becoming the herb woman's (*curandera*) apprentice. In many Mexican American communities as in this book, the *curandera* plays an important role. Yet they seldom make an appearance in literature for young readers. Here is another significant role model capable of instilling pride in children whose heritage is often ignored or marginalized.

Artist Consuelo Mendez uses watercolors with colored pencils, graphite, and collage to create detailed, realistic illustrations that beautifully accompany the text. Children's Book Press has a reputation for publishing exquisitely illustrated books, and this one is no exception. Mendez's pictures authentically depict the plants and animals of the region; a fascinating variety of lizards and other creatures inhabit the pages of this commendable book.

Making Face, Making Soul/Haciendo caras: Creative and Critical Perspectives by Feminists of Color

Lambda Literary Best Small Press Book Award

College–Adult

- Authorship
- Feminism
- Racism
- Women

This book is included as a resource for educators, librarians, and parents; it makes a significant contribution to our understanding of the complexities and corrosive nature of racism. It is filled with new thought and new dialogue—it is a book that will teach in the most multiple sense of the word.

This brilliant collection of creative and theoretical pieces includes poetry, essays, letters, and short stories by emerging voices as well as established writers. Representing diverse backgrounds and shattering the "neat boundaries of the half dozen categories of marginality that define us" (xvi), the writers are of mixed Latina, Native, Asian, and African ancestries, both lesbian and heterosexual and living in a wide variety of places. Many are professors or students at universities as well as writers. Others are involved in a wide variety of fields such as social work, art, carpentry, philosophy, photography, and publishing. The Latinas included in this collection are Norma Alarcon, Gloria Anzaldúa, Judith Francisca Baca, Lorna Dee Cervantes, Sandra Cisneros, Judith Ortiz Cofer, Julia de Burgos, Edna Escamill, Canéla Jaramillo, María C.

Lugones, Lynda Marín, Papusa Molina, Pat Mora, Cherríe Moraga, Carmen Morones, Laura Munter-Orabona, Tey Diana Rebolledo, Catalina Ríos, Elba Rosario Sánchez, Chela Sandoval, Helena María Viramontes, Berniece Zamora, and Maxine Baca Zinn.

In her introduction to the book, Anzaldúa notes that she waited for years for someone to compile a book that would continue the work that she and Cherríe Moraga started in their groundbreaking book *This Bridge Called My Back*. This new collection deepens the dialogue, brings more voices to the foreground, and enhances the legacy of the earlier work. The title, *Making Face*, is Anzaldúa's metaphor for constructing one's identity. "In this anthology and in our daily lives, we women of color strip off the *máscaras* others have imposed on us, see through the disguises we hide behind and drop our *personas* so that we may become subjects in our own discourses" (xvi).

Divided into seven sections, this powerful anthology addresses crucial issues such as the corrosive legacy that racism inflicts, strategies for combating internalized oppression, finding hope through turning the pain around, moving from silence to voice, political art and writing, building solidarity and alliances, and transformation through other modes of consciousness. Varied voices speak of poverty, tokenism, erasure, violence, active and passive devaluation, exclusion, blistering divisions, silencing, exploitation, cultural collisions, abnegation, servitude, classism, homophobia, elitism, and sexism. They explore a full range of concerns, strategies, affirmations, and solutions in over seventy illuminating pieces.

Much of what Chela Sandoval writes in "Feminism and Racism: A Report on the 1981 National Women's Studies Association Conference" is relevant today. She talks about "identifying and dissecting racism at its roots" (57) and "understanding the nuanced and subtle processes which characterize racism" (61). She calls for "collective efforts to imagine a new affirming movement" (61) and the "opportunity to heal the blistering divisions" (69).

In Edna Escamill's powerful piece, "Corazón de una anciana," she writes, "I would spend much of my adult life pulling the thorns from my heart" (137), and "Evil must be named and condemned no matter where it appears" (138). The pattern of sexual assault and harassment of girls and women is the theme of "Her Rites of Passage" by Lynda Marín.

Many pieces are about language: in her poem, "Refugee Ship," Lorna Lee Cervantes laments, "Mama raised me without language/I'm orphaned from my Spanish name" (182). Pat Mora's poem "Elena" is about an immigrant woman who is determined to learn to speak English. Embarrassed at mispronouncing words, she locks herself in the bathroom to study the new language. Some of the pieces in the book are written in both Spanish and English; many works weave the two languages together.

In the fifth section of the book, "Political Arts, Subversive Acts," women consider the meaning of their art and writing and their positions as writers and artists of color. Carmen Morones' short story should be required reading for all teachers and counselors. "Grace" is about a young Latina who has the potential and interest to pursue her gift for art in college. Morones skillfully delineates the forces that keep her down. Her exchange with the school counselor is sadly being repeated all over the country year after year. After the meeting, she leaves feeling "so small. A nobody. A nobody . . . she was angry at herself for having let herself want something so badly that she knew deep within herself that she could never have" (243). How many of these young women are being denied the opportunity to pursue their dreams? What can educators do to stop this tragedy? Reading this illuminating story and sharing it with coworkers is a good place to begin.

In a fascinating interview with Judith Francisca Baca by Diane Neumaier titled "Our People Are the Internal Exiles," we meet the barrio muralist who works with young people in East Los Angeles to create political art. The cover of *Making Faces, Making Soul* is "Triumph of the Heart," from her participatory mural project, "The World Wall: A Vision of the Future without Fear." This 210-foot mural in seven parts addresses contemporary global issues: war, peace, cooperation, interdependence, and spiritual growth. Baca says, "I see myself as an urban artist, using the entire environment that I work in, which includes the people. If I'm talking about transforming an environment—changing, enhancing, making it more beautiful—then I am talking about changing the people who live in that environment as well" (260). Her journey is a fascinating one that will provide inspiration for artists and educators who are searching for ways to address the issues of racism in their communities.

Writers speak of their love of stories, the power of words to exhort, elucidate, and heal. It is important for women of color to search out their literary roots and connect the past with the present. Tey Diana Rebolledo, a critic, cautions, "If we are to diffuse, support, promote, analyze, and understand the work of our writers, we must let them speak for themselves" (354). In her search for the dominant themes and concerns in the writing of Latinas, she examines the scope and complexity of the recurring figure of *abuelitas* and takes a look at the image of La Malinche.

In a letter to Anzaldúa titled "Recognizing, Accepting and Celebrating our Differences," Papusa Molina discusses the work of the Women against Racism Committee in Iowa City. She describes the long, difficult process that they went through to build alliances. The group conducts antioppression workshops, working with others who are involved with antiracism and liberation work. Molina writes about presenting a model where the individual consequences of racism are addressed and a healing process is started. Striving for a new vision, she makes important connections among the myriad exclusions that exist, including those based on race, gender, age, class, sexual orientation, religious/cultural background, physical ability, and mental ability. She believes that "because behaviors and attitudes of oppression are learned, they can be unlearned" (330).

Gloria Anzaldúa, in her deep and prophetic commentary, discusses both intra- and cross-cultural hostilities, calling for greater solidarity and renewed commitment. She feels that a new mestizo consciousness is in the making. In her chosen role as a mediator, she hopes to change culture, to make a profound difference. She writes about recovering ancient identities, of breaking out of old molds, and of finding clarity through building up personal and tribal identities. Anzaldúa speaks compellingly of creating culture, of finding a new way "to explain the world and our participation in it, a value system with images and symbols that connect us to each other and to the planet" (380). Her message is a healing one, filled with hope. She says, "So if we won't forget past grievances, let us forgive. Carrying the ghosts of past grievances *no vale la pena*. It is not worth the grief" (147).

Prietita and the Ghost Woman/Prietita y la Llorona

Smithsonian Notable Book

Américas Honor Award

Grades 3–Up

- Bilingual
- *Curanderas*
- Legendary Characters

Prietita, a young Mexican American girl, becomes lost while searching for an herb to cure her mother and is aided by the legendary ghost woman. This absorbing story begins when Prietita is at the house of her mentor, *la curandera* (the healer). Prietita's younger sister hurries into the yard with the news that their mother is very ill with the old sickness. When Doña Lola, *la curandera*, discovers that she is out of the herb needed, she draws a picture of it for Prietita. As Prietita searches through the woods for the healing plant, she seeks the help of a white-tailed deer, a salamander, a white-wing dove, a jaguarundi, and lightning bugs. As she follows each animal, she journeys deeper into the woods. Several times along the way, she hears a faint crying sound and remembers her grandmother's stories about *la Llorona*, who is said to cry for her lost children and look for other children to steal. Prietita is frightened and lost, but she bravely asks the ghost woman for help. *La Llorona* helps her find the herb and then guides her back to the path.

Gloria Anzaldúa writes that her grandmother used to tell her scary stories about *la Llorona*. In fact, the legends surrounding the ghost woman are well known throughout the Southwest and Mexico. Anzaldúa, like other children, was afraid, but even at an early age, she wondered if there was another side to the ghost woman. Years later, when she studied the roots of her Chicana/*Mexicana* culture, she found that there really is a powerful, positive side to the legendary figure, the female and Indian part of her culture. Anzaldúa, in revealing this positive side of *la Llorona*, hopes to encourage youngsters to be critical thinkers. By looking beyond the surface of things, they may discover hidden truths just as Anzaldúa did with the story of *la Llorona*. Anzaldúa is noted for her groundbreaking vision and writing. Just as she has done in her other fine books, she has opened up a fresh space for new inquiry and thought regarding the legendary character of *la Llorona*. By portraying the ghost woman in a positive way, she is breaking out of a mold that constricts the image of females in literature.

The protagonist of the book is Prietita, who was introduced to readers in Anzaldúa's first book for children, *Friends from the Other Side/Amigos del otro lado*. In the first book, the young Latina took a stand against the prejudice within her own community against recent emigrants from Mexico. Now, in this second book, she bravely searches for the herb that is desperately needed to treat her mother, who is very ill. Once again, Prietita goes against the tide and befriends the unfairly maligned *la Llorona*, and in so doing, illuminates her positive and powerful qualities. Prietita is an exemplary young Latina protagonist. The body of children's literature needs more characters like her who demonstrate that Latinas are courageous, assertive, adventurous, divergent thinkers and good problem solvers and leaders.

As the first book ended, Prietita took an important step toward becoming the herb woman's *(curandera)* apprentice. In many Mexican American communities *las curanderas* play an important role. Yet they seldom make an appearance in literature for young readers. Here is another significant role model capable of instilling pride in children whose heritage is often ignored or marginalized. Now, in the second book, Prietita is working more closely with Doña Lola, learning the traditional healing arts of her people. Anzaldúa notes that, in writing the book, she wanted to convey her respect for *las curanderas*, who know many things about healing that Western doctors are just beginning to learn.

Anzaldúa's story is beautifully complemented by colorful paintings rendered by Christina Gonzales, who is a graphic artist, jeweler, and painter. Her portrayal of Doña Lola is particularly striking with her attractive wrinkles and dignified stance. Here is another rarity in children's literature: a middle-aged woman who is portrayed as a wise, stable leader of the community. In a society that suffers from many prejudices, including looksism, it is refreshing to behold an image of a woman that has not been prettified. The engaging illustrations of the animals and plants of the Southwest add to the appeal of this exquisitely designed book. Children's literature enthusiasts look forward to more innovative books by Anzaldúa in which she encourages us to question the status quo. Her books provide fascinating, well-written stories while breaking stereotypes and shattering myths.

This Bridge Called My Back: Writings by Radical Women of Color

College–Adult

- Feminism
- Women Writers

This powerful collection contains prose, poetry, personal narrative, analysis, interviews, and art by more than fifty African American, Asian American, Latina, and Native American women writers and artists. The book is divided into seven sections: The Roots of our Radicalism; Theory in the Flesh; Racism in the Women's Movement; On Culture, Class and Homophobia; The Third World Woman Writer, The Vision, and Twenty Years Later and includes black-and-white photographs, a full-color art folio, writer and artist biographies, and an extensive bibliography.

Irene Beltrán-Hernández

Mexican American (1945–)
Birthday: April 4
Address: P.O. Box 190
Satin, TX 76685
Irenebhernandez@hotmailcom

For myself, to take away my writing is to take away my spirit.

(*Something about the Author,* 23)

[M]end your ideas and try not to class people into categories. Accept people regardless of skin color or their stations in life.

(*Heartbeat Drumbeat,* 71)

Books by Irene Beltrán-Hernández

Across the Great River. Arte Público Press, 1989.
Heartbeat Drumbeat. Arte Público Press, 1992.
The Secret of Two Brothers. Arte Público Press, 1995.
Woman Soldier/La Soldadera. Blue Rose Books, 1998. Order this book directly from the author.

Writer Irene Beltrán-Hernández is a retired caseworker in adolescent services for Dallas, Texas. She has also worked as an administrative assistant to the mayor of Dallas, a public information assistant, programming director, and vocational counselor. She has been the recipient of a number of awards, including the City of Dallas Service in Excellence Award, San Antonio Writers Festival Award, and a University of Wisconsin Fellowship.

One of eight children, Beltrán-Hernandez was born in Waco, Texas, to Isabelle Quinones Beltrán, a nurse, and Emmett Tovar Beltrán, a mechanic. Their life lacked many material comforts, but young Irene found comfort in books. Her mother encouraged her to read, dropping her off at the public library on Saturday mornings, where she checked out a stack of books large enough to last a week. Reading was her escape from the isolation of the country and the routine of the household. However, she remembers that the books that were available did not have "anything with a Mexican slant or Mexican flavor" (*Metropolitan*, 34). She also enjoyed going to visit her beloved grandmother, with whom she lived until she was five. Her first writing experiences involved keeping a journal, which she wrote on ordinary notebook paper. She wrote late at night by flashlight; as a teenager, she wrote in shorthand to keep her thoughts and feeling private.

Beltrán-Hernández excelled in her studies at Waco High School. She worked as an assistant in the library, one of her favorite places. "My problem was skin color. I was too white for the Chicano kids and too dark for the Anglos" (*Something about the Author, SATA*, 22). Beltrán-Hernández remembers a particularly strict English teacher who ignored her all year except for one telling moment. When he returned a paper that she had written, he looked her right in the eye and said, "Well, well. Someday, you'll be somebody important. Mark my words."

After graduating from high school, she worked at the *Waco News Tribune-Times Herald* as a copy person while attending night school at Baylor University, pursuing a degree in journalism. She later transferred to North Texas State University, where she changed her major to sociology. After college she worked as a school counselor and enjoyed listening to the life stories of her students. A professor at Southern Methodist University invited her to undertake a study dealing with recent illegal immigrants from Mexico. She found the job of interviewing them and compiling the statistics fascinating but tedious. This experience led her to a series of jobs with the city of Dallas. These positions were demanding and sometimes dangerous. "One's life was on the line every minute of the day, but it was also exciting. I quickly learned how to defend my people as well as to stand my own ground within the city network. . . . I turned to writing as my therapy" (*SATA*, 23) She took a number of creative writing classes, joined a local writers' group, and graduated from the Institute of Children's Literature.

Beltrán-Hernández's first book, *Across the Great River*, was rejected numerous times by the major publishing houses. She knew that the book was well written and that the topic, a family's illegal migration from Mexico to the United States across the Rio Grande, was an important one. She tenaciously searched for a publisher. Eventually, the book was published by Arte Público Press and subsequently praised for the contribution that it makes to our understanding of immigration issues. Since then, Beltrán-Hernández has written three additional books. When she isn't writing, she takes time to read her work to students in public schools. She plans to continue to write for young readers. "I write basically for the Chicanito. That's the area I want to stay in" (*Metropolitan*, 34).

More Information about Irene Beltrán-Hernández

Metropolitan: The Dallas Morning News (October, 13, 1992, 27A, 34A).
Something about the Author, Volume 74, 21–23.

Selected Works by Irene Beltrán-Hernández

Across the Great River

Grades 7–Adult

- Illegal Immigration

In her first novel, Irene Beltrán-Hernández chronicles a Mexican family's illegal entry into the United States. Katarina Campos, a young girl, tells the harrowing story of how she crosses the Rio Grande with her parents and baby brother. The border patrol shoots and wounds her mother; her father becomes separated from the others and disappears. The coyotes take Kata, her mother, and brother to the ranchito of Doña Anita, a gifted healer and seer. Mrs. Campos gradually recovers with the help of Anita and finds work in town as a seamstress. Kata begins learning about herbs as she watches Anita treat numerous ill and injured neighbors. As Kata matures and takes a leadership role in helping her family find its way in a strange land, she meets a number of fascinating characters. Each interaction adds to her awareness of herself and others. The family faces new experiences, challenges, and traumas, including violence, illness, and accidents. Finally, they find a way to return to their beloved homeland, where they are reunited with Mr. Campos, who had been jailed by the authorities.

This is a suspenseful novel with well-drawn characters. Against the backdrop of the dangers that illegal immigrant families face, we witness the changes in a young girl as she becomes increasingly aware of the world around her. She learns not to judge people by their appearance; for example, she discovers that her first impression of Anita was completely wrong. Anita is fat and unattractive in the traditional sense; she is also a very loving, strong, resourceful person who provides crucial support for the Campos family. Beltrán-Hernández has created a strong Latina protagonist who learns how to solve problems and take care of herself and those whom she loves; the body of literature for young readers needs more characters like her.

Heartbeat Drumbeat

Publishers Marketing Association Benjamin Franklin Award
Grades 10–Adult

- Death
- Identity
- Navajo/Mexican American Heritage

In her absorbing second novel, Irene Beltrán-Hernández tells the story of Morgana Cruz, the daughter of a Navajo mother and Mexican American father. This is a search for identity; as Morgana says to her mother, "I have a foot in two different cultures and I'm not totally accepted by either race" (89). Heretofore, she has led a sheltered life with her well-to-do parents on a ranch in New Mexico. She speaks Navajo, Spanish, and English, is an accomplished potter, and is confident in any group of people. Early in the book, Isadora, her beloved Navajo mentor, dies. This traumatic loss sets in motion a number of events that quickly change Morgana's life in fundamental ways. She weaves her way through a series of personal, emotional, physical, and cultural challenges. She fights her attraction to Eagle Eyes, an enigmatic Navajo diviner and lawyer, whom Isadora had raised to be her successor. Burial ceremonies, dreams foretelling the future, Rocky Mountain tick fever, herbal medicine, fiestas, a Navajo coming-of-age ceremony, a near-drowning, rape, an attack by a bear, hospitalizations, death, blizzards, loyal horses, wall tapestries, a love triangle, old love letters, and more are all here in this fast-paced, engrossing novel that holds the reader's interest with unexpected twists and turns. This is a well-written book with fine attention to detail. The ending will provide an interesting topic for discussion.

The Secret of Two Brothers

Grades 6–10

- Child Abuse
- Death
- Family Violence
- Prison Life

Twenty-one year-old Francisco "Beaver" Torres is paroled after serving three years in the state penitentiary for being an accomplice in an armed robbery. This solid novel tells the story of his attempt to get back on the right path and to take care of his younger brother, Cande. When he returns home to the barrio in East Dallas, he finds his brother living alone in their run-down house. After years of being abused by her alcoholic husband, their mother died of a stroke while Beaver was in prison. Their father had abandoned Cande but returns periodically to harass and, Beaver finds out later, to beat his younger son. The brothers are overjoyed to be reunited, and Beaver sets out to find a job and to create a decent life for himself and his brother. This readable novel presents serious problems in a realistic way, giving the reader hope that young people like Beaver and Cande do not have to fall through the cracks of the social service and educational systems. Several stereotype-breaking adult role models are featured, including Beaver's tough-minded, but kindhearted, probation officer, Cookie Rodríguez. Beltrán-Hernández has tackled important contemporary issues and produced an encouraging book that will appeal not only to Latino readers but to a wider audience of teenage readers.

Woman Soldier/La Soldadera

Finalist Texas Institute of Letters Best Book for Young Adults
Grades 6–Up

- Career Aspirations
- Gangs

Seventeen-year-old Nico Lorenzo, an underachieving loner, discovers that her high school Reserve Officer Training Corps (ROTC) program offers her hope for a better future. With the support of her loving grandmother, her spirit guide, her ROTC tutor, and a caring librarian, she struggles to turn her life around during her eleventh year of school. She sheds her gang image, fights her attraction to a gang leader, copes with the death of her mother, survives a vicious attack, and dramatically improves her grades. By the end of the book, Nico dreams of being "a woman of strong fortitude. . . . A woman who could do anything if she put her mind to it" (226). Dedicated to "all the *chulas* that belong to Dallas gangs [with] advice to seek a path to a better life," *Woman Soldier* is one of the few young adult novels that deal with the way that gang issues impact the lives of young women.

Carmen T. Bernier-Grand

Puerto Rican American (1947–)
Contact:www.carmen-t.com

I write about the little pieces of my life—the relationships, the social issues, the culture. Writing is a way to make a difference in the world.

(Personal communication)

Books by Carmen T. Bernier-Grand

In the Shade of the Níspero Tree. Orchard Books, 1999; Random, 2001.
Juan Bobo: Four Folktales from Puerto Rico. Illustrated by Ernesto Ramos Nieves. HarperCollins, 1994.
Poet and Politician of Puerto Rico: Don Luis Muñoz Marín. Orchard Books, 1995.
Shake It, Morena! And Other Folklore from Puerto Rico. Illustrated by Lulu Delacre. Millbrook Press, 2002.

Carmen T. Bernier-Grand was born and raised in Puerto Rico. She earned her M.S. degree from the University of Puerto Rico and taught mathematics at the university for seven years. Then she made a decision that surprised her family and friends: she decided to pursue an advanced mathematics degree in the United States. After studying at the University of Connecticut, she moved to Portland, Oregon, where she began writing books for children. She also works in classrooms and libraries, telling stories from around the world.

Bernier-Grand's elementary teachers often told her that she had a vivid imagination, but her sister, Lisette, told her that meant she was a liar. In third grade, she wrote a story about her teacher's chewing gum. When her teacher read the story to the class, Bernier-Grand was afraid that she would be expelled from school for lying. But instead, her teacher arranged for the story to be published in the school newspaper.

Bernier-Grand thinks, writes, and dreams in two languages—Spanish and English. The primary source of her inspiration comes from her vivid memories of her childhood in Puerto Rico. Her editors have advised her to focus on one genre so that her readers can identify her. But she writes what her heart dictates, and thus, her books are all very different. In addition to the awards won by her books, the Portland Public Schools granted Bernier-Grand the Cultural Ambassador Award in 1988.

More Information about Carmen T. Bernier-Grand

www.carmen-t.com
"Adversity and Diversity." *The Oregonian*, November 10, 2001, E1.
"An Interview with Children's Book Author Carmen T. Bernier-Grand" by Cynthia Leitich Smith at www.cynthialeitichsmith.com
Terrific Connections by Toni Buzzeo and Jane Kurtz. Libraries Unlimited, 1999.

Selected Works by Carmen T. Bernier-Grand

In the Shade of the Níspero Tree

A Smithsonian Notable Book of the Year

Oregon Book Award Finalist

A Child Study Children's Book of the Year
Grades 4–7

- Friendship
- Newcomers
- Prejudice
- Puerto Rico
- Socioeconomic Class

Narrator Teresa Giraux recalls her pivotal year in fourth grade, when she struggles to understand prejudice based on race, skin color, and socioeconomic class. Caught between her parents' polarized views, she gradually awakens to the complex subtleties of bigotry expressed in her family, school, and community. Teresa's mother, whose family lost their fortune when she was a child, arranges for her daughter to transfer to a prestigious private school. Here Teresa experiences the sting of discrimination and the pressure to betray her friends that lead to her transformation. *In the Shade of the Níspero Tree* is a courageous book that deals with issues of class and race that are seldom addressed so directly in books for young readers. This book has been praised for its strong characterizations, its well-crafted and educational story, and its clear message about intolerance.

Juan Bobo: Four Folktales from Puerto Rico

Bulletin of the Center of Children's Books Blue Ribbon Award
A Child Study Children's Book of the Year
An Americas Commended Book
Grades Preschool–3

- Folklore
- Humor
- Puerto Rico

Series: *I Can Read.* A lively retelling of four Juan Bobo stories, this collection maintains the immediacy and spirit of the original tales in spite of the simple language used to make it accessible to young readers. Juan Bobo, Puerto Rico's beloved "noodlehead," tries to sell his mother's sugarcane, get water from the stream, and take care of the family pig. This book has been praised for its delicious silliness, brisk dialogue, and authentic depiction of a popular fictional character. A Spanish version of each story is appended.

Poet and Politician of Puerto Rico: Don Luis Muñoz Marín

Grades 5–8

- Biography
- History
- Puerto Rico

Don Luis Muñoz Marín (1898–1980) was the poet-politician responsible for engineering Puerto Rico's status as a commonwealth of the United States and improving living standards for Puerto Ricans. This inspiring biography includes numerous black-and-white photographs, an excellent timeline, extensive chapter notes, a diagrammatical explanation of the sequence of governments of Puerto Rico, a thorough index, and an interesting afterword. *BookList* wrote, "[This] book will be a valuable introduction to an eminent political figure, and it will also raise awareness of the status issue."

Shake It, Morena! And Other Folklore from Puerto Rico

Grades Preschool–3

- Bilingual
- Folklore
- Games
- Music

In this lively potpourri of songs, riddles, games, and stories, we follow a young girl through a school day in Puerto Rico. This entertaining treasure opens with "Waking Up Song," which is sung by the parents to their children and closes with "The Song of El Coquí," about the tiny frog who sings all night. Each entry includes footnotes that provide interesting background information about the topic. In the author's note, Carmen T. Bernier-Grand writes, "It is my hope that educators can use this book to teach Spanish, math (Dos y Dos Son Cuatro), natural science (Puedo o No Puedo), social studies (Playground Passport), reading (The Legend of the Hummingbird), writing (Spelling Game), physical education (Shake It, Morena!)" (3). Artist Lulu Delacre provides colorful illustrations and playfully challenges readers to find the twenty-seven tiny lizards hidden within the pages of this charming book.

Diane Gonzales Bertrand

Mexican American (Tejana) (1956–)
Birthday: March 12
Contact: Arte Público Press
University of Houston
452 Cullen Performance Hall
Houston, Texas 77204-2004

Mexican American people, the young women especially, need to see us reflected in a positive way in books. The focus my works give to Hispanic characters comes more from personal experience than from any desire to convey a political or social statement. I just wanted to write stories about people like myself, and I just happen to be Mexican American.

(Arte Público Press Brochure)

Books by Diane Gonzales Bertrand

Alicia's Treasure. Illustrated by Daniel Lechón. Arte Público Press, 1996.
Carousel of Dreams. Avalon Books, 1992. Out of print.
Close to the Heart. Avalon Books, 1991; Arte Público Press, 2002.
Family/Familia. Illustrated by Pauline Rodriquez Howard. Spanish translation by Julia Mercedes Castillo. Arte Público Press, 1999.
The Last Doll/La última muñeca. Illustrated by Anthony Accardo. Spanish translation by *Alejandra Balestra*. Arte Público Press, 2001.
Lessons of the Game. Arte Público Press, 1998.
Sip, Slurp, Soup, Soup/Caldo, Caldo, Caldo. Illustrated by Alex Pardo DeLange. Spanish translation by Julia Mercedes Castillo. Arte Público Press, 1996.
Sweet Fifteen. Arte Público Press, 1995.
Touchdown for Love. Avalon Books, 1990. Out of print.
Trino's Choice. Arte Público Press, 1999.
Trino's Time. Arte Público Press, 2001.
Uncle Chente's Picnic/El picnic de Tío Chente. Illustrated by Pauline Rodriquez Howard. Spanish translation by Julia Mercedes Castillo. Arte Público Press, 2001.

Diane Gonzales Bertrand, a writer and educator, was born in San Antonio, Texas, in a Westside neighborhood that serves as the setting for many of her books. As a child, she loved to create imaginary playmates and eventually transferred that creativity to the written page. She began writing when she was in fifth grade; her first novel was composed of seventy spiral notebooks written during junior high, high school, and college. She also wrote humorous plays for her drama class, poetry for her relatives, and skits for Girl Scout camp.

Reading was Bertrand's favorite subject in school. "I came from a family of seven children, and the least expensive form of entertainment for us was a weekly trip to the library. Every Saturday my mother or father loaded us into the family station wagon and headed for the library. I started writing because I couldn't find any books about people like me" (Personal Communication).

Bertrand earned college degrees from the University of Texas at San Antonio (B.A. 1979) and Our Lady of the Lake University (M.A. 1992). She taught both middle school and high school and is currently writer-in-residence at St. Mary's University, where she teaches creative writing and English composition. She was selected as a National Hispanic Scholar in 1991 and has been recognized as an outstanding educator and advocate for literacy by San Antonio Youth Literacy Council and the Upward Bound Program.

In addition to her parents, Bertrand acknowledges two teachers who nurtured her passion for writing. A high school English teacher encouraged her to explore new topics and find creative ways to express herself.

Later, a teacher at St. Mary's University inspired Bertrand to write for both children and young adults.

"I have learned to pay attention to the people and places around me and to capture those experiences in my own words, sometimes using the Spanish language that is part of who I am too. . . . I am proud of the fact that my books give readers a sense of pride in their own customs and simple traditions" (*Contemporary Authors Online*. The Gale Group, 2001).

More Information about Diane Gonzales Bertrand

"Author Teaches the Joy of Writing," by Elda Silva. *San Antonio Express-News*. July 13, 1997, 10G.
"College Celebrates Anniversary of Women's Rights Movement," by Michael A. De Leon. *San Antonio College Ranger*. March 6, 1998, n. p.
Contemporary Authors Online. The Gale Group, 2001.
"New Novel Explores Quinceañeras," by Judyth Rigler. *San Antonio Express-News*. May 8, 1995, 6–7C.
"Teacher Turns Author," by Karen Malkowski. *San Antonio Express-News*. October 22, 1991, 12A.
"Writer Creates Strong Mexican American Characters," by Anissa Rivera. *Corpus Christi Caller-Times*. July 20, 1996, C1–2.

Selected Works by Diane Gonzales Bertrand

Alicia's Treasure

Grades 3–6

- Beaches
- Sisters and Brothers
- Vacations

This is the lively story of ten-year-old Alicia Ramos's exhilarating first trip to the beach, where she enjoys many things for the first time and gains new insights into herself, her family, and her relationship with her teenage brother. Full of anticipation, she savors each new sight, sound, smell, and activity, including riding on a ferry, building sand castles, walking on the beach, swimming, and sunset watching. Determined to enjoy the weekend, she finds ways to cope with tar on her new swimming suit, sand in her food, and disagreements with her brother. As she prepares to return home, she reflects on her experiences. "I had all these silly ideas about what a beach is. Then, things weren't like I thought, but it was still terrific" (123).

Family/Familia

First Place in the Latino Literary Hall of Fame's Best Children's Picture Book—Bilingual Category

Grades 1–4

- Bilingual
- Family Reunions

Daniel is a reluctant participant in the Gonzalez family reunion until he discovers who his ancestors were, learns more about his extended family, and finds a new friend, his cousin Brian. This heartwarming story is complemented by attractive, full-page illustrations.

The Last Doll/La última muñeca

Grades 1–4

- Bilingual
- Birthdays
- Dolls
- *Quinceañera*

Sarita, a beautiful old-fashioned doll, sits unnoticed and forlorn on a toy store shelf until the special day when she is given to Teresa Beltrán at her *quinceañera* party. The traditional fifteenth birthday celebration is lovingly detailed through the bilingual text and colorful, full-page illustrations. Later that night, Teresa tells Sarita, "You are my last doll, *la última muñeca*. You will always stay with me, even as I grow into a woman." The author has added a unique dimension to this high-interest story by telling it from the perspective of the doll.

Sip, Slurp, Soup, Soup/Caldo, Caldo, Caldo

Grades K–3

- Bilingual
- Food
- Recipes

The rhythmic text and lively illustrations in this entertaining book sing the praises of a delicious dish that Mamá prepares on rainy Sunday mornings. "Mamá's *caldo* fills up a warm spot inside us. [It] stops the sniffles, softens a cough, slides down a sore throat." This charming book ends with the family enjoying the thick, hot soup with fresh, warm tortillas. Recipe appended.

Sweet Fifteen

Américas Commended Title for Young Adults
Grades 8–Up

- Gender Roles
- Grieving
- *Quinceañera*
- Tradition and Change

Preparations for the traditional *quinceañera* celebration marking Stephanie Bonilla's fifteenth birthday serve as a backdrop for this story about the place of ritual in modern families and communities. Stephanie feels that the *quinceañera* celebration is an outmoded tradition, an archaic custom. The unexpected death of her father and her mother's grief add to her reluctance to go through with plans for her party. But Rita Navarro, the seamstress selected to design Stephanie's *quinceañera* gown, helps her find a way to cherish traditions while adapting to societal changes. This interesting book provides a sensitive examination of the conflicts experienced by teenagers from traditional families as they adapt to the complex realities of modern life. Author Diane Gonzales Bertrand writes, "[Parents have] learned that when a child turns 15, they need all the positive reinforcement they can get. [*Quinceañeras* are] an important way of recognizing that the child is becoming an adult" (*San Antonio Express-News*, May 8, 1995, 6C).

Trino's Choice

Austin Writer's League Teddy Award for Best Children's Book
First Place in the Latino Literary Hall of Fame's Best Young Adult Fiction—English Category
ForeWord Magazine Best Young Adult Book of the Year
Tomás Rivera Mexican American Children Book Award Finalist
Grades 5–10

- Crime
- Death
- Poverty
- Socioeconomic Class

Living in a run-down trailer park with his single mother who struggles to provide for her four children, threatened by a group of bullies, and alienated at school, thirteen-year-old Trino Olivares hates his life. When his little brother gets sick, and there is no money for medicine, he desperately decides to join the bullies in robbing a local car wash. He arrives late, just in time to see one of his friends killed. Devastated, he begins the process of turning his life around. Critics have praised this dramatic novel extensively for its realistic characters and settings, genuine dialogue, and suspenseful writing. It has many other strengths and is perhaps Diane Gonzales Bertrand's most powerful work to date. However, it is also a good example of how one sentence can mar an otherwise excellent book. It happens during one of the most significant events in the book when Trino attends a poetry reading and begins to awaken to his possibilities. Later, the poet, Emilce Montoya, gives the troubled teen some much needed advice. But then Montoya says, "[Do] you think poetry is [only] for queers?" (47). When offensive terms are used by dishonorable characters, it is clear to the reader that they are wrong. But in this case, the word is used by the poet, an otherwise admirable character. Sequel: *Trino's Time*.

Trino's Time

Grades 5–10

- Schools
- Poverty
- Socioeconomic Class

In this solid sequel to the highly acclaimed *Trino's Choice*, seventh-grader Trino Olivares continues his journey of self-awareness and personal growth. Haunted by the memory of his friend's murder and frustrated by his family's financial situation, he finds the strength to face these and other challenges. He becomes more interested in school while working on a report about José Antonio Navarro, one of only two *Tejanos* who signed the Texas Declaration of Independence. Trino improves his grades, finds new friends, and takes on more responsibility for his family. When a fierce storm leaves his family homeless, he risks his life to help his loved ones. *Trino's Time* has been praised for its quick pace, realistic dialogue, likable characters, and engrossing story of perseverance. Prequel: *Trino's Choice*.

Uncle Chente's Picnic/El picnic de Tío Chente

Hispanic Children's Literature Reading with Energy Award
Grades K–4

- Fourth of July
- Picnics
- Uncles

When the Cárdenas family plans a special Fourth of July picnic for Uncle Chente, a trucker who travels around the country, a big rainstorm and power failure threaten to ruin the day. But the children soon discover that it takes more than a change in the weather to dampen their relative's enthusiasm for the party. Soft, full-page illustrations accompany this warm tale filled with delicious food, music, storytelling, and fun.

Alberto Blanco

Reprinted with permission of the publisher, Children's Book Press, San Francisco, CA. www.childrensbookpress.org

Mexican (1951–)
Birthday: February 18
Address: University of Texas at El Paso
Language and Linguistics
El Paso, TX 79968

The artist is not a special kind of human being, but each human being is a special kind of artist.

(Personal Communication)

Books by Alberto Blanco

Angel's Kite/La estrella de Angel. Illustrated by Rodolfo Morales. Children's Book Press, 1994.

Dawn of the Senses: Selected Poems of Alberto Blanco. City Lights Books, 1995.

Dos cuentos con alas. Illustrated by Laura Almeida. Colección Botella al Mar, Editorial Grijalvo, Mexico, 1994.

The Desert Mermaid/La sirena del desierto. Illustrated by Patricia Revah. Children's Book Press, 1992.

Mandalas para iluminar. Colección Letra y Color, Ediciones del Ermitaño and SEP, 1984.

Pájaors, pájaros. Illustrated by Patricia Revah. Editorial Trillos, Mexico, 1990.

Un sueño de Navidad. Illustrated by Patricia Revah. Colección Reloj de Cuentos, Number 6, CIDCLI and SEP, Mexico, 1984.

También los insectos son perfectos. (poetry). Illustrated by Diana Radaviciute. Colección Reloj de Versos, Number 11, CIDCLI and CONACULTA, Mexico, 1993.

Alberto Blanco is considered one of Mexico's most outstanding poets. The recipient of numerous awards, honors, and scholarships, Blanco is also an artist, art critic, musician, and translator and has published more than twenty books. A chemist by profession, he has also studied philosophy and has a master's degree in Asian studies with a specialization in Chinese studies. At the present time, he is a full-time professor in the bilingual master of fine arts creative writing program at the University of Texas at El Paso.

Born in Mexico City to parents who were voracious readers, Blanco started writing as a child and has continued writing throughout his life. His father worked in a factory producing pigments and inks, and Blanco's first toys were the little tin caps of the paint tubes. Blanco says, "When I was a teenager, I began to notice that the books I liked to read had some connection to what I was writing, but it was such a subtle connection like some kind of invisible, unworldly connection until I was twenty or twenty-one" (*Rio Grande Review, RGR*, 38). He goes on to describe attending a literary workshop with a friend where the facilitator, a well-known Mexican writer, encouraged him to have his work published. Blanco realized that he needed to share his work in order to maintain his sense of self. He also knew that he needed to remain true to himself and not let the publishing process distract him from his goals. He has been able to stay in touch with his creativity and in fact has made it the center of his life.

For Blanco, poetry is at the heart of his writing. He has gradually added many other forms of writing, but poetry remains the sustaining, supporting focus of his literary efforts. He is a prolific writer with ten books of poetry, ten books of translations, seven books for children, and hundreds of works in anthologies, magazines, and newspapers to his credit. One of his many fascinating projects is his translations of the poetry of Emily Dickinson. Her poems were difficult to translate because of the contradictions and sensitivity in her work. He notes, "She's a master of rhymes and rhythms, so what I found was that not each and every poem of Emily Dickinson can be translated into Spanish, but I think I have succeeded in some" (*RGR*, 45). Blanco has also translated the works of other poets such as Kenneth Patchen, Allen Ginsberg, and W. S. Merwin. In addition, he translates other genres such as science books and children's books.

Blanco has been a scholar for the Centro Mexicano de Escritores, the Instituto Nacional de Bellas Artes, and the Fondo Nacional para la Cultura y las Artes. His books of poetry include *Cromos*, which won the Carlos Pellicer Poetry Award, and *Canto a la sombra de los animales*, which won the José Fuentes Mares National Prize. His poetry can be found in *Dawn of the Senses*, a bilingual poetry anthology edited by Juvenal Acosta. Blanco's poems have been translated into French, German, Italian, Portuguese, Russian, and, of course, English. Recently, Blanco's work has been collected in an American anthology of Mexican poetry, *Light from a Nearby Window*. He recently spent a year as a Fulbright scholar at the University of California at Irvine, where he completed the work on an anthology of American poetry in Spanish, *Antología de Poesía Norteamericana Contemporánea*. The program in which Blanco is currently involved at the University of Texas at El Paso is the only master of fine arts in creative writing program in the United States in which students write and study in English, Spanish, or both languages.

In addition to writing, Blanco has performed rock and jazz in the bands Las Plumas Atómicas and La Comuna. As a child, he enjoyed listening to his mother play the piano. Now, he continues to play music on his own, but he finds that it isn't the same as being part of a band. So music is gradually appearing with more force in his poems. As he reads his poetry, he sometimes taps his feet and sways to the music of the words. A compact disc has been made featuring some of his poems combined with music.

Another of Blanco's many interests is art. He enjoys painting and has illustrated numerous books and book covers with his collages and designs. He has been writing for many years about Mexican art and artists. He has produced some very interesting books and portfolios in collaboration with Mexican artists such as Rodolfo Morales, Vicente Rojo, and Francisco Toledo. In addition, Blanco often writes essays and catalogs for art museums in Mexico. His wife is tapestry artist Patricia Revah, one of Latin America's most original illustrators of children's books. Born in Mexico of Greek and Russian heritage, she displays her work in Mexico and Europe and is considered an expert in the art of using color dyes from indigenous Mexican plants.

Several of Blanco's children's books have been illustrated by his wife, including two award-winning books, *Pájaros, pájaros* and *Un sueño de*

Navidad. They have collaborated on a bilingual picture book, *The Desert Mermaid*, which was published in the United States by Children's Book Press. In turn, Blanco has illustrated a book written by his wife.

A cultural ambassador, Blanco travels often to Europe and around the United States, teaching, giving lectures, and taking part in conferences and festivals. His interest in philosophy is apparent in a recent interview in which he spoke of paradoxes and contradictions. He also has a great sense of humor, laughing at himself and at life, saying that he changes his opinions often: "I have this feeling that sooner or later we're going to be embarrassed by every opinion we've had . . . I'm pretty serious about the fact that you can't be serious" (*RGR*, 37).

More Information about Alberto Blanco

"Stalking Borders: An Interview with Alberto Blanco." *Rio Grande Review: UT El Paso's Literary Magazine*. Spring 1995.

Fiction International 25. Special Issue: Mexican Fiction by Harold Jaffe. San Diego State University Press, 1994.

First World, ha ha ha!: The Zapatista Challenge, edited by Elaine Katzenberger. City Lights, 1995.

New Writing from Mexico by Reginald Gibbons. TriQuarterly Books, Northwestern University, 1992.

This Same Sky by Naomi Shihab Nye. Four Winds Press, 1992.

The Tree Is Older Than You Are: A Bilingual Gathering of Poems and Stories from Mexico with Paintings by Mexican Artists by Naomi Shihab Nye. Simon and Schuster, 1995.

Selected Works by Alberto Blanco

Angel's Kite/La estrella de Angel

Américas Honor Award

Choices, Cooperative Children's Book Center

All Ages

- Bilingual
- Kites
- Bells

Told in English and Spanish, this is the story of how a young kite maker brought back the missing church bell to his beloved town. There are several theories about what happened to the bell, but no one knows where it was. Most people have gotten used to living without it, but Angel, the kite maker, can't forget. So he decides to make the most beautiful kite in the world to take his mind off the missing bell. What special emblem did he include in the magnificent kite? What went wrong when he went out to fly it on a windy day? Why did Angel and his three trusty dogs spend the night on a cold hilltop? Readers will enjoy finding the answers to these questions and others in this heartening story about the magic of hope and hard work.

Rodolfo Morales, the illustrator of this book, was one of Mexico's greatest artists. The inspiration for this story came from his childhood as a kite maker in Ocotlán, in the state of Oaxaco, Mexico. The exquisitely framed collage pictures are filled with interesting details that readers of all ages will enjoy examining at length. The mystery of the bell will provide an interesting topic for discussion and writing. Drama and art enthusiasts will also be inspired by this beautiful book.

The Desert Mermaid/La sirena del desierto

Prickly Pear Award for Spanish Language Book

All Ages

- Bilingual
- Deserts
- Folklore
- Mermaids
- Music

A contemporary folktale told in English and Spanish, this engaging book tells the story of a desert mermaid who seeks to save her people. O'odham Himdag, an Indian poet of the Sonora Desert, provides the theme for this ecological tale: "The only way to bring water to the desert is to know the old songs." When the story begins, the mermaid is living in an oasis. At first she doesn't know that all the oases are gradually disappearing and that she is the only mermaid left in the entire Sonora Desert. With the help of a magic horse named Silver Star, the mermaid bravely sets out on an epic journey to recover the forgotten songs of her ancestors and thus to secure the future of her people. What roles do the songbirds, the swamp alligators, and other animals play in this drama? Where do the three pearls originate, and how do they help or hinder the courageous duo? What amazing sight awaits the mermaid when she arrives at the sea?

These and other questions will be answered as readers of all ages savor this beautifully written and illustrated book. As a child, Alberto Blanco enjoyed spending time in Mexico's beautiful Sonora Desert. Years later, he was inspired by memories to write this original story in the style of a folktale. His wife, Patricia Revah, lovingly illustrated it with fascinating tapestries. *The Desert Mermaid* is a heartwarming tribute to the ecology of the desert and the importance of music in our lives. The stereotype-shattering portrayal of the mermaid as an ingenious, courageous person is encouraging. The ending is particularly refreshing with its celebration of sisterhood—no mention of the damsel being rescued by a prince and, happily, no impending marriage on the horizon. Like the enchanting songs, this tale has a special rhythm, making it a perfect choice for both reading aloud and reading alone.

María Cristina Brusca

Argentine (1950–)
Birthday: May 4

According to my experience, drawing, writing and illustrating books for children can provide a great joy. Of course, there is a lot of work and patience involved, since not always the ideas find their way into images smoothly. But one should always remember that no matter how difficult the work, the search is in itself a reward. My deepest desire is to continue to have the opportunity of working for such a thrilling audience. . . . If my books contribute to a larger understanding of life and different cultures, I will be more than satisfied.

(Personal Communication)

Books by María Cristina Brusca

Written and Illustrated

The Blacksmith and the Devils. Written with Tona Wilson, Henry Holt, 1992. Spanish version: *El herrero y el diablo*.
The Cook and the King. Written with Tona Wilson. Henry Holt, 1993.
My Mama's Little Ranch on the Pampas. Henry Holt, 1994.
On the Pampas. Henry Holt, 1991. Spanish edition: *En la pampa*.
Pedro Fools the Gringo and Other Tales of a Latin American Trickster. Retold by María Cristina Brusca and Tona Wilson. Henry Holt, 1995.
Three Friends: A Counting Book/Tres amigos: Un cuento para contar. Written with Tona Wilson. Henry Holt, 1995.
When Jaguars Ate the Moon: And Other Stories about Animals and Plants of the Americas. Written with Tona Wilson. Henry Holt, 1995.

Illustrated

Mama Went Walking by Christine Berry. Henry Holt, 1990.
The Zebra-Riding Cowboy by Angela Shelf Medearis. Henry Holt, 1992.

María Cristina Brusca is the accomplished author and illustrator of a number of engaging books for children. Her drawings and paintings have been displayed in various exhibitions and collective shows. She has also illustrated numerous book covers and games as well as other projects such as a serial encyclopedia. She currently divides her time between Argentina and the United States.

Born in Buenos Aires, Argentina, Brusca spent as much time as she could at her grandparents' ranch, La Carlota. She enjoyed spending weekends and summers with her cousin at the large *estancia*, riding horses, helping with the chores, and listening to the stories told by the *gauchos*. "I loved the big, flat extensions of the *pampas*, the creatures that lived there, riding horses for hours, talking to the *gauchos* and learning about their culture, their special way of talking, their clothes, et cetera" (Personal Communication). Brusca has written two fascinating picture book memoirs about these childhood experiences, *On the Pampas* and *My Mama's Little Ranch on the Pampas*. "I've hoped to communicate some of these memories, which time and distance make so fragile, and to share some of my experiences with North American children. I've also hoped to show them a little bit of *gaucho* culture, of the way of life of those who live so close to the land and to nature" (Henry Holt Catalog).

It was also at the ranch that Brusca's father taught her how to draw and to paint with watercolors. At thirteen, she began studying art in the city. As she grew older and became more involved in her art studies, she had less time to spend in the country. Her love of art and reading led her to enter a special high school where she studied drawing, painting, graphic design, and bookbinding.

Brusca graduated from college in 1973 as a professor of graphic design. Between 1973 and 1988, she worked in Buenos Aires designing book covers, illustrating children's books, and collaborating on a number of children's magazines. During that time, she was also drawing and painting her own work and participating in various exhibitions and collective art shows.

In 1988, Brusca moved to the United States and settled in Port Ewen, New York. She gradually established herself as an illustrator and writer of children's books. When her editor suggested that she write a book about her childhood experiences in Argentina, she created *On the Pampas*. This book was received with such enthusiasm that she wrote a sequel, *My Mama's Little Ranch on the Pampas*. The process of creating the books was a very pleasant one for Brusca. "I've had great fun remembering my summers with Susanita—our love of horses, our small adventures, our freedom from being told what to do and what not to do, learning to take care of ourselves. I felt a special emotion drawing my grandmother, the ranch, my friend, Salguero. And going to meet the child that I was" (Henry Holt Catalog).

From 1992 to the present, Brusca has collaborated with Tona Wilson on a number of enchanting picture books, including one featuring Argentine folktales, a collection of stories about plants and animals indigenous to the Americas, and a bilingual counting book. Brusca notes, "When I met Tona Wilson, I discovered that we had the same enthusiasm for folktales and the same curiosity about the flora and fauna of the Americas" (*Junior Library Guild*, 34). In 1995, two of these books were published in Spanish by an Argentine publishing house.

The response to Brusca's work has been very enthusiastic. Indeed, the praise for her clear, captivating text and authentic, distinctive watercolors has been widespread. Her work challenges stereotypes of women and girls, showing them actively engaged in the work involved in running a ranch. Brusca and Wilson's books are noted for their extensive research and loving attention to detail. Together they are making a unique contribution to the field of children's literature.

Brusca concludes, "So far, I have been able to share with American children experiences that come from other parts of the world, particularly the country where I was born. Writing and drawing these books, I had to do a lot of research so I have also learned a lot about myself" (Personal Communication).

More Information about María Cristina Brusca

Dutchess Magazine. Fall 1994, 74–75.
Junior Library Guild. April–September 1995, 34.

Publishers Weekly. March 6, 1995, 70.
School Library Journal. May 1994, 107.

Selected Works by María Cristina Brusca

The Blacksmith and the Devils

Grades 3–Up

- Argentina
- Blacksmiths
- Folklore

María Cristina Brusca and Tona Wilson retell this Argentine folktale based on the version told by the famous *gaucho* Don Segundo Sombra in a novel by Ricardo Guiraldes. It is the tale of Juan Pobreza the blacksmith, known in Argentina as "Miseria" and in Spain as "Pedro de Urdemalas" and by other names in other parts of the Americas. Juan Pobreza's "name suited him perfectly since *pobreza* means 'poverty' in Spanish." Although he was poor, he never turned anyone away even if they couldn't pay. On the day when he fixes the shoe of a *gaucho*'s mule, his life changes in dramatic ways. The *gaucho* claims to be Saint Peter and offers to grant Juan three wishes for his generosity. The story takes an unexpected twist here, leading Juan into a bargain with the devil that results in a series of hilarious events. As the blacksmith matches wits with the underworld, his antics improve the lives of everyone on the *pampas*. Well, almost everyone. "A few greedy people, who had gotten rich from other people's troubles, were not pleased." As the tale unwinds, Juan finds himself in an amazing variety of unexpected places and situations.

In the foreword, the authors explain that folktales change a little with each retelling. They invite us to gather around the campfire and listen to this story and then, in the tradition of oral storytelling, to make the story our own by changing it in any way when we tell it to our friends. Readers might enjoy adapting it to their location, time, gender, or worldview. After examining the detailed, humorous illustrations, they might want to create their own pictures to accompany their version of the folktale. Brusca's amusing watercolors are filled with droll details that will elicit many chuckles as readers pore over the double-spread paintings. The facial expressions on the humans as well as the animals are especially comical. The fact that some people were not happy with the peace and harmony on the *pampas* provides a fascinating topic for critical thinking discussions. Teachers who work in areas where this material might be considered controversial should share the book with their supervisors before introducing it in the classroom. Spanish edition: *El herrero y el diablo.*

The Cook and the King

Nebraska Library Commission's 1993 List of Thirty Best Buys
Grades 2–5

- Culinary Arts
- Folklore
- Judges
- Kings
- South America

The Cook and the King was inspired by a South American folktale. It is the tale of a wise young woman who teaches a selfish, pompous king an important lesson. The story opens with the annual carnival during which the hardworking people of the kingdom thank their *Pachamama*, Mother Earth, for giving them life. Soon afterward, the king demands that Florinda, famous for her *empanadas*, come cook for him. She wisely agrees only after he promises to grant her one wish whenever she asks for it. From her new vantage point in the palace, Florinda watches as the king makes hasty, foolish, and unfair judgments in settling the disputes among the people. Each time she finds a way to make a subtle, but strong, objection. But one day she dishes up a lesson that enrages the king and puts her life in danger. Will Florinda be clever enough to save herself? Will the pattern of injustice ever change in this tiny kingdom high up in the mountains of South America?

María Cristina Brusca and Tona Wilson have teamed up to bring us another humorous and insightful folktale from South America, this time featuring a clever young peasant woman outwitting a powerful king and in so doing replacing strife with harmony. They have created an admirable female protagonist that shatters the stereotypes of women as passive conformists. The authors provide additional information about customs and music in a note at the end of the book. Brusca's amusing illustrations add even more gusto to this engaging story. This folktale lends itself nicely to a variety of forms of drama such as pantomime or readers theater. As the authors note in *The Blacksmith and the Devils*, folktales change a little with each retelling. Storytellers might want to make this story their own by adapting it to their location, time, or interest.

My Mama's Little Ranch on the Pampas

Grades 1–5

- Argentina

- Picture Book Memoir
- Ranch Life

In this captivating sequel to *On the Pampas*, María Cristina Brusca recalls more of her experiences as a young girl in Argentina. This time she chronicles her first year on the small ranch purchased and managed by her mother. She took a very active part in taking care of the farm, opening and closing the windmill, mending fences, caring for the saddles and reins, and riding her horse, Pampero. She helped tend the new cows and their calves and even assisted with the dramatic cesarean delivery of a calf. She celebrated her birthday by driving the sulky into town and dancing the *malambo* at the general store.

Readers of all ages will enjoy this autobiographical reminiscence told through Brusca's authentic voice and distinctive, detailed watercolor illustrations. As she relates "all the funny and scary and wonderful things" that happened that year, the reader experiences them along with her. Brusca's story is refreshingly realistic and includes cow manure, bird droppings, and cattle breeding. The depiction of the emergency cesarean birth of the calf is handled very well, recounting the details of the procedure through text and pictures. Readers from the Northern Hemisphere will be interested in the contrast of the seasons, with spring beginning on September twenty-first. Brusca includes a helpful chart on the seasons in her attractively illustrated glossary, which appears on the inside covers. Regional terms defined in these decorated endpapers and sprinkled throughout the narrative include *pasteles, malambo, rastra*, and *la luz mala*. This is another well-written book with a much-needed, strong Latina protagonist, one who is not afraid to get her hands dirty or to try a new adventure. It challenges stereotypes of females, depicting a woman who manages her own ranch and shares all the chores with her daughter. This book provides fascinating reading for youngsters of all backgrounds from the city or the country.

On the Pampas

Notable Trade Book in the Field of Social Studies
Parents' Choice Picture Book Award
Grades 2–5

- Argentina
- Picture Book Memoir
- Ranch Life

Based on her experiences as a child, María Cristina Brusca has created a delightful picture book about a girl from Buenos Aires, Argentina, who spends her summers at La Carlota, her grandmother's ranch on the *pampas*. The *pampas* are the flat grasslands that stretch for hundreds of miles through central Argentina and Uruguay. The book opens with Cristina's train trip to the *estancia*, where she is met by her cousin, Susanita, who knows "everything about horses, cows, and all the animals that live on the *pampas*." Together the girls ride and groom horses, help with the cattle, read comic books, search for *ñandú* eggs, and listen to the *gauchos* tell tall tales. Ranch life offers plenty of adventures for these two active and tireless cousins, both of whom embrace every experience wholeheartedly. When the summer ends, Cristina has one last surprise before she returns to the city.

María Cristina Brusca has written an outstanding book, noteworthy for its depiction of girls as adventuresome, courageous, and solvers of problems. Cristina and Susanita are both "always ready for an adventure no matter how scary." The body of children's literature is gradually improving due to a growing awareness of the need to portray girls accurately as the active, strong people they are. This book makes an important contribution to that goal. *On the Pampas* is also notable for its captivating text and distinctive, detailed watercolors, which capture the excitement of the story. Especially impressive are the faces and figures of the humans because they look like ordinary people and are not at all prettified. Each animal is given an individual face and personality as well. The inside front and back covers provide a fascinating illustrated glossary of terms such as *recado, mate, bombagha*, and *ñandú*. María Cristina Brusca's autobiographical reminiscence is a very special book, one that brings back memories to those of us who grew up in the country and introduces an interesting way of life to those who have always lived in the city. This fine book earned a starred review in *School Library Journal*. Sequel: *My Mama's Little Ranch on the Pampas*. Spanish edition: *En la pampa*.

Pedro Fools the Gringo and Other Tales of a Latin American Trickster

Grades 3–7

- Folklore
- Trickster Tales

Twelve amusing short stories feature Pedro Urdemales, a cunning trickster who survives by outwitting the rich and powerful. As the authors explain in the introduction, "Some of Pedro's exploits will be familiar from stories about other popular and trickster heroes, such as Coyote and Br'er Rabbit, or the Mayan rabbit Juan Tul." In the first story, a young, poor, homeless Pedro learns to use his wits to keep himself alive. When he finds work with a stingy priest, the lessons that he learns about how to get enough to eat prove to be very useful later. As he travels around Chile, Argentina, Mexico, Guatemala, and other parts of Latin America, he escapes a band of vigilantes, outwits a passing gringo with a get-rich scheme, and even tricks the devil himself. The final story finds him matching wits with San Pedro, trying to find a way to get into heaven.

Trickster stories appeal to people of all ages because they enjoy reading about greedy folks being outwitted by someone who appears to be an ordinary person. The authors inform us that the stories that they have selected are just a sampling of the many that have been told in Latin America and the southwestern United States. Slight variations of the same tales are often told in different locations. The book includes a section telling where these stories came from and a bibliography. Black-and-white illustrations accompany each story and add to the fun.

Three Friends: A Counting Book /Tres amigos: Un cuento para contar

Grades Preschool–3

- Bilingual
- Counting Book
- Cowgirls and Cowboys

When a cowgirl and cowboy set out to catch some cows, there's no telling what adventures await them. Can they outwit a bevy of armadillos, roadrunners, and coyotes? What other critters are out there in the desert plotting against them? As we count our way through this rollicking story, we have a great time learning about tumbleweeds, saguaro cactus, and other flora and fauna of the area. This humorous book will encourage young readers to learn to count in Spanish and English and to enjoy the pleasure of being bilingual. People of all ages will savor the playful illustrations, searching out those mischievous little creatures and checking to see what they will be up to next. As the tuckered-out *vaqueros* retire for the night, can they guess what escapades young readers might cook up for tomorrow? Here is an opportunity for great fun combining bilingual counting with drama, writing, science, and art. The inside back cover provides a glossary of related terms such as *botas, lazo, sartén*, and *chaparreras*.

When Jaguars Ate the Moon and Other Stories about Animals and Plants of the Americas

Selection of the Junior Library Guild
Grades 2–Up

- ABCs
- Animals and Plants
- Folklore
- Indigenous People

Twenty-six tales, featuring an animal or plant for each letter of the alphabet, constitute this fascinating, one-of-a-kind compendium. The authors retell stories about the anteater, iguana, kinkajou, llama, quetzal, tapir, zompopo, and many other fascinating creatures, based on oral traditions, ancient myths, anecdotes, short stories, and parts of longer stories. The people and geographical region where each tale originated are identified. The locations range from all parts of the Americas including Argentina, Paraguay, Guatemala, and Mexico to what is now the United States and Canada. The tales were told by people who have lived on these continents for tens of thousands of years. Some of the stories answer questions such as: How did the Guarani people learn to dance? How did the armadillo get armor? Why do tapirs eat prickly branches and brambles that no other animal will touch? In the title story, "When Jaguars Ate the Moon," burning bits of the moon fall into the forest. The ensuing pandemonium results in the creation of animals, stars, constellations, and an eerie lunar eclipse.

There are many special features about this book. The authors have lovingly interwoven themes about respect for the interdependence of all the people, animals, and plants of the earth into their engrossing tales. Each story is accompanied by an enchanting illustration, and each page is framed with detailed paintings of additional indigenous flora and fauna. The book ends with a map of the Americas identifying the locations of the tales, notes on each of the stories, and an extensive bibliography. Brusca and Wilson are to be commended for the tremendous amount of research that went into creating this beautiful volume. It lends itself perfectly to interdisciplinary studies, combining storytelling, science, social studies, art, and geography. Readers might wish to savor a few pages at a time, stopping periodically for discussion, map study, creative dramatics, or writing.

Omar Castañeda

Photo: Bleu Castañeda

Guatemalan American (1954–1997)
Birthday: September 6

I count myself a feminist, an activist for those who are struggling to break the sometimes oppressive weight of history and find just a little space for themselves where they might have dignity and voice.

(*Something about the Author*, 44)

Because I am Guatemalan American and have always lived in non-Hispanic communities in the U.S., I have had to deal with conflicting views of the world. In my writing, I investigate the individual's search for identity in a changing world. My characters glimpse something other than what is sanctioned by their native culture, and at the same time, they uphold many of their society's values.

(Personal Communication)

To become proud of differences, we have to write through our family and individual histories.

(Personal Communication)

Books by Omar Castañeda

Abuela's Weave. Illustrated by Enrique O. Sanchez. Lee and Low, 1993. Spanish edition: *El tapiz de Abuela*. Film version by Spoken Arts, 1994.
Among the Volcanoes. E. P. Dutton/Lodestar, 1991.
Cunuman. Pineapple Press, 1987.
Dance of the Conquest. Illustrated by Véronique Fontaine. Kane Publishing, 1991.
Imagining Isabel. Dutton/Lodestar, 1994.
New Visions: Fiction by Florida Writers. Edited by O. Castañeda, C. Blackwell and J. Harrington. Arbiter Press, 1989.

Omar S. Castañeda, a writer, educator, and lecturer, lived in Bellingham, Washington, and was an associate professor at Western Washington University, where he taught creative writing, literature of the Mayas, world literature, and other related courses. He served on numerous educational committees, gave a variety of professional presentations, and organized numerous writing conferences. He often served as a jurist for award and residency programs and was a cofounding editor of *Chiricú*. He was the founder and former director of the Hubless Wheel, a reading series that features minority and ethnic writers. On January 11, 1997, Castañeda died of injuries sustained in a car accident in Bellington, Washington. He is remembered for his unique voice and his commitment to broadening the scope of literature for young readers. He donated a portion of the royalties from his books to a humanitarian organization in Guatemala.

The son of Miriam Mendez Castañeda, a sculptor and homemaker, and Hector Neri Castañeda, a philosopher, Castañeda was born in Guatemala City, Guatemala, and raised in Michigan and Indiana. Although he was hungry for information, he was alienated by the regimentation and punitive nature of the schools that he attended. He dropped out of high school for a year and lived on the streets. During this time, he realized the importance of education and returned to school with renewed determination. After high school, Castañeda spent four years in the military. During his first creative writing class in college he immediately knew that he wanted to write. He discovered that writing was a way to work through problems, create possible worlds, and forge identity. If he went several days without writing, he felt strange, dislocated.

Castañeda was often invited to give readings and workshops. The titles of some of his presentations provide a glimpse into Castañeda's interests and concerns: "The Dubious Immigrant," "Mayan Creation Stories," "Borders and Barriers for a Multicultural Society," "Politics in Publishing Ethnic Difference," "Authenticity in Multicultural Children's Literature," "Issues of Multiculturalism for Teachers," and "Looking Out for the Other."

Castañeda taught in Florida, China, Indiana, and Washington. He traveled to South Korea, Hong Kong, Japan, and the Philippines, and he worked in Mexico, Guatemala, and China. Several of his short stories have been translated into other languages and used as material for university courses in other countries.

A prolific writer, Castañeda's short fiction has been widely anthologized and appears in numerous journals. He also wrote essays, articles, poetry, and books for adults, young adults, and children. He was the recipient of a number of awards, grants, and fellowships, including an Indiana University Ernest Hemingway Fellowship, a Fulbright Senior Central American Research Grant, and the Charles H. and N. Mildred Nilon Award for Excellence in Minority Fiction for one of his books for adults, *Remembering to Say "Mouth" or "Face."* (Other awards for his books for children and young adults are listed with the reviews of the books.)

On professional leave during the 1995–1996 academic year, Castañeda was working on a book entitled *Negotiating Values: New Strategies for Fiction Writing Workshops*, which presented not only conventions and techniques of fiction writing but a critique of those conventions to show their history, social biases, and political implications. Another work in progress was a magic-realist novel about a young woman of mixed Guatemalan and American blood who visits Guatemala to learn more about her heritage. Castañeda was also working on two translation projects: one was of the only book on Mayan cosmology written by a Mayan group, and the other was of an ongoing publication of *La Liga Maya Internacional*. He finished writing three picture books featuring newly immigrated children to the United States and issues of bilingual education and two books for adults.

Castañeda's writing is often set in Guatemala or Indiana. He noted,

> I write for children out of political interests and artistic challenge; I write for adults for the very same reasons. My writing is characterized by concerns for Guatemala, socio-political upheaval, racism and biculturality in the United States. I often portray cultural conflict, the twin drives of assimilation and confrontation, and reformation of belief under drastic social changes. I show individuals becoming perverse when desiring too much control over people, emotions, even ideas, and, most of all, by not freely inventing their own identity. My experimentation is usually with unreliable narrators and varieties of irreal modes. My writing for children attempts similar objectives, yet in far less experimental ways. My most recent interest has been to capture young Central American immigrant experiences of erasure of language and culture. (Personal Communication)

Castañeda's bicultural background was central to his writing. He wrote about people experiencing the clash of cultures and how the resulting turmoil contributes to the shaping of identities. His work plays an important role in bringing to light the struggles and issues facing people whose existence is often ignored, erased, or marginalized. This theme of developing identity is especially relevant to young people who are struggling with which parts of their traditions they want to keep and what parts of a new worldview fit for them.

While he thought of himself as mostly an adult fiction writer, Castañeda felt that children's literature is also vitally important. His award-winning books for young readers feature admirable Latina protagonists who provide greatly needed strong role models. He found that young people are often the most open to new ideas that might threaten adults. Because children have not yet established such rigid worldviews, they are flexible readers, able to enjoy a wider range of perspectives. He encouraged teachers to be sensitive and open to the forms that their students' writing takes. He felt that it is important to honor their complicated emotions and the possible violence and other unpleasant topics that may enter into their writing. Students need an avenue for expression; it is crucial that we do not repress the multiplicity of emotions and variety of plots that emerge in their writing.

More Information about Omar Castañeda

"For the Well-Intentioned Multiculturalist." *Children's Book Council Journal*, Spring/Summer 1995.

Contemporary Authors, Volume 135, 77.

Something about the Author, Volume 71, 43–44.

Selected Works by Omar Castañeda

Abuela's Weave

Consortium of Latin American Studies Programs Honoree

Parent's Choice Honoree

Grades K–4

- Art
- Birthmarks
- Grandmothers
- Weaving

This exquisite book tells the story of Esperanza and her grandmother, who live in rural Santa Cruz, Guatemala. The young girl and Abuela work tirelessly on backstrap looms to create handwoven tablecloths, *huipiles* (blouses), skirts, and an exquisite tapestry that blossoms with the images of Guatemala. With Abuela's guidance, Esperanza learns the secrets of making goods that will "pull the wonder right out of people." As they work, Esperanza worries about selling the weavings at the Fiesta de Pueblos in Guate. What if people refuse to buy from Abuela because of her birthmark? What if the shoppers prefer modern, machine-made goods? Will Esperanza have the courage to carry out Abuela's plan? As the story unfolds, a young girl discovers the magic of her grandmother's artistry as well as her own hidden strengths. A woman teaches her granddaughter a lesson about creating from the heart and believing in herself.

Enrique O. Sanchez's brilliantly colored illustrations in this, his first picture book, are rendered in acrylic on canvas. They beautifully complement Castañeda's rich narrative. The text and paintings present a wealth of cultural detail, authentically re-creating images of rural Guatemala. Readers will enjoy discussing Abuela's motivation for hiding her birthmark on this particular day. They will soon realize that since she has been selling her goods for years, she wanted to create a situation where her granddaughter would have to rely on her own wits and, in so doing, develop self-confidence and independence. Thus, she will be prepared to follow her abuela's example in the future. This is a gentle, cheerful story of generational sharing and traditional handicrafts. Spanish edition: *El tapiz de Abuela*. Film: *El tapiz de Abuela*.

Among the Volcanoes

Child Study Association Book of the Year

New York Public Library Best Books for the Teen Age Award

Grades 6–10

- Career Aspirations
- Gender Roles
- Illness
- Tradition and Change

This is a poignant story of a young woman's search for a way to break out of the constricting female role and to follow her dream of becoming a teacher. Isabel Pacay lives with her family in the small village of Chuuí Chopaló, Guatemala. She has long dreamed of finishing school and becoming a teacher. However, this seems like an impossible goal in a community that expects females to follow the traditional path of marrying young and selflessly devoting their lives to their families. Now her mother is ill, and as the oldest child in the Mayan family, Isabel is expected to take on the household responsibilities. Her goals seem more unattainable than ever. She struggles with her ambivalent feelings toward her boyfriend, Lucas Choy, knowing that a traditional marriage would end her chances of doing "what she most dearly wanted and could least explain" (6). When a young American arrives in the village to conduct medical research, the family is faced with an apparent life-or-death decision. Should her mother continue to rely on the local healer, the *sanjorín*, whose treatments seem to be ineffective? Or should she defy local tradition and try Western medicine? What is the meaning of the ominous omens left outside the family hut?

With sensitivity and insight, Omar Castañeda wrote an exceptional story of a young woman searching for her identity in a world fraught with upheaval and change. The multifaceted characterization of the young protagonist is remarkably well drawn and memorable. Strong Latina characters are greatly needed in literature for young readers. Castañeda's passages about Isabel's hopes for the future are poignant: "As a quetzal . . . she would be elegant and nobler than the life she was born into, and she would wing over the vast wall of volcanoes surrounding the lake and discover the world spreading infinitely outward" (8). She hoped to "connect with something important in the world; to feel a part of something larger and more necessary than a single person" (21). She had been "convinced that she could be an exception to the volcanic forces that smelted people into acceptable molds" (58). The conflicts between traditional and Western cultures and the pain of change and loss are presented with depth and insight. Descriptive passages provide a realistic portrait of the complexities of the Mayan culture, the ever-present political unrest of the area, and a strong sense of the natural beauty of the Guatemalan highlands. The betrayal by a best friend, the miscommunication with, and jealousy of, a significant other, the inspiration of a respected teacher, the bumbling insights of a newcomer, the needs and demands of family, and, most of all, the belief in, and love of, self make this a compelling, significant novel. Readers won't want to miss the sequel, *Imagining Isabel.*

The Dance of the Conquest: Spotlight on Readers Theatre

Grades 3–5

- Drama
- Guatemala
- History

This play, written for readers theater, features the history and culture of Guatemala. Every year the Mayas repeat their history in the Dance of the Conquest, which tells the story of the Mayan defeat by the Spanish invaders in 1524. It celebrates the memory of the heroic men and women who fought to defend their country. The Dance of the Conquest is an important part of annual festivals in which each city in Guatemala honors its patron saint. The dancers act out the terrible events that took place over 400 years ago.

Omar Castañeda's interesting play is divided into three acts and has eight major parts plus minor roles. The teacher's name is Teacher Pacay.

(Castañeda has written Isabel Pacay's story in *Among the Volcanoes* and *Imagining Isabel*.) The easy-to-read play emphasizes cooperation and gender-positive assignment of parts. Participants and audience will learn about history, geography, and culture while enjoying readers theater, a significant drama form that lends itself well to a variety of interpretations. A pronunciation key is included. Other readers theater scripts are available from Kane Press, 222 East 46th Street, New York, NY 10017, (212) 986-2240.

Imagining Isabel

New York Public Library Best Books for the Teen Age Award
Grades 6–10

- Career Aspirations
- Gender Roles
- Political Awakening
- Tradition and Change

In this sequel to *Among the Volcanoes*, Isabel Pacay Choy enrolls in a government-run teacher education training program and finds herself involved in the turbulent political and social issues of contemporary Guatemala. Omar Castañeda dedicated this book "To the slain and wounded heroes of the Massacre of Santiago Atitlán, 2 December 1990; and to the more than 220,000 slain or disappeared since the 1954 coup in Guatemala." *Imagining Isabel* begins with sixteen-year-old Isabel's marriage to Lucas and the death of her mother. Her dreams of becoming a teacher seem unattainable until a letter arrives from the National Education Commission inviting her to become a teacher trainee. At first she is filled with doubt and fear. How can she leave her new husband and recently widowed father and both sets of families? Tradition dictates that women lead a selfless life, caring for loved ones. But Isabel has always had a desire to be something other than what she was expected to be. So with her young sister, Marcelina, she attends the eight-week program in the town of Sololá, where she quickly learns more than she ever dreamed possible. As she quietly absorbs the political and philosophical debates between her two very different roommates and observes the people around her, she is at times intimidated and overwhelmed, feeling inadequate, and at times inspired, feeling energized. One day when she goes for a walk, a vaguely familiar figure leads her to the body of a dying man. Terrified, she calls for help and then quietly fades into the background. Aware of the political climate, she wonders if she should tell anyone about the incident. Should she come forward and identify herself as the person who found the body? Should she leave the school and return to the "safety" of her small village? Can she trust anyone at the school, or are they part of the conspiracy? Isabel's political awakening is interwoven with a story of new friendships, family affection, changing customs, and personal growth.

This is a remarkable book about an admirable young woman who has the capacity to "wonder about things of which she has only the barest inkling . . . of the dormant need to rise up and fight for what lies buried in all of them. . . . She has the strength to doubt herself and yet come up again, to worry and to act at the same time. She is not afraid . . . to imagine herself in new ways" (176). One can imagine her returning to Chuuí Chopaló as a teacher who works for both the education and just treatment of her people. Readers not only will be inspired by the strong examples of the women in this story but will learn more about Guatemalan history, politics, and culture. Castañeda deftly probed several significant issues in this book, including gender roles, the search for truth in a confusing political climate, and Guatemala's struggle to balance tradition with change.

Ana Castillo

Photo: © Iwona Biedermann

Latina (1953–)
Birthday: June 15
Contact: Susan Bergholz Literary Services
17 West 10th Street, #5
New York City, NY 10011-8746

When I started taking writing in verse seriously nearly three decades ago, I wrote as a witness to my generation. . . . Poetry, like my painting, was my indulgence. It was also, like my painting, often my companion and my refuge. I was a Chicana protest poet, a complete renegade—and I continue to write that way.

(*I Ask the Impossible,* xv–xvi)

Books by Ana Castillo

Goddess of the Americas: Writings on the Virgin of Guadalupe (Editor). Riverhead Books, 1996. Spanish edition: *La Diosa de las Américas: Escritos sobre la Virgen de Guadalupe.*

I Ask the Impossible: Poems. Anchor Books, 2000.

Loverboys. Norton, 1996; Dutton, 1997.

Massacre of the Dreamers: Essays on Xicanisma. University of New Mexico Press, 1994; Dutton, 1995.

The Mixquiahuala Letters. Bilingual Press, 1986; Doubleday, 1992. Spanish edition: *Las cartas de Mixquiahuala.*

My Daughter, My Son, the Eagle, the Dove: An Aztec Chant. Illustrated by S. Guevara. Penguin Putnam, 2000. Spanish edition: *Mi Hija, Mi Hijo, el Águila, La Paloma: Un Canto Azteca.*

My Father Was a Toltec: Poems. West End Press, 1988; *My Father Was a Toltec and Selected Poems*. Norton, 1995.

Peel My Love Like an Onion. Doubleday, 1999. Spanish edition: *Carmen la Coja.* Vintage Books, 2000.

Sapogonia: An Anti-Romance in 3/8 Meter. Bilingual Press, 1990.

So Far from God. Norton, 1993. *Tan lejos de Dios*. Dutton, 1999.

Third Woman: The Sexuality of Latinas (Coeditor). Third Woman Press, 1989, 1993.

Women Are Not Roses. Arte Público Press, 1987.

One of the most prominent Latina writers in the United States today, Ana Castillo is a poet, novelist, essayist, editor, and teacher. Her body of work is innovative and tremendously varied; it often offers scathing sociopolitical commentary. Indeed, her desire to take risks and find creative alternatives has led to her reputation as one of the most daring and experimental of Latino novelists.

Castillo was born in Chicago on June 15, 1953. She wrote her first poems when she was nine years old after the death of her grandmother. "In high school and college, she was active in the Chicano movement, using her poetry to express her political sentiments" *(Contemporary Authors Online)*. She received her B.A. in art education in 1975 from Northeastern Illinois University, her M.A. from the University of Chicago in 1979, and her Ph.D. from the University of Bremen in Germany in 1991. Castillo was a writer-in-residence, lecturer, and visiting professor at a number of universities until the early 1990s, when her success as a novelist allowed her to turn to writing full-time.

In addition to her poetry collections, novels, and essays, Castillo has edited several books and contributed to numerous anthologies. She has received many awards and fellowships, including honors from the Women's Foundation of San Francisco in 1987 for "pioneering excellence in literature" and National Endowment of the Arts Fellowships for poetry in 1990 and 1995.

Castillo's unique style, feminist themes, and unwavering commitment to social justice have created a tremendous interest in her work. *BookList* wrote, "Whether [she] is writing poetry, essays, or fiction, her work sizzles with equal measures of passion and intelligence."

More Information about Ana Castillo

www.anacastillo.com

Breaking Boundaries: Latina Writings and Critical Readings, edited by Asuncion Horno-Delgado. University of Massachusetts Press, 1989.

Contemporary Authors Online. The Gale Group, 2000.

Dictionary of Literary Biography. Volume 122.

Latina Self-Portraits: Interviews with Contemporary Women Writers, edited by Bridget Kevane and Juanita Heredia. University of New Mexico Press, 2000.

¡Latinas! Women of Achievement, edited by Diane Telgen and Jim Kamp. Visible Ink, 1996.

The Oxford Companion of Women's Writing in the United States, edited by Cathy N. Davidson and Linda Wagner-Martin. Oxford University Press, 1995.

Selected Works by Ana Castillo

I Ask the Impossible

Grades 12–Adult

- Poetry

This energetic collection of more than sixty diverse poems, written between the years 1989 and 2000, celebrates the strength that "is a woman . . . buried deep in her heart." Confirming her unwavering commitment to social justice, Castillo writes, among other things, about the injustices of women's lives, especially the betrayal of church and state. Included are powerful tributes to Anna Mae Aquash, a murdered Micmac Indian rights activist, Sister Dianna Ortíz, an American nun who was captured and tortured by the Guatemalan secret police; and Zapatista leader Comandante Ramona. Several poems are in Spanish with translations by Rosario Ferre. *Library Journal* wrote, "[T]his retrospective provides a delightful and enticing orientation to one of the most outstanding Chicanas writing today."

Massacre of the Dreamers: Essays on Xicanisma

Gustaves Myers Award

College–Adult

- Essays

- Feminism
- Xicanisma

In ten fascinating essays based on her doctoral work, Castillo reflects on the experiences of Chicanas and on the need for Xicanisma, a socially committed and politically active Chicana feminism. She shares much about her experiences as a writer and scholar, her personal life and relationships, and her family and friends. *BookList* wrote, "The sometimes bristly, provocative essays . . . will be a stimulating addition to ethnic and women's studies collections."

The Mixquiahuala Letters

American Book Award
Grades 12–Adult

- Epistolary Novel
- Friendship
- Tradition and Change
- Women

Ana Castillo's first novel explores the changing role of women in the United States and Mexico during the 1970s and 1980s. Utilizing a series of introspective letters written over a ten-year period from Teresa, a Chicana poet, to her white friend, Alicia, the novel has been widely studied as a feminist text and praised for its powerful evocation of warfare between the sexes. "Bound in that yet undefined course known as The New Woman's Emergence" (35), the two women gain strength from each other while confronting the demands and expectations dictated by the men in their lives. Castillo provides three possible arrangements of the forty letters—for the "Conformist," the "Cynic," and the "Quixotic"—by numbering the letters and supplying varying orders in which to read them, each with a different resolution. Spanish edition: *Las cartas de Mixquiahuala*.

My Daughter, My Son, the Eagle, the Dove: An Aztec Chant

Américas Commended List
Grades 4–Up

- Chants
- Folklore
- Guidance
- History

- Mexico
- Poetry

Steeped in the wisdom of the ancients, this radiant title celebrates rites of passage in a young person's life: birth, childhood, adolescence, choosing a life companion, and parenthood. Based on Aztec chants recited by parents or wise elders, these messages are intended to affirm, advise, instruct, and exhort. "Do not stray. /Do not let yourself / fall. Stay on the path. / Oh my daughter, / so tenderly loved." Two sections, one for a daughter and one for a son, share "lessons [that] apply as much to our children today as they did to the indigenous children of Mesoamerica hundreds of years ago," as Castillo states in her afterword. Guevara's beautiful earth-toned paintings combine images of a contemporary girl and boy with Aztec symbols and glyphs. *Voice of Youth Advocates* wrote, "This . . . touching tribute to the years of adolescence . . . radiates devotion, joy, and pride . . . offering time-honored messages of loving guidance." Spanish edition: *Mi Hija, Mi Hijo, el Águila, La Paloma: Un Canto Azteca.*

My Father Was a Toltec and Selected Poems

Grades 12–Adult

- Poetry

In this collection of poetry in English and Spanish, Ana Castillo invokes her origin as the daughter of a member of the Toltec gang in Chicago and examines her own struggles in the schoolyard and into adulthood. Many of her poems address painful, gritty subjects: street violence, poverty, suicide, welfare, affairs, culture clashes, and lives torn apart. These fiery poems are filled with mystery, music, and spirit.

Peel My Love Like an Onion

Grades 12–Adult

- Flamenco Dancers
- Physical Disabilities
- Romance

Carmen Santos, a self-described Chicago Mexican, was once a celebrated flamenco dancer, despite her polio-damaged leg. At forty, she struggles with the reemergence of her devastating disease, the end of her career, and the abandonment of her two lovers. How this indomitable protagonist survives these and other challenges and becomes an overnight celebrity as a singer makes for fascinating reading. This bittersweet novel has been praised for its unflinching verve; observant and witty narrative; and strong-willed, passionate, and realistically flawed protagonist. *BookList* wrote, "Carmen tell[s] the story of her arduous quest in an astringently frank narrative that is punctuated with sharp social commentary and unsparing musings on the vagaries of love." Spanish edition: *Carmen la Coja*.

So Far from God

Carl Sandburg Literary Award for Fiction
Mountain and Plains Booksellers Award
Grades 12–Adult

- Magic Realism
- Mothers and Daughters
- Sisters

Set in a small hamlet in central New Mexico, this brilliant novel follows the fascinating lives of a strong Latina, Sofi, and her four unusual daughters. The book opens with the "death" and subsequent resurrection of the youngest daughter, La Loca, at age three, who later dies of AIDS. The eldest, Esperanza, a Chicana campus radical turned television news anchorwoman, visits her family as a ghost after being killed while covering the Persian Gulf War. Recovering spontaneously after being brutally mutilated by a mysterious *malogra*, Caridad apprentices herself to a *curandera*. Later, she falls in love with Esmeralda, a social worker, and together they fly off the mesa, where they can "be safe and live forever" (211). The fourth daughter, Fe, temporarily loses her mind after being jilted and later dies from cancer caused by working with toxic chemicals in a high-tech weapons plant. Sofi copes with these and other losses by creating an artisans' cooperative and founding an organization MOMAS (Mothers of Martyrs and Saints). "All of this and more is reported by a fast-talking, earthy, feminist, opinionated, and irresistible narrator" *(BookList)*. This inventive novel is filled with tragic events, yes, but they are leavened with wry humor, scathing social commentary, pungent folklore, and of course, magical manifestations. *Choice* praised *So Far from God* for its "high degree of universality" and described it as "an outstanding work of art."

Denise Chávez

Photo: © Daniel Zolinsky

Chicana/Mexican American (1948–)
Birthday: August 15
Contact: Susan Bergholz Literary Services
17 West 10th Street, #5
New York City, NY 10011-8746

My characters are survivors, and many of them are women. I feel, as a Chicana writer, that I am capturing the voices of so many who have been voiceless for years. . . . My work is rooted in the Southwest, in heat and dust, and reflects a world where love is as real as the land. In this dry and seemingly harsh and empty world there is much beauty to be found. That hope of the heart is what feeds me, my characters.

(Contemporary Authors Online)

Books by Denise Chávez

Face of an Angel. Farrar, Straus, and Giroux, 1994.
The Last of the Menu Girls. Arte Público Press, 1986.
Life Is a Two-Way Street. (Editor). Rosetta Press, 1980.
Loving Pedro Infante. Farrar, Straus, & Giroux, 2001. Spanish edition: *Por amour de Pedro Infante*.
Shattering the Myth: Plays by Hispanic Women (Selector), edited by Linda Feyder. Arte Público Press, 1992.
The Woman Who Knew the Language of Animals. Houghton Mifflin, 1992.
Writing Down the River: Into the Heart of the Grand Canyon (Author of Essays), photographed by Kathleen Jo Ryan. Northland, 1998.

Plays by Denise Chávez

The Adobe Rabbit, Elevators, The Flying Tortilla Man, Francis!, The Green Madonna, Hecho en Mexico, How Junior Got Throwed in the Joint, The Language of Vision, The Last of the Menu Girls, The Mask of November, El mas pequeño de mis hijos, La morenita, Nacimiento, Novena narrativas, Plague-Time, Plaza, Santa Fe Charm, El santero de Cordova, Si, hay posada, The Step, The Wait, and *Women in the State of Grace*

Denise Chávez, a renowned Chicana playwright and novelist, is an assistant professor of creative writing, playwrighting, and Chicano literature at New Mexico State University. She earned her bachelor of arts degree in drama from New Mexico State University in 1971. She received a masters of fine arts from Trinity University in San Antonio, Texas, in 1974 and a master's degree in creative writing from the University of New Mexico in 1982.

Born and raised in Las Cruces, New Mexico, Chávez started writing when she was eight years old. She attributes her love for writing to the fact that she spent so much time by herself as a child. "Writing was a way to communicate, explain, understand, and empower myself" (*Latina Self-Portraits*, 34–35). In high school, she discovered that theater was also a powerful way to communicate, and in college she "practically lived in the drama department" (*Latina Self-Portraits*, 35). She wrote her first play when she was a college senior, and since then she has written and produced numerous plays, as well as short stories and novels. Her work has been selected for several anthologies, including *An Anthology of Southwestern Literature, An Anthology: The Indian Río Grande*, and *Voces: An Anthology of Nuevo Mexicano Writers*.

Denise Chávez has been the recipient of many grants, awards, and fellowships, including a 1996 Woman of Distinction Award in Education from the Soroptimist International of the Americas Club and a 1996 Luminaria Award, presented by the New Mexico Community Foundation in Santa Fe. Throughout her career, she has demonstrated a social conscience that has prompted her to present workshops to underserved audiences such as people who are elderly, developmentally disabled, at-risk, and in prison. She is deeply committed to her community in Las Cruces, where she has been the artistic director of the Border Book Festival since its inception in 1994. The festival brings in writers from all over the United States and Mexico. "Expanding the horizons of literature and story and getting people involved is my work as well. I am a community artist, a grassroots person. I hope to leave a legacy of creativity. It's important for me to leave something for those who follow, for posterity" (*Latina Self-Portraits*, 44).

More Information about Denise Chávez

Contemporary Authors Online. The Gale Group, 2001.
Criticism in the Borderlands: Studies in Chicano Literature, Culture, and Ideology, edited by Jose-David Saldivar and Rolando Hinojosa. Duke University Press, 1991.
Dictionary of Literary Biography. Volume 122, 70–76.
Feminist Writers, edited by Pamela Kester-Shelton. St. James Press, 1996.
Latina Self-Portraits: Interviews with Contemporary Women Writers, edited by Bridget Kevane and Juanita Heredia. University of New Mexico Press, 2000.
¡Latinas! Women of Achievement, edited by Diane Telgen and Jim Kamp. Visible Ink Press, 1996.
This Is about Vision: Interviews with Southwestern Writers, edited by William Balassi, John Crawford, and Annie Eysturoy. University of New Mexico Press, 1990.

Selected Works by Denise Chávez

Face of an Angel

American Book Award
Mesilla Valley Writer of the Year Award
Premio Aztlán Award
Grades 12–Up

- Mothers and Daughters
- Socioeconomic Class
- Waitressing
- Women's Roles

Denise Chávez's ambitious first novel centers on the life of Soveida Dosamantes and her connections with a multitude of characters, including extended family members, husbands, lovers, friends, servants, and coworkers. After thirty years of working in a restaurant in the fictional town of Agua Oscura, New Mexico, Soveida is writing a handbook for waitresses called *The Book of Service*. She also takes classes in the Chicano Studies Department at the local community college, where she participates in an oral history project focusing on elderly Chicanas. This 467-page family saga is composed of one rich vignette after another, including stories within stories, passages from Soveida's term papers, letters from her husbands and lovers, and extended dialogues. *Face of an Angel* has been praised for its profound respect for, and understanding of, Chicano/a culture; nontraditional, vibrant protagonist; and humorous, passionate, witty narrative.

The Last of the Menu Girls

Puerto del Sol Fiction Award

Steele Jones Fiction Award for the title story

Grades 11–Adult

- Short Stories
- Authorship

The seven interrelated stories in this first collection feature Rocío Esquibel, a young woman who pushes against the traditional roles that society prescribes for women. As she comes to terms with the issues of her past, she emerges as a writer. Her mother counsels her to write the stories of their lives. In the title story, Rocío works in a hospital as a "menu girl," distributing and collecting menus from the patients. *Library Journal* wrote, "These stories fairly shimmer with the warmth, tones, and language of the Southwest." In 1990, an adaptation of her story cycle, *The Last of the Menu Girls*, was produced as a play by Main Street Theater and the Teatro Bilingue de Houston.

Loving Pedro Infante

Grades 12–Up

- Motion Picture Actors
- Romance

Teresina "Tere" Avila is a divorced, thirty-something Chicana working as a teacher's aide in Cabritoville, New Mexico, a small town near El Paso, Texas. Her life revolves around her job, her best friend, Irma, her lover (a married man), and her membership in the Pedro Infante Club #256. Pedro Infante (1917–1957) was an icon of Mexican popular culture, a onetime carpenter whose career in song and film propelled him to the heights of fame. As secretary of the Pedro Infante Club, Tere is a walking almanac of information about this tragic hero who was killed in a plane crash. According to Irma, "You can learn so about Mejicano culture, class structure, the relationships between men and women, women and women, men and men, as well as intergenerational patterns of collaterality in Pedro's movies" (49). This bittersweet novel unravels the fictions that Tere weaves to justify loving the wrong man. *BookList* wrote, "This thoroughly engaging novel walks the delicate line between comedy and pathos perfectly, using laughter to pull us back from pain but never letting us forget that laughs come with a price." Spanish edition: *Por amour de Pedro Infante.*

Sandra Cisneros

Photo: © Al Rendon

Latina (1954–)
Birthday: December 20
Contact: Susan Bergholz Literary Services
17 West 10th Street, # 5
New York, NY 10011-8746

I always feel such incredible energy about writing about something that has never been set down on paper, hasn't been documented.

(*Authors and Artists for Young Adults*, 76)

When I was 11 years old in Chicago, teachers thought if you were poor and Mexican you didn't have anything to say. Now I think that what I was put on this planet for was to tell these stories.

(*Los Angeles Times*, F1)

Books by Sandra Cisneros

Bad Boys. Mango Press, 1980.
Caramelo. Knopf, 2002.
Hairs/Pelitos. Illustrated by Terry Ybañez. Alfred A. Knopf, 1994.
The House on Mango Street. Arte Público Press, 1984; Vintage Books, 1991; Alfred A. Knopf, 1994. Spanish edition: *La Casa en Mango Street*, translated by Elena Poniatowska. Vintage Books, 1995.
Loose Woman. Alfred A. Knopf, 1994; Vintage Books, 1995.
My Wicked Wicked Ways. Third Woman Press, 1987; Turtle Bay/Knopf, 1992.
Woman Hollering Creek and Other Stories. Random House, 1991; Vintage Books, 1992. Spanish edition: *El arroyo de la Llorona y otros cuentos*.

Sandra Cisneros is the highly acclaimed Chicana author of *The House on Mango Street, Woman Hollering Creek*, and several other superb books. The recipient of numerous honors and awards for her poetry and fiction, her books have been translated into ten languages and published internationally. She also writes essays, articles, book reviews, and interviews. A former high school teacher, counselor, college recruiter, and arts administrator, Cisneros has taught writing at practically every level and worked at several colleges and universities as a writer-in-residence. She has lectured extensively at institutions throughout the United States as well as Mexico and Europe. She currently makes her home in San Antonio, Texas.

Born in Chicago, Cisneros is the daughter of Elvira Cordero Anguiano, a Mexican American, and Alfredo Cisneros del Moral, a Mexican. Because he missed his homeland, her father periodically moved the family from Chicago to Mexico City and back. The frequent upheavals were very upsetting to Cisneros and resulted in her becoming introverted and shy. Being the only daughter out of seven children and spending a lot of time by herself added to her shyness. As a result, she became an astute observer of people and the world around her, a trait that later would contribute greatly to her ability to write with insight, compassion and authenticity: "[T]hat aloneness, that loneliness, was good for a would-be writer—it allowed me time to think and think, to imagine, to read and prepare myself" (*The Mexican American Family Album*, 51).

Cisneros's working-class family moved from place to place, living in poor neighborhoods with empty lots and burned-out buildings. The frequent changing of schools made it difficult for a shy child to make friends. Her early education did not help to build her confidence and self-concept. The Catholic schools that she attended stressed discipline and did not individualize instruction or acknowledge the importance of differences. Afraid to volunteer, she learned to blend into the crowd. Being singled out meant being ridiculed and set up as an example. Cisneros described her schooling as a "rather shabby basic education. If I had lived up to my teachers' expectations, I'd still be working in a factory, because my report card was pretty lousy" (*Authors and Artists for Young Adults, AAYA,* 71).

Escaping into books, Cisneros's imagination created a view of life as a story in which she was the main character. Her love of reading came from her mother, who arranged for her daughter to get her first library card before she learned to read. It wasn't until years later that Cisneros realized that many people actually buy some of their books in addition to borrowing them from the library. She doesn't remember reading poetry; instead, she checked out mostly works of fiction, with Lewis Carroll being one of her favorite authors. An avid reader, she also wrote secretly at home. She modeled her first poems on the rhythmic passages in her reading texts, letting her ear guide her.

When she was twelve, her parents borrowed the money for a down payment on a two-story house in a Puerto Rican neighborhood on the north side of Chicago. Having her own home and being in a stable environment gave Cisneros friends and neighbors who would later provide inspiration for the unique characters in her highly successful book *The House on Mango Street,* which has sold over 500,000 copies and is a part of the curriculum at dozens of schools and universities.

In high school Cisneros first found positive recognition for her creativity. When she read poems aloud in class, her feel for what the writer was saying enabled her to interpret them in a very expressive way. Finally when she was a sophomore, a special teacher came along who encouraged the gifted young student to write. As a result, Cisneros gained confidence, became more public with her work, and eventually was selected as editor of the school literary magazine. During her junior year, she was exposed to the works of established American and British writers. Her elective Spanish class introduced her to the works of Latin American poets whose writing deeply impressed the young writer.

After high school, she attended Loyola University, where she majored in English. Believing that college would be a good place for his daughter to find a husband, her father, an upholsterer, supported her efforts. As Cisneros quipped in *Glamour,* "In retrospect, I'm lucky my father believed daughters were meant for husbands. It meant it didn't matter if I majored in something silly like English. After all, I'd find a nice professional eventually, right?" At Loyola she was reintroduced to the Latin American poets via a generation of American poets influenced by the same. One of her teachers encouraged her to enroll in the poetry section of the University of Iowa Writers' Workshop, a program that led to a master's degree.

The two years at the Iowa Writers' Workshop had a major impact on Cisneros' life and writing. At first the experience was extremely painful, and she found herself alienated from her privileged classmates and surroundings. "In graduate school, what I said was looked at as so wacky that you right away shut up. . . . I became very frightened and terrified that first year. . . . I discovered my otherness and what it was that made me different from everybody else" (*AAYA*, 72). As she became aware of the class, color, and gender differences between herself and the writers represented in the curriculum, her panic turned to outrage. "It was not until this moment when I separated myself, when I considered myself truly distinct, that my writing acquired a voice. I knew I was a Mexican woman, but I didn't think it had anything to do with why I felt so much imbalance in my life, whereas it had everything to do with it! . . . That's when I decided I would write about something my classmates couldn't write about" (*Publishers Weekly*, 74–75).

After she received her master's degree, Cisneros worked as a teacher of literacy skills with people whose first language was English and second language was Spanish and held a position as a college recruiter. In 1982, she received her first National Endowment of the Arts Fellowship for poetry and traveled abroad for one and a half years while she finished *The House on Mango Street*. After her fellowship ended, she took a position in San Antonio, Texas, as arts administrator for a Chicano arts center, a job that she left after a year and a half.

As Cisneros was preparing to leave Texas forever, she learned that she had been awarded the Dobie-Paisano fellowship, an award that included a home for six months. This was 1985, and her flight from Texas was deferred. She left Texas several times, but the "final time" was in 1987 because she couldn't find a job teaching. (She later returned to Texas, where she has made San Antonio her home.) Cisneros accepted a position at California State University in Chico, which acknowledged her small press book as a "real" publication. In 1988, Cisneros met her literary agent, and, as a result, her books were sold to Random House. Her book *Woman Hollering Creek*, a series of short stories published in 1991, received wide distribution and glowing reviews, thrusting her into the national limelight.

Cisneros has been the recipient of many awards and honors, including a second National Endowment of the Arts Fellowship in 1988, an honorary doctor of letters from the State University of New York at Purchase in 1993, and a MacArthur Fellowship in 1995. (Additional awards are listed with the reviews of her books.) Cisneros has surmounted barriers of gender, class, and race to achieve the success that many of her people have been denied. She explains that writers with backgrounds similar to her own have historically been "the illegal aliens of American lit" and "the migrant workers in terms of respect" (*Mother Jones*, 15). But Cisneros, like Esperanza in *The House on Mango Street*, will never forget her roots. As a spokesperson for her people, she introduces mainstream audiences to the complexities of Latina life and breaks down longstanding, debilitating stereotypes. Her writing is her way of making change in the world, of setting things right. "I'm very fierce about people coming from the community having an obligation to the community" (*AAYA*, 76).

In addition to her writing, Cisneros is an annual volunteer lecturer at schools in the San Antonio area. She is a member and organizer of Mujeres por la paz, a San Antonio women's peace group. She recently adapted two stories from *Woman Hollering Creek* to the stage—*Milagritos*, a show that she wrote, directed, and performed. When she gives a reading at a library or school, she frequently passes around her fifth-grade report card, which has mostly Cs and Ds, to demonstrate that schools often do not recognize the talents of students and that grades are not reliable predictors of a person's future. Cisneros is known as a passionate, electric reader with outspoken views, and her audiences hang on her every word. She often talks with students about the omission of works by Chicanos, saying, "How many Latino and Latina writers do you see in your books? Why only one?" She adds, "The whole system in their neighborhoods where they are growing up is created to keep them failing. . . . I tell them they have to be very ferocious to beat those odds" (*The Boston Globe*, 76).

More Information about Sandra Cisneros

Books

Authors and Artists for Young Adults, Volume 9, 69–76.
Contemporary Authors Online. The Gale Group, 2001.
Contemporary Literary Criticism, Volume 69.
Contemporary Novelists. St. James Press, 2001.
Contemporary Women Poets. St. James Press, 1998.
Dictionary of Literary Biography, Volumes 122, 152.
Latina Self-Portraits: Interviews with Contemporary Women Writers, edited by Bridget Kevane and *Juanita Heredia*. University of New Mexico Press, 2000.
¡Latinas! Women of Achievement, edited by Diane Telgen and Jim Kamp. Visible Ink Press, 1996.
The Mexican American Family Album by Dorothy and Thomas Hoobler. Oxford University Press, 1994.
Notable Hispanic Women, Book I, 99–101.
The Oxford Companion to Women's Writing in the United States, edited by Cathy N. Davidson and Linda Wagner-Martin. Oxford University Press, 1995.
Sandra Cisneros in the Classroom: "Do not forget to reach," by Carol Jago. National Council of Teachers of English, 2002.
Sandra Cisneros: Latina Writer and Activist by Caryn Mirriam-Goldberg. Enslow, 1998.
St. James Guide to Young Adult Writers. St. James Press, 1999.
"Truth, Lies, and Memory: A Profile of Sandra Cisneros" by Renee H. Shea. *Poets and Writers*. Sept./Oct. 2002, 31–35.

Videotape

Sandra Cisneros. Lannan Foundation, 1997.

Periodicals

America. July 25, 1992, 39–42.
Boston Globe. May 17, 1994, 73, 76.
Glamour. November 1990, 256–257.
Library Journal. January 1992, 55.
Los Angeles Times. May 7, 1991, F1.
Los Angeles Times Book Review. April 28, 1991, 3.
Mirabella. April 1991, 46.
Mother Jones. October 1989, 15.
Newsweek. June 3, 1991, 60.
New York Times Book Review. May 26, 1991, 6.
Publishers Weekly. March 29, 1991, 74–75.
San Francisco Examiner. December 22, 1994, A17.
VISáVIS. September 1992, 64–65, 121.
Washington Post Book World. June 9, 1991, 3.

Selected Works by Sandra Cisneros

Caramelo

Grades 11–Up

- Family Saga
- Fathers and Daughters
- Identity

This is the long-awaited family saga of a Mexican American family crossing and recrossing the border. "Based on [Cisneros'] life, the book features a large cast of characters who, with humor and tenderness, tell the story of growing up between worlds. . . . [W]ritten in the aftermath of her father's death in the mid-1990s, the book also concerns father–daughter relationships" (*Sandra Cisneros: Latina Writer and Activist*, 97).

Hairs/Pelitos

All Ages

- Bilingual
- Hair
- Differences

This endearing bilingual picture book is excerpted from *The House on Mango Street*. The young narrator describes the different types of hair that each family member has. The locks vary from stiff hair that stands up in the air, to hair that is thick and straight, to hair that is like fur. Then there is the rebellious hair that refuses to accept hair bands or barrettes.

But the most special hair of all smells like fresh bread and symbolizes love, belonging, and security. Vivid illustrations feature the family members on bright backgrounds, each picture framed with playful images of toys, stars, flowers, or birds. Not only do the people have different colors and textures of hair, but their faces are of varying hues, providing an intimate portrayal of diversity. Readers of all ages and backgrounds enjoy studying the pictures and reading or listening to the warm, lyrical bilingual text. A natural extension is to discuss (with sensitivity) the similarities and differences in the hair on the heads of the members of the group, whether it be at home, in the library, or in the classroom. After enjoying this exuberant book, readers will want to check out the other stories in *The House on Mango Street*. Hopefully, more of these precious vignettes will find their way into enchanting picture books. The author of this unique book, Sandra Cisneros, notes that she has cropped, straight, shiny black hair.

The House on Mango Street

American Book Award from the Before Columbus Foundation

Grades 6–Up

- Short Stories
- Identity

Dedicated "To the Women/A las Mujeres," this stunningly eloquent collection of forty-four short, interrelated vignettes tells the story of Esperanza Cordero, a young girl growing up in the Latino/a section of Chicago. With lyrical power and breathtaking imagery, Cisneros captures the pain of the outsider, the yearning and conflict about belonging and independence, and the poignant search for identity. Esperanza, whose name means hope in English and "too many letters" in Spanish, observes the interactions and happenings in her noisy, crowded neighborhood. As she shares her perceptions of the world around her, she gradually matures and becomes aware of her own strength and beauty. She recounts many touching experiences: the deaths of relatives and neighbors; kids without respect for all living things, including themselves; and a humiliating encounter with Sister Superior at school. The lively stories are filled with children jumping rope while making up rhymes, neighbors pitching pennies and playing dominoes, laundry and motorcycles, and coconut and papaya juice. Esperanza describes the girls and women who live on Mango Street: Marin, who is dancing by herself waiting for her life to change; Alicia, who doesn't want to spend her life in a factory or behind a rolling pin; Ruthie, who is a good whistler; Rafaela, whose possessive husband locks her inside their apartment while he plays dominoes; and Sally, who escapes an abusive father into a prison of a marriage. We meet Minerva, who is battered by "her husband who left and keeps leaving," who cries and "writes poems on little pieces of paper that she folds over and over and holds in her hands a long time."

In one of the many eloquent pieces, "Four Skinny Trees," Cisneros writes, "They are the only ones who understand me." She describes the trees as four raggedy excuses with skinny necks who do not belong here. "They send ferocious roots beneath the ground . . . and bite the sky with violent teeth and never quit their anger." When she is too sad, Esperanza finds hope by looking at the trees. Later, after she is raped, she tries to will her heart to stop beating. She begins her own quiet war and vows "not to grow up tame like the others who lay their necks on the threshold waiting for the ball and chain." She is too strong to stay; she plans her escape, knowing that she will never forget who she is and will return someday for the ones she left behind.

Cisneros writes that *The House on Mango Street* started out as a memoir but evolved into a collective story based on people from her past and present. She started writing it when she was twenty-two years old and in graduate school. Surrounded by privileged people, studying the works of white writers, she discovered her otherness. She writes that she chose to use a very antiacademic voice in the book: "It's in this rebellious realm of antipoetics that I tried to create a poetic text with the most unofficial language I could find." Thus she created this tender and fierce book about the transformation of a young woman entangled in roots that both enrich and constrain her.

The House on Mango Street was a National Endowment for the Arts Entry in the 1986 Frankfurt and Barcelona International Book Fairs. It has sold over 300,000 copies and is studied in dozens of schools and universities. Rodney D. Smith, a teacher and writer in Piedmont, California, wrote about his experiences using the book in his ninth grade English class. Before adding the book to the curriculum, he and his colleagues had to overcome criticism from parents, school board members, and coworkers who were concerned that the adoption of the new work would come at the expense of "great literature." They asked what multicultural author could match or excel the works of F. Scott Fitzgerald, Mark Twain, or Shakespeare. Smith responds: "*The House on Mango Street* dispels these criticisms. The book's use of voice, theme, and symbolism, as well as the honesty and clarity of its writing, rival that of the best novels I have ever taught" (*San Francisco Examiner*, A17).

The creativity and power of the stories in *The House on Mango Street* are excellent models for young writers. The juxtaposition of beauty and harsh reality and the strong, angry young voice help students examine their own inner conflicts, family issues, and questions about life. *The House on Mango Street* offers many options for exploring the constraints of class, race, and gender and for increasing awareness about ways of creating change within and without. Spanish edition: *La Casa en Mango Street*. Audiobook: *Woman Hollering Creek and The House on Mango Street*. Sandra Cisneros reads selections from these two books.

Woman Hollering Creek and Other Stories

PEN Center West Award for Best Fiction
Anisfield-Wolf Book Award
Lannan Foundation Literary Award
Quality Paperback Book Club New Voices Award
New York Times Noteworthy Book of the Year
American Library Journal Noteworthy Book of the Year
Los Angeles Times Best Book of Fiction
Grades 10–Adult

- Short Stories

As she drives across the arroyo, Felice "opens her mouth and lets out a yell as loud as any mariachi" (55). Why? Because the name of the creek is Woman Hollering. So every time she crosses the bridge, she hollers. In this evocative collection, Cisneros writes about women's search for independence, for love, for balance. Alternately set in Mexico and the border region of Texas, each story is unique and unforgettable. Cisneros set out to represent her community in an honorable way, stating that she attempted "to populate the book with as many different kinds of Latinos as possible so that mainstream America could see how diverse we are." She continues, "The emotions of almost all the characters are the most autobiographical elements in the stories because I really had to look within myself to make all these characters" (*Authors and Artists for Young Adults, AAYA*, 74).

In the heartrending story "Eleven," Rachel's birthday is ruined by a cruel teacher. As Rachel burns with humiliation, she thinks, "I wish I was invisible but I'm not . . . I want today to be far away already, far away like a runaway balloon." (9). The old red sweater symbolizes all those other hurts and indignities that Rachel has suffered, the ones that resulted in her being silenced, unable to speak up and say that the sweater is not hers. In "Mericans," misogyny rears its ugly head even at an early age when the boys' favorite insult is to call someone "Girl." In "Never Marry a Mexican," the narrator confides, "I'm amphibious. I'm a person who doesn't belong to any class" (71). Some of Cisneros' stories are filled with humor and piercing wit, and others are tender, full of sorrow and so much hurt. These are women who are battered, abandoned, disowned, and shamed, and yet they rise up like Ines, Zapata's common-law wife who has learned how to abandon her body at will and fly away as an owl. She circles above the village, seeing through the ages, from past to future, watching the fate of her family, of her people. She speaks of "How words can hold their own magic. How a word can charm, and how a word can kill" (105). Cisneros draws on Latin American mythology for some of the stories. But she notes, "I'm very intent on revising mythology because it is male. I'm part of a generation of women that is looking at history in a revisionist manner—in a way that is going to help to empower women to rethink history" (*AAYA*, 75). Another narrator writes a letter to Virgencita in which she says that "those who suffer have a special power, don't they? The power of understanding someone else's pain. And understanding is the beginning of healing" (128). *Woman Hollering Creek* and Cisneros' other books offer much in the way of understanding and healing. Spanish edition: *El arroyo de la Llorona y otros cuentos*. Audiobook: *Woman Hollering Creek and The House on Mango Street*. Sandra Cisneros reads selections from these two books.

Judith Ortiz Cofer

Photo: John Cofer

Puerto Rican American (1952–)
Birthday: February 24
Contact: The Chelsea Forum
420 West 23rd Street, #5D
New York, NY 10011
(212) 243-4400

My aim as a teacher is to expose students of whatever age to model works of literature that are interesting and accessible, but at the same time I want them to find their own individual voices. My aim is to convince those who want to write that their own lives are the raw material. I show them how they can begin to understand themselves and the world around them by writing about it, as I have done.

(Brochure published by Milledgeville-Baldwin County Allied Arts)

Books by Judith Ortiz Cofer

An Island Like You: Stories of the Barrio. Orchard, 1995.
The Latin Deli: Prose and Poetry. University of Georgia Press, 1993.
The Line of the Sun. University of Georgia Press, 1990.
Peregrina. Riverstone Press, 1986.
Reaching for the Mainland. Bilingual Press, 1987.
Silent Dancing: A Partial Remembrance of a Puerto Rican Childhood. Arte Público Press, 1991. Spanish edition: *Bailando en silencio: Escenas de una niñez puertorriqueña*.
Sleeping with One Eye Open: Women Writers and the Art of Survival, coedited with Marilyn Kallet. University of Georgia Press, 1999.
Terms of Survival. Arte Público Press, 1987.
Woman in Front of the Sun: On Becoming a Writer. University of Georgia Press, 2000.
The Year of Our Revolution: New and Selected Stories and Poems. Arte Público Press, 1998.

Judith Ortiz Cofer, a professor of English and creative writing at the University of Georgia, is widely recognized for her poetry, fiction, short stories, and essays. Her work has appeared in numerous journals and anthologies. She has won a number of awards for her writing, including the Anisfield Wolf Book Award for *The Latin Deli* and a PEN/Martha Albrand Special Citation for *Silent Dancing*. She has received fellowships from the National Endowment for the Arts, the Witter Bynner Foundation for Poetry, and the Bread Loaf Writers' Conference.

Born in the Puerto Rican town of Hormigueros, Ortiz Cofer was raised in Paterson, New Jersey, and Puerto Rico. Her parents were married when her mother was not quite fifteen years old. Her father joined the U.S. Army a few months after the wedding and was transferred to Panama, where he stayed for the next two years. Judith was born a year after the wedding and enjoyed the adoration of her mother, grandmother, and aunt for those first few years. Then the family started a pattern that would continue for the remainder of her childhood of moving back and forth between New Jersey and Puerto Rico. The experience of growing up in two worlds was often bewildering, frustrating, and painful. However, this unique heritage has become Ortiz Cofer's literary inspiration: her poetry and prose spring from her experiences as a bicultural and bilingual person. These two parts of herself have contributed substantially to her ability to write poetry and prose that are unique.

Ortiz Cofer's parents, as different as fire and ice, symbolize the dichotomies of her childhood. Her father, quiet and serious, was obsessed with getting out of the barrio and proving that his family was not like other Puerto Ricans. Her mother, earthy and ebullient, reluctantly moved her children back and forth between Puerto Rico and New Jersey, always yearning for her beloved homeland. When they were on the mainland, the children learned to be quiet and inconspicuous and to keep to themselves. Their father was excessively protective and anxious for them to assimilate. Meanwhile, their mother suffered from "*La Tristeza*, the sadness that only place induces and only place cures" (*Silent Dancing*, 61). Ortiz Cofer became an avid watcher of television programs, from which she learned about middle America. She also became an insatiable reader and soon became addicted to fairy tales.

As her family moved from the cold city to the tropical island and back again, Ortiz Cofer became a "cultural chameleon, developing early the ability to blend into a crowd, to sit and read quietly in a fifth story apartment for days and days . . . or, set free, to run wild in Mamá's realm" (*Silent Dancing*, 17). But in either place, she felt like an "oddball". Her peers made fun of her two-way accent: a Spanish accent when she spoke English, and when she spoke Spanish, she was told she sounded like a "Gringa." A humiliating experience with a teacher in New Jersey taught her that language is the only weapon that a child has against the power of adults. She quickly began building up her arsenal of words. She served as interpreter and buffer to the world for her mother. Ortiz Cofer was the one who faced store clerks, doctors, and landlords because her mother believed that her exile from Puerto Rico was temporary and therefore did not learn to speak English.

Each time that they returned to Puerto Rico, Ortiz Cofer felt "freed . . . like pigeons from a cage" (*Silent Dancing*). Her maternal grandmother was a great storyteller; often her stories were cautionary parables from which her grandchildren were to learn the truth as she saw it. Ortiz Cofer viewed her as her model and liberator. She states that her grandmother's "*cuentos* are forever woven into the fabric of my imagination" (*Silent Dancing*, 19). At her grandmother's knee, she learned about strength and the power of storytelling, as well as much about her culture and heritage. Her grandmother's stories presented contrasting views of women's roles. First, a woman might be like the mythical María Sabida who slept with one eye open, always alert and never a victim. Or she might be like María La Loca, who gave everything up for love and became a victim of her foolish heart. The choices were to get married or become a nun or a prostitute. A woman might become a teacher or nurse until she found a man to marry. But the worst fate of all, according to her grandmother, would be to end up alone.

When Ortiz Cofer was fifteen years old, she went to Puerto Rico for the last time as a child. During her stay there, she realized that she felt smothered by the familial press of her grandmother's home. Resentful at being yanked once again from her life on the mainland, where she felt that she was finally beginning to learn the rules, she once again learned a number of valuable lessons from her grandmother. She watched as Mamá followed a routine of labor and self-sacrifice. She became aware of the new contours and biological changes in her body. During this summer as a *quinceañera,* she thought about the many directions that a woman's life might take. Perhaps this is when she decided to pursue her dream of becoming a writer and educator.

Earlier in New Jersey, Ortiz Cofer had entered a high school where she was the only Puerto Rican student. Having gotten into the school after taking a rigorous academic test, she again felt lost. "Everyday I crossed the border of two countries." At the time, she didn't realize that this experience would later provide inspiration for her writing. She learned to depend on knowledge as her main source of security. She loved libraries; they contained the information that she needed to survive in two languages and two worlds. She read to escape and also to connect. She notes, "Even now, a visit to the library recharges the batteries in my brain . . . there is no subject I cannot investigate, no world I cannot explore. Everything that is is mine for the asking. Because I can read about it" (*The Latin Deli,* 134).

Her final two and a half years of high school were spent in Augusta, Georgia, where her family moved in search of a more peaceful environment. Her father had retired from the army, and relatives in Georgia convinced him that it was a better place to raise teenagers. Ortiz Cofer recalls, "For me it was a shock to the senses, like moving from one planet to another" (*The Latin Deli,* 127). She was the only Puerto Rican in a school of nearly 2,000 students. She excelled academically, but her social life was largely uneventful.

She won a scholarship to college and earned a bachelor of arts degree in English from Augusta College in 1971 and a master of arts in English from Florida Atlantic University in 1977. Subsequently, she has been a bilingual teacher, an instructor of both English and Spanish, and a lecturer and has conducted poetry writing workshops. Her many writer-in-residence assignments include Sweet Briar College in Virginia, a women's prison in Georgia, the Guadalupe Cultural Arts Center in San Antonio, and Westchester University in Pennsylvania.

"I came to writing instinctively, as a dowser finds an underground well. . . . I had found poetry, or it had found me, and it was demanding a place in my life" (*The Latin Deli,* 167). Ortiz Cofer reflects that she felt that something was missing in her life until she started writing. So in order to fit it into her busy schedule, she got up at 5:00 A.M. every day and wrote for two hours. After nearly ten years of writing poetry, her first book was published. She wrote two pages a day for three and one-half years to complete her first novel, *The Line of the Sun*. This incredible need to write taught her the discipline of art. Painfully aware of the crucial need for social change, she states, "My personal goal in my public life is to try to replace the old pervasive stereotypes and myths about Latinas with a much more interesting set of realities. Every time I give a reading, I hope the stories I tell, the dreams and fears I examine in my work, can achieve some universal truth which will get my audience past the particulars of my skin color, my accent, or my clothes" (*The Latin Deli*, 154).

In *Silent Dancing*, Ortiz Cofer writes about her visits to Puerto Rico as an adult. These yearly pilgrimages to her mother's town, the place where she was born, are symbolic of the clash of cultures and generations that mother and daughter represent. In a poem titled "So Much for Mañana," printed in *Terms of Survival*, her mother urges her to put away the heavy books and return to Puerto Rico. Perhaps she will return someday, but for now she is busy writing books that have been described as "treasures," "stellar," "distinguished," and "magical."

Judith Ortiz Cofer told *Contemporary Authors*: "The place of birth itself becomes a metaphor for the things we must leave behind; the assimilation of a new culture is the coming into maturity by accepting the terms necessary for survival. My poetry is a study of this process of change, assimilation and transformation."

More Information about Judith Ortiz Cofer

Contemporary Authors, Volume 32, 88–89.
Contemporary Authors, Volume 115, 97–98.
Contemporary Authors Online. The Gale Group, 2001.
The Hispanic Literary Companion, edited by Nicolás Kanellos. Visible Ink Press, 1997, 229–236.
Latina Self-Portraits: Interview with Contemporary Women Writers, edited by Bridget Kevane and Juanita Hereida. University of New Mexico Press, 2000.
The Latin Deli by Judith Ortiz Cofer.
¡Latinas! Women of Achievement, edited by Diane Telgen and Jim Kamp. Visible Ink Press, 1996.
Notable Hispanic American Women, 103–104.
The Oxford Companion to Women's Writing in the United States, edited by Cathy N. Davidson and Linda Wagner-Martin. Oxford University Press, 1995, 645.
Silent Dancing: A Partial Remembrance of a Puerto Rican Childhood by Judith Ortiz Cofer.

Selected Works by Judith Ortiz Cofer

An Island Like You: Stories of the Barrio

Pura Belpré Award

American Library Association Best Book for Young Adults

Horn Book Fanfare Award

Hungry Mind Review Book of Distinction

Grades 5–10

• Short Stories

Twelve vibrant stories portray the diverse world of Puerto Rican American teenagers in a New Jersey barrio; these sensitive explorations of adolescence provide insight into the complex experience of growing up in two cultures. Dedicated to the author's family here and on the island, the book opens with a lively poem, "Day in the Barrio." We hear the cinder-block jukebox of El Building blasting salsas, we cross the treacherous bridge of a wino's legs, and we stop at Cheo's bodega for plantains and gossip. We climb the seven flights to the roof, where we watch the people below, realizing that each one is "an island like you." The interconnected stories introduce likable, interesting young people. In "Bad Influence," Rita's parents send her to Puerto Rico for a summer with her grandparents to get her away from her boyfriend. Much to her surprise, Rita ends up having one of the best summers of her life. In "Arturo's Flight," the protagonist, ridiculed by his macho classmates for being different, plans to run away. He finds comfort in poetry and the company of an old man who cleans the church. Doris, in "The One Who Watches," feeling scared and invisible, decides she has to start figuring out who she is. She reappears in a later story, "White Balloons," and plays a major role in starting a barrio theater group; she gradually starts feeling fully three-dimensional. "White Balloons" also introduces two gay men, one of whom had grown up in the barrio, escaped to Broadway to become a celebrated actor, and returned to start a theater group for young people when he discovered he was HIV-positive.

Written with humor, authenticity, and compassion, the stories in this collection deal with intergenerational issues, eating disorders, peer pressure, death and dying, looksism, sexism, shoplifting, gangs, drugs, mentally challenged people, homosexuality, socioeconomic class, and more. The spirited adolescent characters learn to examine people carefully, begin to ask whose opinion is important, and learn not to judge people by their age, appearance, disability, gender, language, occupation, or sexual orientation.

The Latin Deli: Prose and Poetry

The Anisfield Wolf Book Award
Grades 12–Adult

- Short Stories
- Poetry
- Biographical Essays
- Women

By blending fiction, poetry, and autobiographical essays, Judith Ortiz Cofer offers her readers a smorgasbord of the sights, smells, tastes, sounds, emotions, and experiences of Puerto Rican women adjusting to life on the mainland. Winner of the Anisfield Wolf Book Award to honor books "which contribute to . . . our appreciation of the rich diversity of human cultures," *The Latin Deli* is rich in retrospective detail and universal truths. The alternating sections of prose and poetry begin with a portrait of life in El Building in the barrio of Paterson, New Jersey. A sixteen-year-old copes with her excessively protective father's rules by reading. "I felt like an exile in the foreign country of my parents' house. Books kept me from going mad" (16). In another piece, a young woman deals with the racist rejection by her new white boyfriend's mother while the adults around her are mourning the assassination of President Kennedy. In "The Witch's Husband," set in Puerto Rico, Ortiz Cofer's grandmother shares the story of her own flight for freedom while telling her granddaughter an old, old story of a woman who flew away each night to join other women in a ritual of independence. Other pieces explore themes of death and grieving, adultery, self-sacrificing women and patriarchal men, generational conflicts, age, family secrets, and dreams of returning to Puerto Rico after retirement.

A number of the pieces in *The Latin Deli* are autobiographical and along with *Silent Dancing* provide insight into the life and writing of Judith Ortiz Cofer and her early struggles to consolidate her opposing cultural identities as well as her need and determination to write. She elaborates on the role that literature has played in her life. As a youngster, she discovered fairy tales: "It was the way I absorbed fantasy in those days that gave me the sense of inner freedom, a feeling of power and the ability to fly that is the main reward of the writer" (132). She escaped the turmoils of her nomadic life by turning to books; this insatiable reading, in turn, helped her become more adept with her second language.

Ortiz Cofer also shares her experiences with a dictatorial and straying father, anti-Puerto Rican prejudice, Roman Catholic contradictions regarding the spirit and flesh, and the degradation of African Americans by the educational system. In an especially poignant piece, "The Story of My Body," she describes her physical self; this essay provides a powerful, albeit implicit argument for judging people by their character, not their skin color, size, or appearance. The concluding pieces in this moving book provide a glimpse into this gifted author's adult life as a writer, educator, and advocate for communication between, and respect for, all people.

The Line of the Sun

New York Library's List of the 25 Most Memorable Books of 1989
Grades 12–Adult

- Fiction

Judith Ortiz Cofer's first novel is an eloquent chronicle of the lives of three generations of a Puerto Rican family. It begins in the village of Salud, Puerto Rico, where Mamá Cielo and Papá Pepe are raising their three children, Carmelo, Guzmán, and Ramona. Carmelo, like his father, is a lover of books and solitude. When village gossip reveals that he is gay, he escapes by joining the army and is killed in Korea a short time later. Ramona is the quiet, obedient daughter who helps take care of the household. She marries Guzmán's best friend, Rafael, who joins the navy soon after the wedding. Guzmán is an exuberant, wild boy whose boundless energy and curiosity constantly propel him into trouble. After a number of escapades, he finally escapes to the United States, where the family loses track of him for a number of years.

Years later, the admiration of Ramona's daughter, Marisol, for her adventurous uncle Guzmán and her telling of his life story contrast the world of rural Puerto Rico with that of metropolitan Paterson, New Jersey. The young narrator and secret biographer pieces together the story of her uncle's life through conversations around her mother's kitchen table in their apartment in El Building. Marisol, who has a rebellious streak herself, is elated when the hero of her imagination finally drops in on her family one Christmas Eve. He tells the family how he ended up a prisoner in a labor camp and eventually escaped to become a subway warrior. Marisol, who is feeling alienated from her parents and is frustrated with living in a state of limbo between two cultures, identifies with her uncle and his restless spirit. When he is injured, she becomes his confidante and personal spy, reporting on the imminent labor strike, spiritist meetings, and police surveillance of El Building. The inevitable tragedy results in Guzmán's return to Puerto Rico. Marisol continues to tell his story as she follows her line of the sun, her future as read in the lines in her hand.

In this extraordinary first novel, Judith Ortiz Cofer's brilliant use of the technique of the narrator telling her uncle's story before she introduces herself is an inspired way to contrast and bridge two cultures and three generations. Marisol confides, "In my mind I had made his story mine . . . drawing excitement from all he represented to me" (282). Through Guzmán's example, she is able to begin consolidating two very different worlds, one that represents the past in the beloved homeland of Puerto Rico and the other, her future as a Puerto Rican woman in a society that does not value her cultural heritage. She muses that, "though I will always carry my Island heritage on my back like a snail, I belonged in the world of phones, offices, concrete buildings, and the English language" (273). As many first novels do, *The Line of the Sun* has autobiographical elements. Marisol's experiences are similar in many ways to those of the author. Uncle Guzmán's character is based on her uncle Hernán, whom she describes in *Silent Dancing*. Readers examining this book within the context of Ortiz Cofer's complete body of work will find other similarities and a number of interesting differences.

In *The Latin Deli*, Ortiz Cofer noted that in order to find time to write *The Line of the Sun*, she got up at 5:00 A.M. and wrote two pages a day for three and a half years. Her determined effort to write her first novel is a splendidly successful one in which she draws the reader into an intriguing landscape where the settings are authentic, the language is resonant, the narrative is multidimensional, and the characters are fully realized.

Silent Dancing: A Partial Remembrance of a Puerto Rican Childhood

New York Library Best Books for the Teenage
PEN Martha Albrand Special Citation for Non-Fiction
Pushcart Prize for the essay "More Room"
Grades 10–Adult

- Autobiography

These beautifully written memoirs eloquently express the complex experience of growing up in two worlds, of learning to be a "cultural chameleon." Judith Ortiz Cofer relates the story of the first fifteen years of her life through prose and poetry, revealing the ways in which her bicultural/bilingual childhood shaped her identity and contributed to her development as a writer and teacher. Her literary mentor, Virginia Woolf, provided inspiration for her process of reclaiming memories to discover meaning and truth in ordinary events. With insight and sensitivity, Ortiz Cofer addresses the themes of female roles and conditioning, dual existence, and the clash of culture and age.

Ortiz Cofer's parents, as different as fire and ice, symbolize the dichotomies of her childhood. Her father, quiet and serious, joined the navy before Judith was born. He was obsessed with getting out of the barrio and proving that his family was not like other Puerto Ricans. Her mother, earthy and ebullient, reluctantly moved her children back and forth between Puerto Rico and New Jersey, always yearning for her beloved homeland. Ortiz Cofer portrays her maternal grandmother, Mamá, a storyteller and the family matriarch, with admiration and sensitivity. One of Mamá's stories is included in the book; the tale of María Sabida provides a model of the "prevailing woman" who was always alert and never a victim. Grandmother's *cuentos* fired her granddaughter's imagination and are "forever woven into the fabric of my imagination." Ortiz Cofer includes a María Sabida fable that she embroidered to entertain herself when she was quite young.

Ortiz Cofer fell in love with reading at an early age; she learned to cope with the quiet, indoor New Jersey life imposed by her excessively protective father by becoming an insatiable reader. She discovered the power of language as she learned to negotiate her way between the two parts of her life.

In the title essay, "Silent Dancing," which was included in the 1991 *Best American Essays*, Ortiz Cofer writes about a five-minute home movie that ends with people dancing in a circle. She notes that these images provide a significant visual aid to her first memories of life in Paterson. As she examines her thoughts and feelings about the images on the screen, memories come flooding back. Perhaps, the silent dance also symbolizes her internal struggles to understand her world as a child living simultaneously in two cultures. Spanish edition: *Bailando en silencio: Escenas de una niñez puertorriqueña.*

Terms of Survival

Grades 10–Adult

- Poetry

In these fifty moving poems, Judith Ortiz Cofer explores the process of change, assimilation, and transformation. In "El Olvido," she cautions that it is dangerous to forget the climate of one's birthplace. She writes about her family, both the ones who came to the United States and those who remained on the island of Puerto Rico. Wanting to be released from rituals, she writes about faith, madness, wickedness, always and never, poverty, prostitutes, and dreams, as she confronts customs, rites of passage, and cultural icons. In "So Much for Mañana," her mother urges her to return to the island before her brain splits from all her studying. Writing poetry is her way of recovering the past and creating the future. She wrote most of these poems during a residency at the Virginia Center for the Creative Arts. Ortiz Cofer elaborates on the themes of some of these poems in her autobiography, *Silent Dancing: A Partial Remembrance of a Puerto Rican Childhood*. A glossary of Spanish words and terms is provided.

Woman in Front of the Sun: On Becoming a Writer

College–Adult

- Authorship

In this fascinating collection of essays woven with poems and folklore, the author tells the story of how she became a poet and writer and explores her love of words, her discovery of the magic of language, and her struggle to carve out time to practice her art.

The Year of Our Revolution: New and Selected Stories and Poems

Grades 9–12

- Autobiography
- Poetry
- Short Stories

In this kaleidoscopic collection of interconnected poems and stories about growing up during the turbulent 1960s, the author examines tensions between Puerto Rican immigrant parents and their American-raised children. The revolution implied in the title is one that takes place when the daughter struggles for independence, rebelling against her parents' rules. In "Gravity" the daughter removes her parents' religious artifacts from her bedroom wall. "I was taking a stand by refusing to decorate with angels and saints, and by disdaining everything my parents loved" (41). Other pieces detail battles over clothes, music, friends, and behavior. *The Year of Our Revolution* has been described as radiant, lyrical, and sophisticated.

Lulu Delacre

Puerto Rican American (1957–)
Birthday: December 20

Contact: Publicity
Scholastic Inc.
555 Broadway
New York, NY 10012-3999
(212) 343-4468
luludela@erols.com

Anything you want, you can achieve, as long as you work hard for it.

(Personal Communication)

I believe childhood should be a wonderful stage in a person's life, and if my drawings add a little happiness in a child's day, I consider my life fulfilled.

(*Something about the Author,* Volume 36, p. 67)

Books by Lulu Delacre

Written and Illustrated

Arroz con Leche: Popular Songs and Rhymes from Latin America. Scholastic, 1989.
Golden Tales: Myths, Legends, and Folktales from Latin America. Scholastic, 1996. (Spanish edition: *De oro y esmeraldas*. Scholastic, 1996.)
Las Navidades: Popular Christmas Songs from Latin America. Scholastic, 1990.
Nathan and Nicholas Alexander. Scholastic, 1986.
Nathan's Balloon Adventure. Scholastic, 1991. (Book Club Edition)
Nathan's Fishing Trip. Scholastic, 1988. Out of Print.
Peter Cottontail's Easter Book. Scholastic, 1991. Out of Print.
Salsa Stories. Scholastic, 2000.
Time for School, Nathan. Scholastic, 1989.
Vejigante Masquerader. Scholastic, 1993.

Illustrated

The Bossy Gallito/El Gallo de Bodas: A Traditional Cuban Folktale retold by Lucía M. Gonzáles. Scholastic, 1994.
Los zapaticos de rosa by José Martî. Lectorum, 1997.
Señor Cat's Romance and Other Favorite Stories from Latin America retold by Lucía M. González. Scholastic, 2001.
Shake It, Morena! And Other Folklore from Puerto Rico compiled by Carmen T. Bernier-Grand. Millbrook, 2002. (See Bernier-Grand's chapter for more information.)

Lulu Delacre is the accomplished author and illustrator of a number of award-winning books for young readers. A multitalented artist and writer, she speaks three languages fluently: Spanish, English, and French. Her work has been exhibited in the United States, Puerto Rico, and Paris. Sought after as a speaker, she has given presentations at numerous schools, conferences, and institutes. She has been honored as a Maryland Woman in the Arts and as a Write from Maryland Author.

Born in Rio Piedras, Puerto Rico, Delacre is the middle child in a family of three daughters. Her parents, Marta Orzabal Delacre, a French professor, and Georges Carlos Delacre, a philosophy professor, are from Argentina. Delacre has fond memories of growing up on the sunny, hot island. She often climbed a tamarindo tree with a friend to eat the fruit. On weekends, her father frequently took his three daughters to the beach, where they enjoyed watching the small tropical fish among the rocks along the shore.

Delacre's earliest memory of drawing takes her back to her grandmother's house. Her grandma, who was from Uruguay, took care of the children while their parents taught at the University of Puerto Rico. Delacre spent many happy hours lying on the floor, drawing as they listened to classical music on the record player. Her grandmother saved all her drawings and neatly stacked them in a corner of her closet. The children also loved disguising themselves with their grandmother's scarves and hats and dancing in front of an old mirror in her room.

When she was ten years old, Delacre's family spent a year in Buenos Aires, Argentina, where her father was on sabbatical leave. There she had her first formal art training. One of her mother's friends, who was a fine artist and who gave lessons to adults, encouraged the talented young artist to join her class. Delacre learned to draw from real life, and her joy in being able to create intensified. Her parents encouraged her to pursue her artistic abilities, and she enjoyed withdrawing into her own private world of dreams as she drew.

By the time she entered the Department of Fine Arts at the University of Puerto Rico, Delacre knew that she wanted to be an artist. At nineteen, she was in Paris, France, where she had been accepted on full scholarship at the distinguished art school L'Ecole Supérieure d'Arts Graphiques. She spent three years of intensive study of photography, typography, design, and illustration. During her second year there, she was very impressed with an exhibit of the work of Maurice Sendak. Her honors thesis was an audiovisual project illustrating Carnival of Animals by Saint Saëns. Her hard work combined with her talent resulted in her graduating first in her class. By then she knew she wanted to become a children's book illustrator.

"Being an author-illustrator is the most challenging and rewarding work I've ever done" (*Scholastic* Brochure) Delacre has a reputation for high standards in both text and art, often thoughtfully appending fascinating background information such as author's and artist's notes, recipes, pronunciation guides, and bibliographies to her books. She creates books inspired by the folklore from her childhood and the traditions that were a part of her life on the island. One of her favorite mediums is color pencil, and she loves spending hours working on a drawing. She sometimes playfully hides tiny lizards within the pages of a book, adding to the appeal of her already engrossing titles. She notes, "If painting the people and places of Latin America true to their own beauty fosters respect, or if sharing some of the golden tales builds bridges among children, I want to keep on doing it. Because for me, that is the true measure of success. *¡Viva nuestra herencia!*" (*Scholastic* Brochure).

Delacre enjoys getting to know the people and traditions of different countries and has traveled to Egypt, Turkey, Spain, Mexico, Israel, Greece, Italy, and England. She has lived in Puerto Rico, Argentina, France, and the United States. In addition to writing and illustrating children's books, her work has been featured in *Sesame Street Magazine* and other magazines and textbooks. She enjoys walking the cobblestone streets of Old San Juan, Puerto Rico, with her children. As they stroll along the cobblestones, she tells them the legends and tales that were told to her when she was a child.

More Information about Lulu Delacre

www. childrensbookguild.org/luludelacre.html
School Library Journal. February 1993, p. 71.
Something about the Author. Volume 36, pp. 65–67.

Selected Works by Lulu Delacre

Arroz con Leche: Popular Songs and Rhymes from Latin America

Horn Book Fanfare Book
Grades Preschool–3

- Bilingual
- Music
- Nursery Rhymes

This merry bilingual collection of twelve rhymes from Mexico, Puerto Rico, and Argentina features the original Spanish versions and rhyming English translations. Musical notations for nine of the rhymes are appended, and games or fingerplays associated with several of the selections are described at the bottom of the pages. Lovely detailed pastel illustrations accompany each of the rhymes, often portraying actual places such as Old San Juan Cathedral in Puerto Rico. The playful elephants who balance so nimbly on the spider's web in "The Graceful Elephant" are enchanting! Tiny lizards mischievously hide amid many of the pictures. Lulu Delacre includes an informative Artist's Note, a bibliography, and a tasty recipe for *arroz con leche* (rice and milk). She learned these songs when she was a child and created this book because she wanted to share her favorite childhood poems and music with her two daughters. The cheerful kaleidoscope of songs and rhymes from the oral tradition will be enjoyed by those who know them and provide a pleasurable introduction to those for whom they are new. The positive response to this title inspired Delacre to create a second book of songs with a similar format, *Las Navidades*. Cassette available from Scholastic.

The Bossy Gallito/El gallo de bodas: A Traditional Cuban Folktale

Notable Trade Book in the Field of Social Studies
Aesop Accolade List
New York Public Library Best Book for Reading and Sharing
Pura Belpré Honor Book for Text and Illustration
Grades Preschool–3

- Birds
- Cumulative Tales
- Folklore
- Roosters

An overbearing rooster finds that others do not care for his bossy ways. On his way to his uncle's wedding, he discovers that he needs assistance. Will he make it to the wedding on time? What is the magic word that will summon forth help? This is the Cuban version of a traditional story that came to Cuba and other Latin American countries from Spain long ago. Many other versions of this popular tale are found in various cultures around the world. One is the traditional passover song, "Had Gadya," which is believed to have roots in French nursery songs dating back many hundreds of years. Another version is "The Old Woman and the Pig." The author, Lucía M. Gonzales, grew up in Cuba listening to her *abuela* Nena tell stories. *El gallo de bodas* became the author's favorite story, as she listened to her aunt tell it many times. She notes that it is known by most Cuban children on the island, and she hopes that traditional stories such as this one will continue to be told to Latina/o children in the United States. Spanish edition: *El gallo de bodas.*

Golden Tales: Myths, Legends, and Folktales from Latin America

A CCBC Choices Book

Grades 4–Adult

- Art
- Folktales
- History
- Legends
- Myths

Twelve classic tales come together in one volume, bringing thirteen countries and four native cultures from which they emerged into a vivid new perspective. This sparkling treasury combines folklore, history, geography and art, celebrating the many-faceted cultures of Latin America. Author/artist Lulu Delacre remembers listening to spellbinding tales as she was growing up in Puerto Rico. Years later, she searched for an illustrated collection to share with her own children. Unable to find a volume that conveyed the beauty, complexity, and depth of the stories that she knew as a child, she decided to create one herself. This magnificent labor of love, then, is the result! After years of extensive research, writing, and painting, Delacre has succeeded in creating an exquisite volume filled with grace, beauty, drama, and strength.

Each of the sections, featuring the Taino, the Zapotec, the Muisca, and the Inca, is prefaced with an introductory passage that provides historical and cultural information about the group. Fascinating stories explain such phenomena as how the rainbow was born, why the sun is brighter than the moon, how the sea was born, and why you can see a rabbit's picture in the full moon. Here we read about changing cultures, miracles, tragic romance, lightning gods disguised as lizards, a lagoon serpent, the sun who loved all the people and animals who inhabited the earth, messages hidden in a code of colored yarns and knots, and much more. These are the poignant stories of the native peoples of the Americas who found themselves conquered and ruled by Spain, and this is a glimpse of the literature that emerged during this turbulent time of change.

Delacre's vibrant oil paintings convey the mystery and magic of these compelling tales. Her distinctive linocuts enable her to get even closer to the art forms used by some of the indigenous cultures, authentically portraying early design motifs based on realia such as a solar disk from a gold pendant, a funerary vessel, a gold and turquoise earring, the Inca zodiac, a chief's wooden stool, a carved face from a Taino bone vessel, and an early colonial Peruvian tunic. Delicate linocut borders adorn the pages, adding to the beauty of this exquisite book. Delacre's respect for the tales of her childhood, extensive research, loving attention to detail, and imaginative approach to art, design, and storytelling have culminated in her most powerful work to date. She thoughtfully includes detailed notes and sources for each tale, early and modern maps, and an extensive pronunciation guide. Spanish edition: *De oro y esmeraldas.*

Las Navidades: Popular Christmas Songs from Latin America

Grades Preschool–3

- Bilingual
- Christmas
- Epiphany
- Music
- Nursery Rhymes

Thirteen holiday songs from Puerto Rico, Santo Domingo, Mexico, and Venezuela are presented in Spanish and English. Following the same format as the earlier collection, *Arroz con Leche,* this title features the illustrated rhymes in the first section of the book followed by the musical arrangements for the songs. Arranged chronologically, beginning with Christmas Eve to New Year's and Epiphany on the sixth day of January, the order of the songs will help the reader travel through the holidays. Lulu Delacre went to the countryside of Puerto Rico to research the illustrations for this project. She notes, "In the process, something wonderful happened. As nostalgic memories of Christmas on the island came to me, I rediscovered the traditions from my childhood." She adds that because some of these customs are slowly disappearing, she created this book in an attempt to preserve them. As she has done in her other well-researched books, she has added creative touches to this title that make it all the more noteworthy. Many of the rhymes are accompanied by notes depicting traditional activities associated with the holidays. Information about, and drawings of, the musical instruments traditionally used to accompany the songs are included. A bibliography, artist's note, a mouthwatering picture and recipe for *Rosca de Reyes* (Three Kings Cake), and Delacre's special hidden lizards are all tucked inside this beautifully illustrated book. Cassette available from Scholastic.

Salsa Stories

A CCBC Choices Book
An IRA Notable Book for a Global Society
IRA List of Outstanding International Books
CBC Notable Social Studies Trade Book for Young People
An Américas Highly Commended Title
Grades 3–7

- Food
- Holidays and Customs
- Short Stories

This cleverly conceived collection of seven heartwarming short stories is enhanced by intriguing, full-page, black-and-white linocuts, seventeen mouthwatering recipes, and a useful glossary and pronunciation guide for the Spanish words used in the text. Inspired by the idea that certain foods could unlock memories from the past, Delacre introduces readers to a symphony of fascinating stories set in Argentina, Cuba, Guatemala, Mexico, Peru, and Puerto Rico. The book opens with a New Year's celebration at Carmen Teresa's house, during which a family friend gives her a beautiful journal. After listening carefully to the childhood stories told by her extended family and friends, Carmen Teresa decides to use her new journal to record the recipes for the special foods mentioned in the stories. In the Author's Note, Delacre writes, "All the recipes included have been tested in my kitchen. Many have been favorites of my family for generations" (99). Spanish edition: *Cuentos con Sazón*.

Vejigante Masquerader

National Council of Teachers of English Notable Children's Book
Américas Book Award
American Bookseller Pick of the Lists
Grades 2–5

- Bilingual
- Carnival
- Fiestas

A boy fulfills his dream of masquerading with the older boys at Carnival. Each year in February, Carnival brings throngs of masqueraders to celebrate in the streets of cities in Latin America and Spain. The *vejigantes* of Ponce, Puerto Rico, celebrate for the entire month of February, before and after Carnival. This year, Ramón is so determined to take an active role in the festivities that he has secretly made his own costume. He has worked hard to save his earnings from running errands for Doña Ana, who has taken time to teach him how to sew. Now, in disguise, he can join El Gallo's group as they play the traditional, good-natured pranks, and no one will recognize him. What problem does Ramón encounter that threatens to ruin his plan? Who steps in to help remedy the situation? Will Ramón have to wait another year to fulfill his dream? These and other questions are answered as readers enjoy this bilingual story about traditions and persistence.

Lulu Delacre has created a well-researched, fascinating book, made all the more interesting by the creative touches that she adds. Early in the book, she challenges her readers to find twenty-eight lizards, one for each day in February, hidden in the pictures. Some are easy to find, but others are well hidden and provide an amusing challenge. This playful strategy encourages readers of all ages to scrutinize the illustrations closely. She also includes background details about *vejigantes*, information about other masqueraders from Latin America and Spain, a glossary, a bibliography, and *vejigantes* chants. Directions for making your own *vejigante* mask are well thought out and easy to follow. The bilingual text and the detailed illustrations pull the reader into the story, capturing the ups and downs of the drama. Readers will enjoy discussing the book, possibly recasting it in the good news/bad news motif. They might even try hiding little lizards or other creatures in their next drawing.

Cristina García

Photo: Norma I. Quintana.
Courtesy of Alfred A. Knopf

Cuban American (1958–)
Birthday: July 4
Contact: Ellen Levine Agency
15 East 26th Street, #1801
New York, NY 10110-1505

When I was growing up, I was in a virulently anti-Castro home, so Cuba was painted for me as a very monstrous place, an island prison. . . . Writing [has] helped me understand my parents and their generation a little better.

(*Contemporary Literary Criticism*, Volume 76, 167)

Books by Cristina García

The Agüero Sisters: A Novel. Knopf, 1997. Spanish edition: *Las hermanas Agüero: Una novela*.

Dreaming in Cuban: A Novel. Knopf, 1992. Spanish edition: *Soñar en Cubano: Novela*.

After working as a reporter, correspondent, and bureau chief for *Time* magazine from 1983 to 1990, Cristina García decided to change career paths and write not about news and world events but from her own imagination and experience. Keenly aware of how her life had been shaped by the relationship between the United States and Cuba, García, who was living in Miami at the time, found "all the issues of [her] childhood bubbling up" (*The Hispanic Literary Companion*, 93). Her exploration into these issues resulted in her first novel, *Dreaming in Cuban*, which was published in 1992. Writing the book gave her insight into her parents' experiences as first-generation Americans, "cut-off from a homeland [they] cannot forgive and their new country forbids them to visit" (*Contemporary Literary Criticism*, 167).

García was born on July 4, 1958, in Havana, Cuba. Two years later she was brought to the United States when her parents went into exile after the Cuban revolution. She grew up in New York City; English was her primary language. She earned her B.A. in political science from Barnard College in 1979 and went on to graduate from the Johns Hopkins University School of Advanced International Studies in Latin American studies in 1981.

When her first novel, *Dreaming in Cuban*, was published, the *New York Times* called García "a magical new writer . . . completely original." The book was nominated for a National Book Award and has been widely translated. García has been a Guggenheim Fellow, a Hodder Fellow at Princeton University, and the recipient of a Whiting Writers' Award.

More Information about Cristina García

Contemporary Authors. Volume 141, p. 151.

Contemporary Authors Online. The Gale Group, 2001.

Contemporary Literary Criticism. Volume 76, p. 167.

The Hispanic Literary Companion, edited by Nicolás Kanellos. Visible Ink Press, 1997.

Notable Hispanic Women. Gale, 1993.

Selected Works by Cristina García

The Agüero Sisters

Grades 12–Up

- Cuba
- Family Secrets

- Mothers and Daughters
- Sisters

In her widely anticipated second novel, Cristina García writes about the power of family myth to mask, transform, and finally reveal the truth. Half sisters Reina and Constancia Agüero have been estranged for thirty years. Free-spirited Reina lives in Cuba, where she is an electrician, and urbanized Constancia lives in New York City and later in Miami, where she establishes a successful cosmetics business catering to Cuban American women. The sisters' complex story is braided with the voice of their father, Ignacio, who secretly murdered his wife, Blanca, and committed suicide when their daughters were young. This tragedy provides the central mystery of the novel, one that has haunted Reina and Constancia all their lives. Finally, in midlife, they are drawn together by the need to establish the truth about their parents. *The Agüero Sisters*, which includes Santeria rituals and animal sacrifices, has been praised for its powerfully imagined characters, vivid mystical parallelisms, and insights into difficult questions of identity. Spanish edition: *Las hermanas Agüero: Una novela*.

Dreaming in Cuban

American Book Award Finalist
Grades 12–Up

- Cuba
- Mothers and Daughters

In her highly acclaimed debut, Cristina García tells the complex story of three generations of Cuban women divided politically, philosophically, and geographically by the Cuban revolution. Shifting the narrative from third to first person, moving from the past to the present, and shifting from character to character, she explores the dreams, dislocations, and disillusionments of a family at home and in exile. Weaving narratives, letters, incidents, memory, and visions, she provides insight into the inner lives of various members of the del Pino family. Widowed matriarch Celia lives near Havana and devotes herself to the revolution by guarding the coast, working in the sugarcane fields, and serving as a judge in the People's Court. Daughter Felicia, who suffers episodes of amnesia and insanity brought on by her husband's "gift" of syphilis, seeks healing through Santeria rituals (which include animal sacrifices). Celia's second daughter, Lourdes, who was raped by a soldier and vehemently opposes the revolution, flees to New York City, where she opens the Yankee Doodle Bakery. Her daughter, Pilar, an artist and student, feels a profound connection with her grandmother, even though she hasn't seen her for seventeen years. "[She] left me her legacy . . . a love for the sea . . . an appreciation of music and words, sympathy for the underdog, and a disregard for boundaries" (176). *Dreaming in Cuban* has been praised for its haunting narrative, its perceptive realism, and the illumination that it brought to bear on the intricacies of family life. Spanish edition: *Soñar en Cubano.*

Carmen Lomas Garza

Photo: Helleah Tsinhnahjinnie

Chicana (1948–)
Birthday: September 12
Contact: P.O. Box 881683
San Francisco, CA 94188-1683
lasecretaria@carmenlomasgarza.com

From the time I was a young girl, I always dreamed of being an artist. I practiced drawing every day.

(Family Pictures)

If you see my heart and humanity through my art then hopefully you will not exclude me from rightfully participating in this society.

(*A Piece of My Heart*, 13)

Books by Carmen Lomas Garza

Family Pictures/Cuadros de Familia. Children's Book Press, 1990.
In My Family/En mi familia. Children's Book Press, 1996.
Magic Windows/Ventanas mágicas. Children's Book Press, 1999.
Making Magic Windows: Creating Papel Picado/Cut-Paper Art. Children's Book Press, 1999.
Papel Picado: Paper Cutout Techniques. Xicanindio Arts Coalition, 1984.
A Piece of My Heart/Pedacito de mi Corazón: The Art of Carmen Lomas Garza. Laguna Gloria Art Museum, 1991; New Press, 1994.

Video by Carmen Lomas Garza

Homenaje a Tenochtitlan: An Installation for Day of the Dead. Call (512) 467-7306.

Carmen Lomas Garza was born September 12, 1948, in Kingsville, Texas, near the border with Mexico. From the time that she was a young girl she dreamed of becoming an artist. Her mother inspired her to follow her heart and helped her plan her future. At the age of thirteen Garza made a commitment to pursue a career in art and taught herself elements of drawing.

In *A Piece of My Heart*, Garza describes the pain and discrimination that she and her older brother suffered at school. She has vivid memories of the day her brother came home crying because his teacher had hit him with a ruler for speaking Spanish. Later, Garza also suffered many emotional and physical punishments. "Each time I spoke Spanish I was ridiculed for my accent and made to feel ashamed. By the time I graduated from high school I was confused, depressed, introverted and quite angry" (12). The university classes available to her excluded information about the rich art and history of her people, and her own work was criticized for being too political, too primitive, and not universal. Garza turned to her art to heal the wounds inflicted by years of exclusion and humiliation. The Chicano movement for civil rights also nourished her and helped her find her voice.

Garza earned her B.S. at the Texas Arts and Industry University in Kingsville, Texas; her M.A. in education at Juarez-Lincoln/Antioch Graduate School in Austin, Texas; and her M.A. in art at San Francisco State University in California. She has won many awards, grants, and fellowships for her art. She has had numerous solo exhibitions as well as group exhibitions. Her work is displayed in museums, libraries, and schools, including the Smithsonian Institution in Washington, D.C. Garza works in a wide variety of media, including oil on canvas, acrylic on canvas, gouache on arches paper, *papel picado* (paper cutouts), lithographs, and metal cutouts.

Garza presently lives in California. She is considered one of the major Mexican American painters in the United States. She is also an art instructor and curator. Some of her posters, videos, and cards are available through A Medio Dia Productions, P.O. Box 140304, Austin, TX 78714; (512) 467-7306.

More Information about Carmen Lomas Garza

www.carmenlomasgarza.com

Newspapers and Journals

Brown, Betty Ann. "A Community's Self-Portrait." *New Art Examiner*. December 1990, 20–24.
Crohn, Jennifer. "What's the Alternative?" *The East Bay Guardian*. March 1991, 41.
Kutner, Janet. "Art with Roots." *Dallas Morning News*. February 17, 1990, 1C–2C.
Lewis, Valerie. "A Celebration of Family." *San Francisco Chronicle*. July 29, 1990, 9.
Matthews, Lydia. "Stories History Didn't Tell Us." *Artweek*. February 14, 1991, 1, 15–17.
Santiago, Chiori. "Mano a Mano: We Have Come to Excel." *The Museum of California Magazine*. March/April 1989, 8–13, back cover.
Santiago, Chiori. "The Mexican Museum." *Latin American Art*. Fall 1990, 95–98.
Van Proyen, Mark. "To Touch Both Body and Soul." *Artweek*. April 11, 1991, 11–12.
Wasserman, Abby. "The Art of Narrative." *The Museum of California Magazine*. Winter 1991, 24–28, front cover.
Woodard, Josef. "Not So Naive After All." *Artweek*. April 14, 1991, 9–10.

Books

Multicultural Voices in Contemporary Literature by Frances Ann Day. Heinemann, 1999.
A Piece of My Heart/Pedacito de mi Corazón by Carmen Lomas Garza. New Press, 1994.
¡Latinas! Women of Achievement edited by Diane Telgen and Jim Kamp. Visible Ink, 1996.

Videos

Maldonado, Betty. *Hispanic Artists in the United States—The Texas Connection*. De Colores Productions, 1988.
Rodríguez, Laura. "*Aqui y Ahora/Female Creators: A Profile of Carmen Lomas Garza*. KTVU, Channel 2, Oakland, CA, 1982.

Selected Works by Carmen Lomas Garza

Family Pictures/Cuadros de familia

American Library Association Notable Book
Texas Bluebonnet Award
Pura Belpré Honor Award

Parents' Choice Approved Book
Library of Congress "Best Books of the Year" Selection
School Library Journal "Best Books of the Year" Selection

- Art
- Artists
- Bilingual
- Autobiography
- Traditions

In My Family/En mi familia

Américas Picture Book Award
Hungry Mind Review Children's Books of Distinction Award
Skipping Stones Book Award
International Reading Association Notable Book
Pura Belpré Honor Award for Illustration
Tomás Rivera Children's Book Award
Texas Bluebonnet Master List
Choices: Cooperative Children's Book Center
All Ages

- Art
- Artists
- Autobiography
- Bilingual
- Traditions

Carmen Lomas Garza's memories of her childhood in a rural Mexican American community in Kingsville, Texas, near the Mexico border inspired her to create these two magnificent books. Her engaging, detailed pictures and accompanying bilingual text portray the day-to-day experiences of her early years such as making tamales, going to a fair in Mexico, picking cactus, participating in a cakewalk, picking oranges, and celebrating birthdays. Garza elaborates on her great dream of becoming an artist and how her mother inspired and supported this aspiration. These are excellent books for studying traditions as well as for inspiring young artists and writers to follow their dreams. *In My Family* includes a fascinating section: "Carmen Lomas Garza Answers Questions from Children." *Family Pictures* is also available in Big Book format

Magic Windows/Ventanas mágicas

Pura Belpré Illustrator Award
Américas Honor Award
Skipping Stones Honor Award
Carter G. Woodson Honor Book
Parents' Guide to Children's Media Outstanding Achievement
Parents' Choice Picture Book
All Ages

- Art
- Bilingual
- Papel Picado

Through the magic windows of her intricate cut-paper art *(papel picado),* Carmen Lomas Garza depicts exquisite scenes from her family life, her community, her work as an artist, and legends from her Aztec past. Each full-page reproduction is accompanied by a bilingual narrative that explains the cultural history explored in the scene.

Making Magic Windows: Creating Papel Picado—Cut-Paper Art

All Ages

- Art
- *Papel Picado*

This user-friendly workbook introduces readers to the traditional Mexican craft of *papel picado*. Step-by-step directions and illustrations are provided for creating beautiful designs and banners by folding and cutting tissue paper. After sections on scissors safety and how to hold and cut the paper, instructions are provided for eight different *papel picado* designs. For more advanced students, there is a section on using a craft knife safely and a sample sunburst project.

A Piece of My Heart/Pedacito de mi Corazón: The Art of Carmen Lomas Garza

All Ages

- Art
- Artists
- Autobiography

This beautiful book gathers thirty-seven vivid, full-color and black-and-white reproductions of Carmen Lomas Garza's work. It includes a poignant autobiographical piece by the artist; an interpretive essay by Amalia Mesa-Bains, a nationally known artist, curator, critic, and scholar of Latino art; a biographical listing of Garza's grants, fellowships, awards, exhibition history; and an extensive bibliography.

In her autobiographical essay, Garza describes the pain and discrimination that she and her brother suffered at school. "By the time I graduated from high school I was confused, depressed, introverted and quite angry" (12). The university art classes offered to her excluded information about the rich art history of her people, and her work was criticized as being too political, too primitive, and not universal.

Garza turned to her art to heal the wounds inflicted by years of exclusion and humiliation. She had decided at the age of thirteen to become an artist. The Chicano movement for civil rights also nourished her and helped her find her voice, enabling her to start the long process of self-healing. Today, she is one of the most loved and distinguished painters of Chicana/o life. She writes, "If you see my heart and humanity through my art then hopefully you will not exclude me from rightfully participating in this society" (13).

The works of art presented in *A Piece of My Heart/Pedacito de mi Corazón* take us into the heart of one of the most distinguished chroniclers of Chicano life. Her canvases preserve the traditions and practices of daily life among families, friends, and neighbors in southern Texas. As we enter the world of Garza's paintings, we are struck by the intricate details and the empowerment of the familiar. Each piece invites the viewer to study the central figures, the paintings on the walls, the furniture, dishes, and curtains. The pieces depicting outdoor scenes pay special attention to the flora and fauna of the area, and the centralized positioning of women in her work is noteworthy. They are actively engaged in healing, preparing food, storytelling, and nurturing. Garza's pictures often show the whole family involved in projects such as making tamales, preparing empanadas, painting Easter eggs, and eating watermelon. For readers interested in interpretations of the paintings, Mesa-Bains' analysis of each is placed on the same page. This beautifully designed book makes Garza's art available to a wider audience. Art enthusiasts of all ages, interests, and backgrounds will be enriched by the heartfelt work of this gifted artist.

Juan Felipe Herrera

Photo: Mayela Padilla.
Courtesy of Children's
Book Press

Mexican American (1948–)
Birthday: December 27
Contact: Children's Book Press
2211 Mission Street
San Francisco, CA 94110

At this point, I am writing more comedy with a dash of mystic sauce. My books for children have opened up a new path for me, a more fully dimensional human direction.

(Contemporary Authors Online, unpaged)

Books by Juan Felipe Herrera

For Children

Calling the Doves/El canto de las palomas. Illustrated by Elly Simmons. Children's Book Press, 1995.
CrashBoomLove: A Novel in Verse. University of New Mexico Press, 1999.
Grandma and Me at the Flea/Los meros meros remateros. Illustrated by Anita De Lucio-Brock. Children's Book Press, 2002.
Laughing Out Loud, I Fly/A carcajadas yo vuelo: Poems in English and Spanish. Illustrated by Karen Barbour. HarperCollins, 1998.
The Upside Down Boy/El niño de cabeza. Illustrated by Elizabeth Gomez. Children's Book Press, 2000.
Welcome to Salsaland. AOL Time Warner, 2002.

For Adults

Akrílica. Alcatraz Editions, 1989.
Border-Crosser with a Lamborghini Dream. University of Arizona Press, 1999.
Exiles of Desire. Lalo Press, 1983; Arte Publíco Press, 1985.
Facegames. Dragon Cloud Press, 1987.
Giraffe on Fire. University of Arizona Press, 2000.
Loteria Cards and Fortune Poems: A Book of Lives. City Lights, 1999.
Love after the Riots. Curbstone Press, 1996.
Mayan Drifter: Chicano Poet in the Lowlands of America. Temple University Press, 1997.
Memoria(s) from an Exile's Notebook of the Future. Santa Monica College Press, 1993.
Night Train to Tuxtla: New Stories and Poems. University of Arizona Press, 1994.
Notebooks of a Chile Verde Smuggler. University of Arizona Press, 2002.
187 Reasons Why Mexicanos Can't Cross the Border. Borderwolf Press, 1995.
Rebozos of Love. Toltecas en Aztlan, 1974.
The Roots of a Thousand Embraces: Dialogues. Manic D. Press, 1994.
Thunderweavers. University of Arizona Press, 2000.

Juan Felipe Herrera, a renowned poet, actor, musician, and educator, was born in Fowler, California, to farmworker parents. His interest in poetry began as a child and was encouraged by his mother, who loved words. As they followed the crops, she recited poetry and sang songs, and his father told stories. When he was eight years old, they settled in a city so he could attend school, where he pursued his interest in music, poetry, and art.

Herrera has degrees from the University of California in Los Angeles, Stanford University, and the University of Iowa. He has taught creative writing to students from third grade to university level. He often performs with a theater troupe and gives readings at elementary schools and bookstores. He has served as editor of a number of groundbreaking small press magazines such as *Red Trapeze, El Tecolote Literario, Gato's Jour-*

nal, Bovine Interventions, and *Citybender* and university reviews, including *Vortice* and *Metamorfosis.*

Herrera has been the recipient of many awards, fellowships, and grants, including the Before Columbus American Book Award for *Facegames.* Currently, he is a professor of Latin American Studies at California State University in Fresno, California.

More Information about Juan Felipe Herrera

Calling the Doves/El canto de las palomas. Illustrated by Elly Simmons. Children's Book Press, 1995.
Contemporary Authors. Volume 131, 237.
Contemporary Authors Online. The Gale Group, 2001.
Contemporary Authors New Revision Series. Volume 96, 158–161.
Mayan Drifter: Chicano Poet in the Lowlands of America. Temple University Press, 1997.
The Upside Down Boy/El niño de cabeza. Illustrated by Elizabeth Gomez. Children's Book Press, 2000.

Selected Works by Juan Felipe Herrera

Calling the Doves/El canto de las palomas

Ezra Jack Keats Award
Américas Commended Title
International Reading Association Notable Book
Cooperative Children's Book Center Choice
Hungry Mind Review Children's Book of Distinction Award
School Library Journal Best Book
Smithsonian Notable Book
Grades K–Up

- Autobiographical Picture Book
- Bilingual
- Migrant Farmworkers

Juan Felipe Herrera tells the story of his childhood as the son of migrant farmworkers. He shares his experiences of eating breakfast under the open sky, listening to his mother recite poetry and sing songs, and hearing his father tell stories and call the doves. Rudolfo Anaya praised this beautifully illustrated book, saying that it is "a sensitive story of a family who comes from Mexico to work in the fields of California. Juan Felipe's parents teach him a love for the land, and they give him the precious gift of poetry."

CrashBoomLove: A Novel in Verse

Américas Award
New York Public Library Books for Teens
Finalist for Los Angeles Times Young Adult Fiction Prize
Grades 8–12

- Alienation
- Divorce
- Newcomers
- Peer Pressure
- Poverty
- Schools

Fifteen-year-old César García narrates this gritty, hard-hitting story about a traumatic period in his life after his father left the family. Hurt, angry, and alienated, César yields to self-destructive peer pressure to fight, sniff airplane glue, shoplift, and ditch school. The turning point comes when his friend is killed, and he is injured in a car accident. With a metal rod in one leg, he begins the tough job of turning his life around through journal writing, music, art, and a renewed connection with his mother. This book has been praised for its inventive use of language, powerful imagery, and ebullient portrait of hope and survival.

Grandma and Me at the Flea/Los meros meros remateros

Grades K–Up

- Bilingual
- Community
- Flea Markets
- Grandmothers

Every Sunday Juanito helps his *abuela* at the flea market, where they enjoy seeing old friends. Together they fulfill grandmother's vision of the market as a sharing community of friendly exchanges. Herrera brings his boyhood memories of the *remate* to life with his exuberant bilingual prose, and the luminous paintings draw the reader into the vibrant world of the flea market.

Laughing Out Loud, I Fly/A carcajadas, yo vuelo: Poems in English and Spanish

Pura Belpré Honor Award
Grades 5–Up

- Bilingual
- Poetry

Twenty-two imaginative bilingual poems pulse with the joy and laughter and sometimes the confusion of growing up between two cultures. This sometimes startling collection (which may confuse literalists) has been praised for its musicality, sensual imagery, and vibrant tone. In the author's note, Herrera writes, "At the age of seventeen . . . when I first opened Picasso's tiny book of poems, *Hunk of Skin*, I was immediately bathed in sunlight. The words had the aromas of morning pears and fresh oranges, their perfume pulled me along familiar gold-filtered landscapes." Inspired, Herrera invites readers to join in and play, laugh out loud, and fly!

The Upside Down Boy/El niño de cabeza

Texas Bluebonnet Master List
Smithsonian Notable Book
Grades 2–Up

- Autobiographical Picture Book
- Bilingual
- Newcomers
- Schools

After years of working in the fields, eight-year-old Juan Felipe Herrera's migrant family decides to settle in one place so he can go to school. Bewildered by the new school, routine, and language, Juanito worries, "Will my tongue turn into a rock?" (7). But a sensitive teacher and his loving family help him make a place for himself through music, art, and poetry. This treasure has been praised for its upbeat tone, playfulness, and enchanting illustrations. Herrera dedicated this memoir to his third grade teacher, Mrs. Lucille Sampson, "who first inspired me to be a singer of words, and most of all, a believer in my own voice" (32).

Lyll Becerra de Jenkins

Photo: Natalie Stultz

Colombian (1925–1997)

I am glad that I write novels for young adults. I feel that, in some small way, I'm endowed with a certain responsibility. Perhaps, through my stories, I can illuminate their lives and stimulate their compassion and understanding, their love for the universal family.

(Lodestar Brochure)

Books by Lyll Becerra de Jenkins

Celebrating the Hero. Lodestar Books, 1993; Penguin, 1995.
The Honorable Prison. Lodestar Books, 1988; Penguin, 1989. Spanish edition: *La prision de honor*.
So Loud a Silence. Lodestar Books, 1996.

Lyll Becerra de Jenkins, the author of the widely acclaimed *The Honorable Prison*, dedicated her writing career to broadening the scope of literature for young adults. Her short stories appeared in periodicals and books around the world, including *The New Yorker*, the *New York Times*, and *Best American Short Stories*. Jenkins died of cancer on May 7, 1997, in Fripp Island, South Carolina. She is remembered as a wise and perceptive chronicler of the human condition.

Born and raised in Colombia, South America, Jenkins' first school was in a convent with Benedictine nuns on the islands of San Andres y Providencia. When her parents moved the family to Colón, Panama, she was enrolled in a bilingual American school inside the Canal Zone. Later, she attended the Convent of Maria Auxiliadora in Soacha, a town to the north of Bogotá. When her family moved to the coastal town of Cartagena, she attended Colegio Biffi, where she was taught by German Franciscan nuns. After graduation, she trained to be a bilingual secretary. Jenkins acted in Teatro Municipal of Bogotá, under the direction of Alejandro Acevedo, a Spanish director from Madrid exiled in Colombia. She also took dancing lessons in Escuela de Danza Jacinto Jaramillo, where she specialized in flamenco.

After she and her husband and their five children were settled in the United States, Jenkins began writing fiction. She remembered her first lesson in fiction when she was a young girl and had no idea that she would someday become a writer. It was customary for her family to have discussions after meals in what was called *la sobremesa*. One day, as Jenkins was sharing an incident that had taken place that day at the convent, her sister kept interrupting, saying that she was exaggerating. Their father intervened, encouraging Jenkins to continue expressing her perceptions of what had happened. Years later, when she sat down to write her first stories, she recalled her father's words. She soon learned that facts do not make good fiction. She noted, "It's in the reinvention of the truth that I, as a writer, find the dimensions of my experiences and their full essence and significance."

Jenkins enjoyed writing about family relationships, their joys, pain, and conflicts. Her first short story, a sad tale about one of her brothers, was accepted and published by *The New Yorker*. By fictionalizing the story, Jenkins gained insight into his true character and his motivations. Her next story was about a family living under a military dictatorship.

After it too was published in *The New Yorker*, Jenkins received several letters asking what happened to the people in the story. This was the beginning of her first book, the award-winning *The Honorable Prison*, which is a fictionalized account of her personal experiences. Her second book, *Celebrating the Hero*, is also based on family events. Her third book, *So Loud a Silence*, grew out of the experiences of her brother-in-law, who was kidnapped and held for ransom.

Being bilingual, Jenkins found it interesting that she instinctively wrote in English when she was in the United States and in Spanish when she visited her relatives in South America. When one of her editors told her that they wanted to preserve her accent in her stories, she felt a strong incentive to share her experiences and insights. Jenkins' books give a fresh perspective to the traditional coming-of-age novel and bring the country of her birth to life in all its complexity. Reviewers praised her powerful novels, noting that they will grip the attention of young adults and inject their thinking with new awareness. The *Christian Science Monitor* recommended that if we read one young adult book, it should be *The Honorable Prison*. Similarly, the *Chicago Sun-Times* proposed that it be required reading for high school students. The response to Jenkins' second novel, *Celebrating the Hero*, was equally enthusiastic, calling it an eloquent contribution to the growing body of immigrant literature. *MultiCultural Review* described Jenkins' third book, *So Loud a Silence*, as a realistic and finely crafted novel. These three remarkable books established Lyll Becerra de Jenkins' reputation as an important contributor to literature for young adults.

Selected Works by Lyll Becerra de Jenkins

Celebrating the Hero

Children's Book of the Year, Bank Street College
Parents' Choice Story Book Honor Award
New York Public Library Book for the Teen age
Consortium of Latin American Studies Award Nominee
Grades 7–12

- Colombia
- Family Secrets
- Gender Roles
- Grandparents
- Grieving

After her mother's death, seventeen-year-old Camila Draper travels to San Javier, Colombia, to attend a ceremony honoring her late grandfather and, while trying to learn more about her mother's relatives, uncovers disturbing family secrets. During her early years, Camila had enjoyed listening to her mother reminiscing about her childhood, her homeland, and her father. But as she grew older, she became tired of these stories and told her mother to stop talking about the past. After her mother's unexpected death, she is haunted by the silences that she imposed on her mother. She is filled with "questions I want to ask that I cannot formulate to myself, in English or Spanish. I know only that the questions are there, within me, weighty as rocks" (7). As she searches for the truth, she is met with evasions, riddles, hints, and hostility. She wonders if there is a conspiracy to keep her from learning about her grandfather. Was he really the Illustrious Son, the hero he is purported to have been? As she unravels the tangled threads of the past, she learns some painful, but important, truths about the subjugation of women, the lengths to which relatives and community members will go to protect prominent men, and the abuses of power, loyalty, and trust within a family and a community. This is a perceptive novel about grieving, denial, contradictions, silences, misogyny, fabricated truths, remorse, and illusions.

Lyll Becerra de Jenkins noted that *Celebrating the Hero*, her second novel, like her first, is based on family history. Even though her grandmother had a beautiful voice and studied singing and piano in an exclusive music school in Bogotá, Colombia, her husband had prohibited her from singing. Jenkins didn't know all the details because she, like Camila, had been bored with stories about her relatives and had not listened attentively. When she began writing the book, she struggled to remember everything that she had heard about her grandmother. Then she realized that the facts did not matter—that the creative process involves sorting out and choosing the ideas that fit the work. The book has been praised by critics as a beautifully crafted novel that makes an eloquent contribution to the growing body of immigrant literature. Reviewers saluted Jenkins' skill and insight in bringing the country of her birth to life in stories that give a new perspective to the traditional coming-of-age novel. Written in fluid prose and with remarkable insight, the novel's suspense is derived from the gradual accretion of facts garnered from innuendo, rumor, and bits of evidence. Camila is spurred on "to learn about the past, the legacy my mother left to me. She was obsessed with her family, San Javier, her country. She passed her virus to me" (119). With her mother's presence within her, Camila returns home, saddened and wiser, ready to begin the difficult, complex journey that lies ahead of her.

The Honorable Prison

Scott O'Dell Award for Historical Fiction
Booklist Best Book of the Decade
Booklist Children's Editors' Choice

Parents' Choice "Shoe-in Winner"
New York Public Library 100 Titles for Giving and Sharing
ABA-CBC Children's Books Mean Business
National Conference of Christians and Jews Recommended Book
Zilveren Griffel for the Best Book Published in the Netherlands
Grades 7–12

- Historical Fiction
- Freedom of Speech
- Political Prisoners
- South America

Because of the political stand taken by her father, a newspaper editor who persistently opposes the military dictatorship of their unnamed country, Marta Maldonado and her family are imprisoned by the government. Seventeen-year-old Marta, her thirteen-year-old brother, and their parents are preparing to flee the country when they are taken from their home and jailed in an isolated pueblo near a military outpost in the Andes. Marta's first-person narrative provides an unflinching portrayal of the traumatic year that they spend in the "honorable prison," as well as her own personal growth and political awakening. As the family struggles with the cold, damp climate, the shortage of food and medicine, the fear of impending violence, and the isolation and monotony of their imprisonment, Marta gradually realizes that she has lived a privileged, self-absorbed life. She reexamines her resentment of the position that Papa has taken against the atrocities committed by their government, and she tries to hold on to her dream of freedom as her father's chronic lung condition deteriorates, and they all face starvation.

The Honorable Prison is a gripping story that reveals the devastating impact of political repression on one family. It is an eloquent tribute to all those courageous individuals who have opposed social injustice and human rights abuses. As Papa taught Marta to understand and respect the campesinos, so will this poignant book inspire readers to educate themselves about the injustices of class oppression. Jenkins, who grew up in Colombia, wrote the book as a "fusion of personal experiences and invention." She noted that while she was writing the novel, she "was full of doubts. Was I properly conveying to American readers the meaning of living in house imprisonment under a dictator general? I never expected my novel to be so well received or so fully understood" (Lodestar Brochure). Indeed, the critical response to her book has been overwhelmingly positive, praising it as a stunning and brilliantly crafted novel rendered more vivid by the understatement of its prose. Reviewers noted that Jenkins' writing has a subtle beauty and that even her minor characters are multidimensional. *Horn Book* stated, "Like *The Diary of Anne Frank,* it is a stern reminder of the dangers inherent in government gone mad and a celebration of the best in our common humanity—the spiritual triumph of those refusing to be subjugated." *The Honorable Prison* has been translated into twelve languages. Spanish edition: *La prision de honor*. Curriculum Unit: *Journey of the Sparrows & The Honorable Prison*. The Center for Learning, 1995.

Francisco Jiménez

Mexican American (1943–)
Birthday: June 29
Contact: Santa Clara University
Department of Modern Languages and Literatures
500 El Camino Real
Santa Clara, CA 954053

The school curriculum is a mirror of our society. If you don't see yourself in the curriculum, then you see a distorted image of yourself . . . or you feel invisible.

(*Sacramento Bee*, March 20, 1999, H7)

Books by Francisco Jiménez

For Children and Young Adults

Breaking Through. Houghton Mifflin, 2001. Spanish edition: *Senderos fronterizos.*
The Christmas Gift/El regalo de Navidad. Illustrated by Claire B. Cotts. Houghton Mifflin, 2000.
The Circuit: Stories from the Life of a Migrant Child. University of New Mexico Press, 1997; Houghton Mifflin, 1999. Spanish edition: *Cajas de carton: Relatos de la vida peregina de un niño campesino.*
La Mariposa. Illustrated by Simón Silva. Houghton Mifflin, 1998. Available in both Spanish and English editions.

For Adults

Francisco Jiménez is the editor, author, or coauthor of many scholarly books.

Francisco Jiménez is an educator, writer, scholar, university administrator, and advocate for bilingual education. He is the author of several award-winning books for young readers and the editor, author, or coauthor of many books for adults ranging from literary criticism, to textbooks, to collections of contemporary Latino writing. A professor of modern languages at Santa Clara University in California, Jiménez has served on various professional boards and commissions and has been the recipient of many honors, awards, grants, and fellowships, including the 2001 Reading the World Award, presented by the Center for Multicultural Literature for Children and Young Adults, University of San Francisco.

Jiménez was born in the small village of San Pedro Tlaquepaque, Mexico, and emigrated with his family to the United States when he was four years old. Over a period of ten years marked by poverty, impermanence, and fear of deportation, they traveled from one labor camp to another, picking cotton, grapes, and strawberries. Jiménez was unable to begin his studies each year until the harvests were completed; his attendance in school was irregular because the family was constantly moving. The family language was Spanish, and the language used in the schools was English. As a result, he was held back in first grade and even labeled mentally retarded. With extraordinary tenacity, he persisted, overcame many obstacles, and went on to earn his Ph.D. from Columbia University.

Jiménez elaborates on these and other early experiences in his eloquent books for young readers. He writes to pay tribute to his family, document his history, and voice the experiences of many children who confront obstacles in their efforts to become educated. His inspiration for writing comes from his teachers and the community of his childhood. "I am particularly inspired by the courage, tenacity, and unwavering hopes and dreams of migrant farm workers, in the midst of adversity, for a better life for their children and their children's children" (unpublished interview).

Even though some of his teachers were cruel and others were insensitive, some were supportive and helped him overcome formidable odds. One of these teachers encouraged him to read *The Grapes of Wrath*, a book that introduced him to the power of literature to touch hearts and minds. Years later, this quiet, unassuming professor has become an eloquent spokesperson for migrant farmworkers. "What I'm doing with my writing now is trying to awaken compassion for those who work hard for very low wages to put food on our table" (*Miami Herald*, August 12, 2001, B6).

More Information about Francisco Jiménez

Books

Authors and Artists for Young Adults, Volume 32, 47–52.

Breaking Through. Houghton Mifflin, 2001. Spanish edition: *Senderos fronterizos*.

The Circuit: Stories from the Life of a Migrant Child. University of New Mexico Press, 1997; Houghton Mifflin, 1999. Spanish edition: *Cajas de Carton: relatos de la vida peregina de un niño campesino*.

Contemporary Authors, Volume 131, 259–260.

Contemporary Authors New Revision Series, Volume 90, 177–179.

Notable Latino Americans: A Biographical Dictionary, 212–215.

Something about the Author, Volume 108, 120–123.

Articles

"*Boston Globe–Horn Book* Award Acceptance Speech for *The Circuit*," by Francisco Jiménez. *Horn Book*. January/February 1999.

"Out of Cardboard Boxes" by Judy Green. *Sacramento Bee*. March 20, 1999, H1, H7.

"Secrets Shared: A Conversation with Francisco Jiménez" by Rosalinda B. Barrera. *The New Advocate*. Winter 2003, 1–8.

"Sequel Tells Story of Migrant Life," by Sue Corbett. *Miami Herald*. August 12, 2001, B6.

"Talking with Francisco Jiménez," by Chris Liska Carger. *Book Links*. December 2001/January 2002, 14–19.

Selected Works by Francisco Jiménez

Breaking Through

Américas Award for Fiction

Pura Belpré Author Honor Award

Junior Library Guild Book Club Selection

Grades 5–Up

- Autobiographical Short Stories
- Immigration
- Migrant Farmworkers

This poignant sequel to *The Circuit* is a memoir of the author's teenage years in the late 1950s, when he struggled to complete junior high and high school while working long hours to help his family. Twenty-five independent, intertwined short stories chronicle the grinding poverty, hard labor, and prejudice that the family endured as well as their resilience, goodheartedness, and hope. One inspiring vignette features a caring teacher who encouraged Panchito to write and loaned him *The Grapes of Wrath*, a novel that introduced him to the joys of reading. This important book ends with black-and-white family photographs and a moving note from the author, in which he pays tribute to his family and teachers. Spanish edition: *Senderos fronterizos.*

The Christmas Gift/El regalo de Navidad

American Library Association Notable Book
Américas Commended List
Grades K–4

- Autobiographical Picture Book
- Bilingual
- Christmas
- Migrant Farmworkers

This lovingly illustrated bilingual picture book is adapted from one of the stories in the author's autobiographical collection *The Circuit: Stories from the Life of a Migrant Child*. In order to find work, Panchito's family has to move again a few days before Christmas. With no work and no money for presents, he worries that he will not receive the red ball that he has been wanting. When Christmas Day finally arrives, Panchito learns an important lesson about love and sharing. In the Author's Note, Jiménez writes that this experience was so special that he vividly remembers it every year on December 25.

The Circuit: Stories from the Life of a Migrant Child

A *Booklist* Editors' Choice
Boston Globe–Horn Book Award for Fiction
Américas Award Winner for Children and Young Adult Literature

A Smithsonian Notable Book for Children
Jane Addams Children's Honor Book
California Library Association's John and Patricia Beatty Award
New York Public Library Books for the Teen Age
American Library Association Best Book for Young Adults
Grades 5–Up

- Autobiographical Short Stories
- Immigration
- Migrant Farmworkers

Twelve independent, intertwined short stories follow the author's migrant farmworker family through their circuit, picking cotton, strawberries, and grapes, thinning lettuce, and topping carrots—and back again—over a period of ten years. In spite of poverty, impermanence, and fear of deportation, the family manages to survive through resourcefulness, solidarity, and backbreaking work. This is an important book not only because the understated writing touches the heart but because there has been so little published for young readers about the experiences of migrant farmworkers. Indeed, this award-winning book is a significant social document that gives voice to an important group of people who have been too long ignored, unrecognized, and underappreciated. Spanish edition: *Cajas de cartón: Relatos de la vida peregina de un niño campesino.*

La Mariposa

Parent's Choice Award
Smithsonian Notable Book for Children
Américas Commended List
Grades K–4

- Autobiographical Picture Book
- Schools
- Second Language Acquisition

Dedicated "to my teachers, whose faith in my ability and guidance helped me break the migrant circuit," this richly illustrated picture book is a gentle reminder that schools must nurture a child's first language. The son of migrant workers, Francisco, who speaks only Spanish, struggles to adjust during his first year of school. Because English is the only language permitted, Francisco copes by watching a caterpillar in a jar next to his desk and by drawing butterflies. "Sometimes he imagined himself flying out of the classroom and over the fields where Papá worked." Poignant and honest, *La Mariposa* reveals how Francisco's imagination sustained him during a needlessly painful time in his life. Spanish edition: *La Mariposa*.

Ofelia Dumas Lachtman

Mexican American (1919–)
Birthday: July 9
Contact: Arte Público Press
University of Houston
Houston, TX 77204-2090

She was deeply tired but at peace, as if a storm had caught her in its vortex, whirling her around and around and finally tossing her on to a sheltered, tranquil place. . . . Maybe life had to come to a standstill to be grasped at all. Maybe life had to come to a standstill for it to start.

(*A Shell for Angela*, 213)

Books by Ofelia Dumas Lachtman

Big Enough/Bastante grande. Illustrated by Enrique O. Sánchez. Spanish translation by Yanitzia Canetti. Arte Público Press, 1998.
Campfire Dreams. Harlequin Books, 1987. Out of print.
The Girl from Playa Blanca. Piñata Books: Arte Público Press, 1995.
A Good Place for Maggie. Arte Publico Press, 2002.
Leticia's Secret. Arte Público Press, 1997.
Pepita Finds Out/Lo que Pepita descubre. Arte Público Press, 2002.
Pepita Takes Time/Pepita siempre tarde. Illustrated by Alex Pardo DeLange. Spanish translation by Alejandra Balestra. Arte Público Press, 2001.
Pepita Talks Twice/Pepita habla dos veces. Illustrated by Alex Pardo DeLange. Arte Público Press, 1995.
Pepita Thinks Pink/Pepita y el color rosado. Illustrated by Alex Pardo DeLange. Spanish translation by Yanitzia Canetti. Arte Público Press, 1995.
A Shell for Angela. Arte Público Press, 1995.
The Summer of El Pintor. Arte Público Press, 2001.
Tina and the Scarecrow Skins/Tina y las pieles de espantapájaros. Arte Público Press, 2002.

The daughter of Mexican immigrants, Ofelia Dumas Lachtman is a native of Los Angeles. She attended Los Angeles city schools and later Los Angeles City College. After studying at the University of California in Los Angeles for a brief period, she got married and moved to Riverside, California.

During World War II, Dumas Lachtman worked as a medical stenographer. Later, she became a group worker and eventually assumed a position as the executive director of the West Los Angeles-Beverly Hills Young Women's Christian Association (YWCA). She retired from that position in 1974 and devoted herself full-time to writing.

Dumas Lachtman's interest in writing started when she was a child. Her first publication came at age twelve, when her work appeared in an anthology of children's poetry. Her writing credits include publication in the *Chicago Tribune*, the *Christian Science Monitor*, the *Boston Globe*, the *Washington Times*, *Newsday*, the *St. Petersburg Times*, the *Dallas Morning News*, the *Detroit News*, *Michigan Magazine*, *Green's Magazine*, and numerous other periodicals.

Recently, a number of Dumas Lachtman's picture books and young adult novels have been published by Arte Público Press. Her work explores a variety of important themes including bilingualism, identity, loss, internalized racism, and women's roles. Her books feature Latina protagonists who are resourceful, assertive, and likable. She has a unique way of writing that leads readers to look forward to her next book.

Ofelia Dumas Lachtman makes her home in Los Angeles, where she writes novels and stories. She is a member of the Society for Children's Book Writers, International PEN, and Sisters in Crime, a group for women mystery writers.

More Information about Ofelia Dumas Lachtman

The Hispanic Literary Companion, edited by Nicolás Kanellos. Visible Ink, 1997.

Selected Works by Ofelia Dumas Lachtman

Big Enough/Bastante grande

Grades K–3

- Bilingual
- Mothers and Daughters
- Piñatas
- Size

Every time Lupita offers to help out at the restaurant that Mamá runs all by herself, Mamá just sighs, "Muy, muy chica." But when a treasured piñata is stolen from the restaurant, little Lupita proves that she is big enough to help get it back. Like many of Ofelia Dumas Lachtman's books, this delightful title features a resourceful young Latina who solves a problem.

Call Me Consuelo

Grades 4–7

- Grandmothers
- Moving
- Mystery

After her parents die in an automobile accident, twelve-year-old Consuelo reluctantly leaves her home in the small mining community of Dos Palos, California, to live with her Anglo grandmother in the suburbs of Los Angeles. However, when she solves a real-life mystery in a nearby deserted movie lot, she surprises everyone by accepting her new life. This intriguing story has many strengths, including an adventurous, likable protagonist, a quirky cast of secondary characters, and an element of suspense. It is a story about loss, change, differences, new friendships, intergenerational relationships, and heroism.

The Girl from Playa Blanca

Benjamin Franklin Award for Young Adult Literature

Grades 5–9

- Mystery
- Immigration

When Elena and her little brother, Carlos, leave their seaside village in Mexico to search for their immigrant father in Los Angeles, they encounter intrigue, crime, mystery, and friendship. The story that unfolds entails stolen letters, an old deed, a mysterious storeroom, a bungled kidnapping, hidden treasure, and a fatal accident. As Elena meets a devious gang member, a taciturn restaurant owner, a mysterious archaeologist, a seemingly kind employer with a puzzling vision impairment, an enigmatic law student, and a household of perplexing servants, she struggles to unravel the tangles of the web. Elena is a resourceful, likable protagonist whose sleuthing skills improve as the story progresses. Ofelia Dumas Lachtman, who has an ear for dialogue and a talent for suspense, has written a fascinating book.

Leticia's Secret

Grades 4–8

- Cancer
- Dying and Death
- Friendship

Leticia is a terminally ill preteen whose family tries to keep her illness a secret. Her cousin, eleven-year-old Rosario Silva, is determined to solve the mystery. Why does everyone pamper Leticia? As the story unfolds, the two become close friends, sharing their love for reading and writing. Finally, Rosario learns that her cousin is dying of cancer. This interesting book ends with Rosario's planting a rose bush in memory of Leticia. Much of the book focuses on Rosario and her adventures at school and her interactions with classmates. Secret notebooks, poetry contests, mental messages, and a fast-paced robbery attempt add intriguing elements to this poignant examination of family dynamics, dying and death, and grief.

Pepita Takes Time/Pepita siempre tarde

Grades K–3

- Bilingual
- Tardiness

Pepita is back, and this time she has developed the habit of dawdling. So what if she's a little late to breakfast and to school? When confronted, she shrugs, "It doesn't hurt anyone if I'm late." But eventually she learns the hard way that "taking time" not only means inconveniencing others but can result in her missing important events.

Pepita Talks Twice/Pepita habla dos veces

Skipping Stones Book Award
Grades K–3

- Bilingualism
- Problem Solving
- Canine Companions

Pepita, a little girl who can converse in Spanish and English, decides not to "speak twice" until unanticipated problems cause her to "think twice." Pepita has grown accustomed to using her bilingual skills to help those around her. It seems that everyone calls upon her for assistance. The corner grocer, neighbors, relatives, and teachers are always asking her to translate. Finally, one day she becomes frustrated with her role as translator and decides that she is never going to speak Spanish again. She maintains her position through a number of situations until her canine companion, Wolf/Lobo helps her reconsider her decision.

Ofelia Dumas Lachtman has created an engaging story about the benefits and challenges of bilingualism. Her gentle message is that it is a fine thing to know two languages. Pepita is an assertive, resourceful girl who is gaining skill in solving problems, and young readers will enjoy discussing other options that she might consider in dealing with the constant requests for help. The book might serve as a reminder to adults to spread the translating tasks around so that one child is not overwhelmed.

Pepita Thinks Pink/Pepita y el color rosado

Grades K–3

- Bilingual
- Differences
- Prejudice

Pepita likes every color but pink. She just can't bring herself to make friends with her new neighbor, Sonya, a girl with a pink dress, pink balloons, and pink skin. But finally she remembers that Tía Rosa said that people come in many colors and that Papá told her that people may be different on the outside but that inside they are very much the same. This lively book ends happily with Pepita and Sonya going to the corner store to buy more pink balloons.

A Shell for Angela

Grades 11–Adult

- Identity
- Internalized Racism
- Death
- Grieving
- Passing for Anglo

This poignant novel traces the emotional and cultural journey of a woman whose traumatic childhood experiences lead her to reject her Mexican heritage and family. At the age of nine, living in a barrio in Los Angeles during the depression era, Angela Martín witnesses the beating and arrest of her father by immigration officials. The wounds inflicted by this and other experiences are compounded by the racist messages that she receives at school and in the community as well as the internalized racism at home. Angela has no one to answer her questions, no one to tell her that her people are beautiful, strong, and good, so she internalizes the lies that society teaches about Mexican Americans and spends many years denying her heritage. She tries to live the life of a perfect suburban housewife and passes as an Anglo for many years. But a new crisis in her life leads her to revisit her early experiences and decisions. As she begins her troubled journey to the past, she struggles to unravel the painful threads of her life. Ofelia Dumas Lachtman has beautifully captured the complexities, paradoxes, and poignancy of Angela's dilemma. This fine book explores issues of exploitation of farmworkers, unresolved grief, self-abnegation, the constricting roles open to women, identity confusion, class upward mobility, and life-threatening illnesses. Note: The one flaw in the book is the use of the offensive term "Japs." When an epithet is used by a racist person and is rebutted within the text, it is clear to the reader that the person is wrong. But in this case, the offensive term was used by Angela, an otherwise admirable character.

The Summer of El Pintor

Grades 6–Up

- Grandfathers
- Mystery
- Socioeconomic Class

When sixteen-year-old Monica Ramos reluctantly moves from her private school to live in the Los Angeles barrio where her deceased mother grew up, she finds an old, unopened letter to her mother from El Pintor, the painter. Monica, who loves a mystery, is quickly drawn into a web of questions about the disappearance of the enigmatic El Pintor. Following clues from the artist's paintings, she discovers that he is suffering from amnesia. When his memory returns, they finally open the mysterious letter, which reveals that El Pintor is Monica's grandfather. This interesting book is especially important because it is one of the few young adult mysteries featuring Latino/a characters. *Voice of Youth Advocates* wrote that "this readable novel features realistic characters and believable situations with elements of Latino culture skillfully interwoven. Teen readers, regardless of cultural background, should enjoy this engaging mystery."

Victor Martinez

Chicano (1954–)

Contact: Susan Bergholz Literary Services
17 West 10th Street, #5
New York City, NY 10011-8746

If you want to learn how art enriches life, read. If you want to develop capabilities and powers you never thought imaginable, read. . . . Reading is a great task, a great discipline. . . . Language and reading, when I was a boy, became a way of escaping [poverty]. When I read, I was transported somewhere else.

("People in Books: Writing from the Heart," *American Bookseller*, January 1997, 72)

Books by Victor Martinez

Caring for a House. Chusma House Publications, 1992.
"The County Fair," in *One Hot Second: Stories about Desire,* edited by Cathy Young. Knopf, 2002.
A la conquista del corazon, written with Juan Antonio Diaz. Uruguay, 1993.
Parrot in the Oven: Mi Vida. HarperCollins, 1996, 1998; Turtleback Books, 1998. Spanish edition: *El loro en el horno: Mi vida.*

Victor Martinez, a poet and novelist, received the 1996 National Book Award for Young People's Literature for his coming-of-age novel *Parrot in the Oven: Mi Vida.* Joyce Carol Thomas, the committee chairperson, presented the prestigious award with these words, "The language of the winning book—at once original, musical, compelling—recalled now the complex layers of a gospel song moving down the spine, now a *mariachi* melody winging into the heart" (*American Bookseller,* January 1997, 72).

Born in Fresno, California, the fourth of twelve children, Martinez once picked crops in the Central Valley. "I come from a very poor background. I've lived in labor camps, project houses, and cheap apartments, and everything that helped me develop a way of understanding where I was and how I related to society and how I should move within it came from reading literature" (*American Bookseller,* January 1997, 72).

At age fourteen, Martinez suffered the beginnings of a recurring throat ailment that he thinks is related to breathing in pesticides from the fields where he worked. (Several times a year he has surgery to remove the tiny papillomas on his vocal cords, and his voice retains a perpetual hoarseness.) Because he couldn't talk, he didn't participate in extracurricular activities during high school. Isolated, he turned to books for solace.

After high school, Martinez studied creative writing at California State University at Fresno with poet Philip Levine, who encouraged him to write. "He told me I had talent. No one ever told me that before—it was a revelation in my life. I fell in love with poetry in a big way" (*Publishers Weekly,* December 16, 1996, 32). Martinez's poetry helped earn him a graduate fellowship in creative writing at Stanford University and later a position teaching for the Poetry in the Schools program in San Francisco.

Martinez also worked as a welder, truck driver, firefighter, and office clerk, while writing at night. When he received the National Book Award, he accepted it for all the other Chicano writers who are struggling to find a publisher for their work. He is currently working on a book about his years of struggling as a writer.

More Information about Victor Martinez

Contemporary Authors Online. The Gale Group, 2001.
"Finding His 'Real Job,'" by Sara McGuire. *Madera Tribune*. February 11, 1998, 1, 7.
"Flying Starts," by Shannon Maughan. *Publishers Weekly*. December 16, 1996, 32.
"Fresno Native Wins Literary Prize," by James S. Howard. *Fresno Bee*. November 8, 1996, A1, A6.
"Parrot in the Oven: Mi Vida," by Virginia Madrid-Salazar. *San Joaquin Vida en el Valle*. December 4, 1996, A1, A9.
"People in Books: Writing from the Heart." *American Bookseller*. January 1997, 72.
"TimeOut," by Joe Garofoli. *Times*. January 5, 1997, 1–2 H.

Selected Work by Victor Martinez

The Parrot in the Oven: Mi Vida

National Book Award for Young People's Literature

Horn Book Fanfare Book Award

Grades 6–Up

- Alcoholism
- Family Life
- Farmworkers
- Gangs
- Socioeconomic Class

"*Pericho*, or parrot, is what Dad called me sometimes. It was from a Mexican saying about a parrot that complains about how hot it is in the shade, while all along he's sitting in an oven" (51–52). Based in part on the author's experiences, this extraordinary debut novel details the events in the life of a young Latino during a pivotal year filled with pain, tension, awkwardness, and excitement. Fourteen-year-old Manuel "Manny" Hernandez, who narrates the story in a series of loosely connected vignettes, searches for his place in the world while struggling with family problems, economic challenges, and social humiliations. His unemployed, alcoholic father spends most of his time at the local pool hall and is eventually jailed after threatening his mother with a rifle. Other vignettes detail Manny's experiences during an Immigration and Naturalization Service (INS) raid on a field where he is picking pesticide-coated chili peppers, his sister's miscarriage, and his grandmother's funeral. Shortly after being initiated into a gang, Manny finds the strength to change his mind and maintain his personal integrity. *Parrot in the Oven* is an important book, distinguished by its endearing protagonist, its compassionate story, and, most of all, its striking use of language. "Dad lifted his eyes and gave me a look that could crack concrete" (47). "The lightbulb in the bathroom was blazing a white star in the mirror, and looking at it, I was surprised by how much pleasure and agony could burst from one's heart at the same time" (197). *Publishers Weekly wrote*, "Martinez maintains the authenticity of his setting and characterization through a razor-sharp combination of tense dialogue, coursing narrative and startlingly elegant imagery."

Nicholasa Mohr

Puerto Rican American (1938–)
Birthday: November 1

Because of who I am, I feel blessed by the work I do, for it permits me to use my talents and continue to "make magic." I can recreate those deepest of personal memories as well as validate and celebrate my heritage and my future.

(Bantam Brochure)

Books by Nicholasa Mohr

All for the Better: A Story of El Barrio (Stories of America Series). Illustrated by Rudy Gutierrez. Steck-Vaughn, 1993. Spanish edition: *Para una vida mejor.*
El Bronx Remembered. HarperCollins, 1993.
Felita. Illustrated by Ray Cruz. Dial, 1979; Bantam Skylark, 1990.
Going Home. Dial, 1986; Bantam Skylark, 1989.
Growing Up Inside the Sanctuary of My Imagination: A Memoir. Messner, 1994.
In Nueva York. Arte Público Press, 1988.
The Magic Shell. Illustrated by Rudy Gutierrez. Scholastic, 1995. Spanish edition: *El Regalo Magico.*
A Matter of Pride and Other Stories. Arte Público Press, 1997.
Nilda. Harper & Row, 1973.
Old Letivia and the Mountain of Sorrows. Viking, 1996. Spanish edition: *La vieja Letivia y el monte de los pesares.*
Rituals of Survival: A Woman's Portfolio. Arte Público, 1985.
The Song of El Coqui and Other Tales of Puerto Rico. Written with Antonio Martorell. Viking, 1995. Spanish edition: *La canción del coquí y otros cuentos de Puerto Rico.*

Plays by Nicholasa Mohr

El Bronx Remembered
I Never Even Seen My Father
Nilda
Zoraida

Nicholasa Mohr is the highly acclaimed author of numerous picture books, short story collections, novels, essays, and plays. She was born in New York City's oldest Spanish-speaking community known as El Barrio (the neighborhood), or Spanish Harlem. When she started school, she moved with her family—mother, father, and six older brothers—to the Bronx, where she spent most of her growing-up years. "Growing up in a household of six older brothers, and being part of a family who still held old-fashioned Puerto Rican concepts about the male and female roles, was often a struggle for me" (Bantam Brochure). Mohr elaborates on some aspects of this struggle in her books.

From the beginning, she found magic in creating pictures and writing letters. Her art provided adventure, freedom, and space in the small crowded apartment where she lived with her extended family. Her mother lovingly provided support and encouragement for Mohr's achievements. (Mohr's father died when she was eight years old.)

Drawing and painting sustained Mohr through otherwise depressing conditions in both her home and school life. By using her imagination, she was able to create something pleasing and interesting. She used her skills and imagination to further develop her creativity, first in visual arts and later in her writing.

Mohr wanted to attend a college preparatory high school, but due to the intervention of a bigoted guidance counselor, she attended a trade school instead. She writes about the racism of the counselor and other teachers in her memoir, *Growing Up Inside the Sanctuary of My Imagination*. At the trade school, she majored in fashion illustration. After she graduated, she attended the Art Students' League in New York City, where she studied drawing and painting. Her love for books led her to discover the work of Mexican artists; she later studied art and printmaking in Mexico. Subsequently, she has taught art in colleges in New York and New Jersey.

As Mohr's art developed, her feelings and experiences as a Puerto Rican woman born in the United States came through. This led to a publisher asking her to write about her life. She was aware of the lack of Puerto Rican literature, so she eventually agreed to the suggestion. "I was well aware that there were no books published about Puerto Rican girls or boys. . . . I was also reminded that when I was growing up, I'd enjoyed reading about the adventures of many boys and girls, but I had never really seen myself, my brothers or my family in those books. We just were not there" (Bantam Brochure). In her memoir, she elaborates on her love for books and libraries. She writes, "One of the most thrilling events I can recall was when I got my first library card" (61). The library became a home away from home for Mohr, providing a quiet place where she could study, read, and write.

Years later, writing her first books was difficult, but with her characteristic determination and by applying some of the techniques that she had developed as a visual artist to her new challenge as a writer, she has become a successful author. Mohr writes about the ongoing struggles of the Puerto Rican people on the mainland to gain their basic human rights. Her work, often incorporating a strong social statement, reflects the perspectives of the Puerto Rican people in all their complexity and variety. She has won many awards and honors, and in 1989 she was awarded an honorary doctorate from the State University of New York. The National Hispanic Academy of Media Arts and Sciences honored her with the Annual Achievement in Literature Award in 1996. She recently moved back to El Barrio, East Harlem, where she was born.

More Information about Nicholasa Mohr

Authors and Artists for Young Adults, vol 8, 161–167.
Contemporary Authors Online. The Gale Group, 2001.
Dictionary of Literary Biography, vol 145, 170–177.
Hispanic, Female and Young: An Anthology, edited by Phyllis Tashlik. Arte Público Press, 1994.

Growing Up Inside the Sanctuary of My Imagination by Nicholasa Mohr. Julian Messner, 1994.
The Hispanic Literary Companion, edited by Nicolás Kanellos. Visible Ink Press, 1997.
Latina Self-Portraits: Interviews with Contemporary Women Writers, edited by Bridget Kevane and Juanita Heredia. University of New Mexico Press, 2000.
¡Latinas! Women of Achievement, edited by Diane Telgen and Jim Kamp. Visible Ink Press, 1996.
Multicultural Voices in Contemporary Literature by Frances Ann Day. Heinemann, 1999.
The Oxford Companion to Women's Writing in the United States, edited by Cathy N. Davidson and Linda Wagner-Martin. Oxford University Press, 1995.
"Puerto Rican Writers in the United States, Puerto Rican Writers in Puerto Rico: A Separation beyond Language," by Nicolasa Mohr, in *Barrios and Borderlands: Cultures of Latinos and Latinas in the United States*, edited by Denis Lynn Daly Heyck. Routledge, 1994.
Something about the Author, vol 8, 138.

Selected Works by Nicolasa Mhor

All for the Better: A Story of El Barrio

Grades 2–5

- Biography
- Boycotts
- Depression Era
- Moving
- Puerto Rico

This is the touching biography of Evalina Lopez (Antonetty) (1922–1984). The book focuses on her early years, but the epilogue and afterword provide information about her later years. In 1933, when Evalina was eleven years old, her mother was forced by economic hardship to send her daughter to live with her aunt in New York City. The Great Depression had brought hard times to everyone, but things were even worse in Puerto Rico. With many tears, Evalina reluctantly bid her family good-bye and bravely traveled by ship to live in Spanish Harlem's El Barrio. There she gradually adjusted to a new city, new home, and new school as well as a new language. She pitched in and helped her relatives and neighbors whenever she could. When she realized that many of her neighbors were too ashamed to apply for the government food packages that were available, she was determined to find a solution. Meanwhile, she saved her money, and with the help of her aunt, her mother and sisters were eventually able to join her in New York.

Evalina Lopez Antonetty became an activist on behalf of her community; she founded the United Bronx Parents Group. Through her leadership, determination, and ingenuity, she made a difference; her life serves as an inspiration to those who hope that one person can improve things.

Nicholasa Mohr has written an easy-to-read, inspiring biography of a truly special person. The black-and-white detailed drawings add to the warmth of the story. *All for the Better* is one of twenty-eight books in the Stories of America Series, edited by Alex Haley. Spanish edition: *Para una vida mejor*.

El Bronx Remembered

National Book Award Finalist
New York Times Outstanding Book
School Library Journal Best Book for Fall
Grades 7–12

- Bronx
- Short Stories

Nicholasa Mohr's second book, a memorable collection of eleven short stories and a novella, *Herman and Alice*, eloquently captures the joy, tragedy, humor, and irony of life. Depicting Puerto Rican life in the Bronx in New York City, she describes the struggle to find meaning in spite of the cultural contradictions faced by her characters. Taking place during the postwar years from 1946 to 1956, the focus is on rural Puerto Ricans adjusting to the big city. The introduction states: "These migrants and their children, strangers in their own country, brought with them a different language, culture and racial mixture. Like so many before them, they hoped for a better life, a new future for their children, and a piece of that good life known as the 'American dream.'" Mohr explores a number of significant themes, including cultures in transition, dreams and disillusionments, cross-cultural interactions, family fortunes and hard times, class structure and social mores, and intergenerational conflicts. Her novella, *Herman and Alice*, is one of the earliest U.S. Latino works to deal with the topic of homosexuality. When gay, thirty-eight-year-old Herman Aviles and pregnant fifteen-year-old Alice get married, they agree that they are not interested in a physical relationship. After the baby is born, Alice's feelings change, and she starts going out with her old friends. Eventually, Herman decides to return to Puerto Rico and to try to contact his former lover, Daniel. In another piece, Uncle Claudio decides to return to Puerto Rico because "there he is Don Claudio and in New York, he is Don Nobody." Other *El Bronx Remembered* stories deal with a mother who is accused of dealing drugs; a valedictorian who suffers the embarrassment of wearing his uncle's "roach killer" shoes to graduation; three girls who find a dead man in an abandoned building;

a lonely elderly Jewish man who is welcomed into the home of his generous Puerto Rican neighbors; a Catholic girl who wants to eat lunch with her Jewish friend during Passover; and a young girl who experiences the death of a beloved dog because of the stinginess of adults. *El Bronx Remembered* is a significant work, exploring the circumstances and values of an emerging culture.

Felita

Notable Children's Book in the Field of Social Studies
Grades 4–7

- Death
- Gender Roles
- Grandmothers
- Moving
- Newcomers
- Nonviolence

Eight-year-old Felita Maldonado loves her neighborhood in New York City. To her disappointment, her parents decide to move. "We're off to a better future," her father announces. Only her wise and loving grandmother, Abuelita, who moved to New York from Puerto Rico, understands how much Felita will miss her old neighborhood and Gigi, her best friend. The people in the new neighborhood taunt and tease Felita, yelling, "Go on back to your own country" (37). Faced with unrelenting prejudice in their new location, Papi, Mami, Felita, and her two brothers finally decide to return to their old neighborhood. Felita finds that many things have changed while she was gone, and some of the most significant changes are within herself. She has learned much about her heritage and about how to deal with the prejudice that the family has faced. When her beloved Grandmother dies, Felita vows to visit Puerto Rico—a trip that she had long hoped to take with her Grandmother.

In her first book for this age group, Mohr not only provides information about the pain of discrimination as experienced by a young girl but offers insight into how one might cope with such bigotry. In Abuelita's words, "Felita, it is important for you to know that no one is better than anyone else because they have a lighter skin or a different kind of hair. Inside, you must know this and feel strong" (61). As Felita talks with her grandmother, she is able to sort out her feelings. Readers who are experiencing similar discrimination will be heartened by the sensitive way in which Felita's experiences are handled. Perhaps, the ones who are mistreating their classmates will understand that what they are doing is wrong and begin to change their attitudes and behavior. The book also provides important information on Puerto Rico, including the fact that Puerto Ricans, whether they are born on the island or on the mainland, are American citizens. Children will find much to discuss and write about in this engaging book, including the ups and downs of Felita's friendship with Gigi.

In her memoir, *Growing Up Inside the Sanctuary of My Imagination*, Nicholasa Mohr reveals that *Felita* was based on her own family's experiences. She writes, "That experience—when in my young life I witnessed hatred, abuse, brutality, and xenophobia based solely on the fact that we were Puerto Ricans—will remain with me for the rest of my life" (52). Sequel: *Going Home*.

Going Home

Parents' *Choice Remarkable Book for Literature*

Notable Trade Book in the Field of Social Studies

Grades 4–7

- Puerto Rico
- Travel
- Identity
- Gender Roles

Before reading this book, read the prequel, *Felita*. At the end of *Felita*, when her beloved Abuelito dies, Felita Maldonado vows to visit Puerto Rico. In *Going Home*, twelve-year-old Felita takes this important journey, the one that she had long hoped to take with her Grandmother. The first half of the book is devoted to the period before the trip to Puerto Rico and describes Felita's family, friendships, neighborhood, and school. Since her eleventh birthday, her parents have become increasingly protective, and her brother, Tito, has picked on her and become even more bossy than ever. Supervised and chaperoned, Felita says, "Sometimes I feel like I am in jail" (66). Frustrated with her parents' double standard for their sons and daughter, she longs for Abuelita and their heart-to-heart talks. When school is out, the family leaves for the long-anticipated trip to Puerto Rico. But the experience is not quite what Felita expected. She is surprised that she is considered an outsider and called a Gringita. "All my life I've been Puerto Rican, and now I'm told I'm not. . . . At home I get called a "spick" and here I'm a Nuyorican" (122). Even her aunts and uncles are a disappointment. As Felita becomes involved with a community play, she is met with both admiration and jealousy. However, by summer's end, she has made a close friend, used her creativity and talent, developed more insight into human interactions, and learned about her heritage. She goes home with a richer understanding of herself and an increased appreciation of life on the island.

Felita's first-person narrative is lively and straightforward; her colloquial, spirited language brings an exuberance and veracity to her experiences in New York City and Puerto Rico. Mohr skillfully continues her character development of the maturing protagonist, sensitively depicting her emotions, reactions, and increasing awareness. The author has a keen sense of the strict rules imposed on young Puerto Rican women and a sharp eye for the ups and downs of friendships among adolescents. Readers of all backgrounds will relate to the need to develop independence and to shape one's own identity. In addition, they will meet an admirable Latina character, learn more about Puerto Rico, and perhaps begin to perceive their relatives and friends with new insight.

Growing Up Inside the Sanctuary of My Imagination

Grades 4–Up

- Art and Artists
- Autobiography
- Death
- Teachers

In this compelling memoir, Nicholasa Mohr shares the poignant story of her first fourteen and half years growing up Puerto Rican, poor, and female in the 1940s in Spanish Harlem in New York City. The youngest of seven children and the only girl, she learned early to create her own space in the crowded, noisy environment. She describes slipping consciously into the world of her imagination, erasing the dissonance from her mind. This is an inspiring portrayal of a creative mind and the blossoming of a young girl's imaginative powers.

Mohr introduces us to her brothers, her wonderfully eccentric aunt, her father, and, most importantly, her beloved mother, who provided the emotional support for her hopes and dreams. She remembers her mother's generosity, always making room for relatives and friends who needed a place to stay. She credits her mother with teaching her to love and respect animals, noting, "It is one of the many precious things she gave me from her treasure chest of human values" (83). Her father and mother were very different in their beliefs and behavior; Mohr feels that their opposing points of view helped her to look at all sides of an issue and to seek out her own truth. She notes that "to this day I can empathize with both sides and have learned to celebrate my own relationship to humankind" (7).

The chapters that deal with Mohr's experiences at school should be required reading for all educators. Starting in kindergarten with a rigid, cruel teacher, her years in school were, for the most part, demoralizing and stifling. During her thirteen years in elementary and high school, she found only two teachers who were caring and supportive. She and her classmates were routinely chastised and punished for speaking Spanish, even informally at recess. Mohr notes that the school system seemed to have no place for children like her. Her experiences with the heartless guidance counselor who ignored her request to attend the High School of Music and Art are appalling. This is a chilling example of how institutional racism works to ignore and stifle the talents and dreams of young people of color.

Mohr was dealt another crushing blow when her mother died of cancer at the young age of forty-nine. The passages that describe her last pain-filled weeks and especially their last loving talk are beautifully written. Mohr writes, "There are two major components that have helped me survive and thrive. The first was my imagination and the powers of my inner life. The second was my mother's faith in me and her determination that I succeed" (111). In spite of the harsh realities of her childhood, Mohr believed in herself and ultimately was able to follow her dream of being an artist and, later, a writer. In the introduction, Mohr shares that as she wrote this book, reliving the early stages of her evolution, "I enlightened my own consciousness and healed some of my latent wounds" (ix).

A list of published works by the author and black-and-white photographs of Nicholasa Mohr and her relatives are included. *Growing Up Inside the Sanctuary of My Imagination* is part of the In My Own Words Series, which features memoirs by authors of books for young readers. Television adaptation: *The Dignity of the Children*, ABC Documentary, Winter/Spring 1996.

In Nueva York

Notable Trade Book in the Field of Social Studies
American Library Association Best Books
New York Times Outstanding Book of the Year
School Library Journal Best Book
Grades 9–12

- Lower East Side, New York
- Short Stories

This is a moving collection of eight, interrelated short stories that depict life in Losaida, one of New York City's Puerto Rican communities. Writing candidly, sympathetically, and with wry humor, Mohr portrays her characters with warmth and sophistication. Some of the same characters appear in several stories, sometimes as major characters and in other stories in a minor role.

In Nueva York is Mohr's third book; it is a significant contribution of humor and pathos to the usual bleak depiction of life on the Lower East Side. She portrays authentically the pull of the two cultures that are present in the lives of her characters: the culture of the big-city neighborhood with its deterioration and danger contrasted with the generous, caring people who remember their lives on the island of Puerto Rico, where the way of life was much different.

In "The Perfect Little Flower Girl," Mohr writes about Johnny and Sebastian, two gay men. Johnny is concerned about providing for Sebastian, who is disabled with asthma and migraine headaches. Finally they find a way around the homophobic system by arranging a marriage to a lesbian friend with the agreement that benefits will go to Sebastian. Mohr also shows insight into size discrimination in her portrayal of Chiquitín, a very small person who appears throughout the book. She writes, "Chiquitín had learned early that because he was physically different from the average person, life for him would have limits. From the simple tasks of buying clothing that fit,. . . . being able to speak face to face with people without being ignored, to the more serious task of getting a job, commanding respect as an adult, and speaking another language, life for Chiquitín was a series of obstacles to be overcome" (141). Mohr's portrayal of these characters as complex, honorable people is a step forward in shattering the stereotypes that surround them.

Mohr uses Spanish liberally throughout the text. Instead of setting these words off in italics and repeating with English, the translation is embedded in the context of the stories. Perhaps Mohr intended her readers to feel the connection between the two cultures through the languages. Indeed, she succeeds admirably in drawing her readers into her stories and the lives of her characters. In this book as in several others, she continues to explore the themes of a community overcoming prejudice—ethnic, gender, racial, and heterosexist. Play: "I Never Even Seen My Father."

The Magic Shell

Grades 2–5

- Dominican Republic
- Emigration and Immigration
- Moving
- Newcomers

When Jaime reluctantly moves with his parents from the Dominican Republic to New York City, he has a difficult time adjusting. The problems in his new environment seem endless: the noise, the cold weather, the heavy winter clothing, being cooped up in an apartment, and a new language, and, most of all, he misses his old friends. Just when he thinks things can't get any worse, he remembers the conch shell his great-uncle gave him as a going-away present. The magic of the shell transports him back to his beloved homeland, where he was free to play in the warm out-of-doors with his friends. These magic times with the shell provide enough comfort and time for him to start learning the new language, make new friends, and gradually adjust to his new home. By the time that his family is ready for a visit to the Dominican Republic, Jaime would rather attend the Discovery Summer Day Camp with his new friends. But once he gets back to his old home and reunites with his old friends, he remembers the joys of life on the island. When he visits his great-uncle and discusses the magic of the shell with him, Jaime realizes that the magic was really within himself.

Nicholasa Mohr has created a touching story of a child learning to live within two cultures; she eloquently captures the pain and frustration felt by the newcomer, the outsider. She portrays the new children whom Jaime meets as welcoming and friendly; unfortunately, this is quite often not the case. Spanish edition: *El regalo magico.*

Nilda

School Library Journal Best Book

New York Times Outstanding Book of the Year

American Library Association Best Book of 1973

Jane Addams Children's Book Award of U.S. Women's International League for Peace and Freedom

Society of Illustrators Citation of Merit for Art

Grades 7–12

- Art
- Barrio
- Death
- Mother–Daughter Relationship

Nicholasa Mohr dedicated *Nilda,* her first novel, with love to the children of El Barrio—and of all the many barrios all over the world. As is often the case with first books, this novel includes autobiographical elements. It is the story of three years in Nilda's life—from age ten to thirteen—and takes place in the barrio in New York City from 1941 to 1945. It chronicles the day-to-day experiences of a poor Puerto Rican family.

When her father's heart attacks and eventual death force the family into the welfare system, Nilda finds that this social service organization is indeed a fearsome institution. She tells about going to the welfare office with her mother and then later having their apartment inspected by the social worker. Her humiliation is further compounded when officials at the health office inspect her head for lice.

School provides no sanctuary. Students have their hands rapped with a ruler for speaking Spanish. One teacher makes no attempt to understand Latino mourning customs; another who teaches Spanish demands Castilian accents from Puerto Rican students. Nilda suffers many losses during these three years. The most devastating is the death of her mother. Subsequently, the family is separated, and Nilda goes to live with her aunt in the Bronx. The young woman copes with all these problems by escaping into her art: "she lost herself in a world of magic achieved with some forms, lines and color."

This is an exceptional story of hardship, family ties, and neighborhood interactions. It is rich in detail, full of a child's thoughts and feelings. Fascinating and frank, humorous and sad—a classic coming-of-age story. Note: Contains strong language.

Old Letivia and the Mountain of Sorrows

Grades K–4

- *Curanderas*
- Folklore

To end the fierce winds that threaten a Puerto Rican village, Letivia and her friends set out on a dangerous odyssey to break an ominous spell cast by the Mountain of Sorrows. Letivia is granted four wishes, but she learns that "one cannot get everything and give nothing in return." This captivating, original tale is rich in Puerto Rican language, culture, and symbolism. Themes explored include courage, friendship, change, healing, prejudice, and respect for, and appreciation of, nature. Mohr's portrayal of Letivia as a wise, heroic healer contrasts with the negative images of witches found in European folklore. Note: Cervantes, the whistling turtle magician, was transformed into a wandering star. Some reviewers interpreted this as self-sacrifice and death. Spanish edition: *La vieja Letivia y el monte de los pesares*.

Rituals of Survival: A Woman's Portfolio

Grades 10–Adult

- Short Stories

This fine collection of five short stories and a novella provides inspiration to women everywhere who are trying to break out of the restrictive roles in which society has placed them. Nicholasa Mohr offers powerful portraits of six New York Puerto Rican women who are, each in her own way, issuing declarations of independence and pursuing domestic and social revolutions. Facing isolation, poverty, illness, depression, demanding relatives, death of loved ones, and lack of support for their dreams, they somehow persevere. Zoraida, resilient and shy, finds a way to deal with her controlling husband and interfering family. When they take away her beloved rocking chair, "the one place where she felt she could be herself, where she could really be free" (29), she retreats further within herself. After her husband dies, sixty-six-year-old Carmela asserts her independence and finds a way to make her own life at last. After a brief return home, Virginia, a bisexual textile designer, leaves to continue her wanderlust ways. Amy, isolated and poverty-stricken after the accidental death of her husband, finds a way to bring a little joy into the lives of her four children on Thanksgiving Day. A former prostitute, Lucia celebrates her twentieth birthday in the hospital on Welfare Island, where she is dying of tuberculosis.

In the novella, Inez struggles to follow her dream of going to art school. When her parents die, she goes to live with her pernicious aunt. She cherishes and keeps alive the memories of her mother, who told her, "Someday you must study so that you can become an important artist . . . make an important contribution to the world and really be somebody" (106). After six years of neglect and emotional abuse in her aunt's home, Inez enters into a marriage as a passport to freedom. However, she soon realizes that she has jumped from the frying pan into the fire; her new husband is insanely jealous and violent. She finds a creative, albeit unusual, way to disentangle herself from this abusive relationship and with great determination follows her dream of attending art school. In all of these stories, the women struggle to remain true to themselves. Their rituals of survival serve as guides for those who follow in their footsteps. Mohr has a unique way of telling her stories from the perspectives of several of the characters so the reader knows what everyone is thinking. She dedicated this book "To the memory of Evalina Lopez Antonetty, a beloved and valiant sister." Years later, Mohr wrote a biography as further tribute to Evalina's life: *All for the Better: A Story of El Barrio.*

The Song of el Coquí and Other Tales of Puerto Rico

All Ages

- Folklore
- Frogs
- Guinea Hens
- Mules
- Slavery

Dedicated "to the children of the barrios who live far away from the Caribbean magic that weaves the stories of this book," this engaging collection of three folktales was written with respect and affection for the rich and complex ancestral traditions that make up Puerto Rican culture. In the first tale, the god Huracán enjoys his mountain home on the beautiful island of Borinquén. However, he soon becomes sad because there is no music, so he creates a storm that lasts for a million years. Soon after the cataclysm subsides, the air is filled with the sweet song of the tiny coquí. The second tale, "La Guinea, the Stowaway Hen," begins in West Africa, where slave traders are kidnapping people. La Guinea, seeking refuge, ends up on the slave ship en route to Puerto Rico. She finally finds a new home where she provides inspiration for Don Elias, a mask maker. In the final folktale, "La Mula, the Cimarron Mule," Mula is worked to near exhaustion by Spanish bandits until she escapes and joins a community of *cimarrones* (escaped slaves) in the hills. Each of the animals represents a group of people in Puerto Rico. El coquí represents the indigenous Tainos, La Guinea symbolizes the African people who were brought to the island as captive slaves, and the story of La Mula is a parable about the Spaniards who conquered the island. Together, the three folktales form a composite of a culture comprising of three very different and very special strands.

The paintings in this book are extraordinarily exquisite! The resplendent art combined with the fascinating stories make this a book that will jump off the bookshelves and into the hands of readers of all ages and backgrounds. Spanish edition: *La canción del coquí: Y otros cuentos de Puerto Rico.*

Pat Mora

Mexican American (1942–   )
Birthday: January 19
Contact: Arte Público Press
University of Houston
Houston, TX 77204-2090
1-800-633-ARTE

Cultures can be bridges. They're not walls. When we learn about other cultures, we realize how much alike people are.

(*Experience Exchange*, 1)

We have a whole generation growing up without ever seeing themselves in print. What does it mean if you don't see yourself in books? There is a strong connection between images and identity.

(*Albuquerque Journal*)

I began writing picture books because I am drawn to the form, but also because I believe there was and is a great need for such books written by Latinas and Latinos describing our values, customs, realities. Not only Latino youngsters need and deserve such books—all young people do in our multicultural society.

(*The Horn Book Magazine*, 299)

Books by Pat Mora

Agua, Agua, Agua. (Let Me Read Series) Illustrated by José Ortega. Good Year Books, 1994.
Agua Santa/Holy Water. Beacon Books, 1995.
A Birthday Basket for Tía. Illustrated by Cecily Lang. Macmillan, 1992. Spanish edition: *Una canasta de cumpleaños para Tía.*
Aunt Carmen's Book of Practical Saints. Beacon Press, 1997.
The Bakery Lady/La señora de la panadería. Illustrated by Pablo Torrecilla. Arte Público Press, 2001.
This Big Sky. Illustrated by Steve Jenkins. Scholastic, 1998.
Borders. Arte Público Press, 1986.
Chants. Arte Público Press, 1994.
Communion. Arte Público Press, 1991.
Confetti: Poems for Children. Illustrated by Enrique O. Sanchez. Lee and Low, 1996.
Delicious Hullabaloo/Pachanga deliciosa. Illustrated by Francisco X. Mora. Arte Público Press, 1998.
The Desert Is My Mother/El desierto es mi madre. Illustrated by Daniel Lechon. Arte Público Press, 1994.
Doña Flor. Knopf, forthcoming.
The Gift of the Poinsettia/El regalo de la flor de Nochebuena. (Written with Charles Ramirez Berg) Illustrated by Daniel Lechon. Arte Público Press, 1995.
House of Houses. Beacon Press, 1997.
A Library for Juana. Illustrated by Beatriz Vidal. Knopf, 2002. Spanish edition: *Una biblioteca para Juana.*
Listen to the Desert/Oye al desierto. Illustrated by Francisco X. Mora. Clarion, 1994.
Love to Mamá: A Tribute to Mothers. Illustrated by Paula S. Barragán M., Lee and Low, 2001.
Maria Paints the Hills. Illustrated by Maria Hesch. Museum of New Mexico Press, 2002.
¡Marimba! Animales A–Z. Clarion, 2002.
My Own True Name: New and Selected Poems for Young Adults. Arte Público Press, 2000.
Nepantla. Essays from the Land in the Middle. University of New Mexico Press, 1993.
The Night the Moon Fell: A Maya Myth. Illustrated by Domi. Groundwood Books, 2000.
Pablo's Tree. Illustrated by Cecily Lang. Macmillan, 1994.
The Race of Toad and Deer. Illustrated by Maya Itzna. Orchard, 1995. Spanish edition: *La carrera del sapa y el venado.*
The Rainbow Tulip. Illustrated by Elizabeth Sayles. Viking, 1999.
Tomás and the Library Lady. Illustrated by Raul Colón. Knopf, 1997.
Unos, Dos, Tres. One, Two, Three. Illustrated by Barbara Lavallee. Clarion Books, 1996.

Pat(ricia) Mora has earned distinction as both a writer and an educator. In each of these fields, she has gained a reputation as a strong advocate for cultural conservation. A former teacher, university administrator, museum director, and consultant on United States–Mexico youth exchanges, Mora now spends her time writing and speaking to audiences of all ages. Best known for her award-winning poetry, she also writes children's books and essays. She was instrumental in establishing April 30 as Día de los niños/Día de los libros, a yearly celebration of childhood, books, languages, and cultures.

Mora was born in El Paso, Texas; she grew up in this border city to which her grandparents came during the Mexican revolution. Her parents, Raul Antonio Mora, an optician, and Estella Delgado Mora, a homemaker, were very supportive. At considerable personal sacrifice, they sent their children to Catholic schools where her mother was a president of the Parent–Teacher Association (PTA). Even though she had been an excellent student, she had to go to work right after high school due to the depression. Books were an important part of Mora's childhood; her mother took the children to the library regularly and encouraged them to read and write. Mora credits her mother with being her first and best editor. In "My Fierce Mother" printed in *Nepantla*, Mora affectionately describes her as a woman who is determined to be treated fairly. No one, no matter how powerful, can intimidate her. "She read every paper I wrote" and "saves every piece I write and any piece written about me."

Mora grew up in a society that did not value her cultural heritage, and so, like most young people in a similar situation, she tried to fit in. She writes that her personal experience with internalized racism now helps her understand how young people may be feeling even today. As a child, she couldn't have known that assimilation means a loss of cultural identity. She spoke Spanish at home with her parents, grandmother, and aunt, but at school the pressure to conform led her to ignore her ethnicity.

Until she was seventeen, she never considered being anything but a nun. Then she became interested in being a physician, but at that time women were not encouraged to enter that male-dominated field. So, like many women before her and since, she went into teaching. She was an English major and a speech minor in both her bachelor's and master's programs. She notes that the university virtually ignored her cultural heritage while she was a student there. Even though she grew up in a middle-class family and neighborhood, she was the first in her family to graduate from college. She soon married and began teaching at a high school in the El Paso Independent School District.

During the ensuing years, Mora earned her master's degree, had three children, and worked as a teacher, lecturer, university administrator, and museum director. She hosted a radio show, *Voices: The Mexican American in Perspective* on KTEP, a National Public Radio affiliate. She began making time for writing in 1980, and in 1983 she received the first of many awards when she was recognized by the National Association for Chicano Studies. Her career as a writer and an advocate for cultural conservation blossomed during the 1980s; the recipient of a Kellogg National Fellowship as well as many other honors and awards, Mora continued her work as an educator and museum director until 1989.

For the first thirty-seven years of her life, Mora lived in El Paso, Texas. In September 1989 she moved with her new husband, an archaeologist, to Cincinnati, Ohio, where she spends her time writing, speaking, facilitating workshops, and traveling. She continues to create poetry but also writes picture books and prose. She has become increasingly aware of the absence of the U.S. Latina voice in American literature. She longs for a world free of the pollution of bias and bigotry. She believes in the power of words to awaken, to heal, and to create change.

In her writing and lectures, she describes and questions our national patterns of discrimination and prejudice. She notes, "I want to hear that which is part of me but which was silenced through both ignorance and prejudice. . . . Like many Latinas in this country, I was educated with few if any references to my Mexican American history, to part of my literary and human heritage" (*Nepantla*, 39). To help remedy this deplorable situation, Mora has written numerous outstanding books for young readers and has plans to write many more. She believes that writers have a responsibility to struggle against injustice, to speak out for cultural conservation and social change.

More Information about Pat Mora

www.patmora.com

Albuquerque Journal. February 24, 1995, page numbers unavailable.

Contemporary Authors. Volume 129, 306.

Contemporary Authors Online. The Gale Group, 2001.

Dictionary of Literary Biography. Volume 209, 160–163.

Experience Exchange. Houghton Mifflin Newspaper, 4–5.

The Hispanic Literary Companion, edited by Nicolás Kanellos. Visible Ink Press, 1997.

House of Houses. Beacon Press, 1997.

"A Latina in Kentucky." *Horn Book Magazine*. May/June 1994, 298–300.

¡Latinas! Women of Achievement, edited by Diane Telgen and Jim Kamp. Visible Ink Press, 1996.

Nepantla: Essays from the Land in the Middle by Pat Mora.

Notable Hispanic American Women, edited by Diane Telsen and Jim Kamp. Gale Research, 1993, 280–282.

"Talking with Pat Mora." *Book Links*. September 1997.

Selected Works by Pat Mora

Agua Agua Agua

Preschool–K

- Aesop's Fable
- Crows
- Water

In this charming little book, Crow finds a way to relieve her thirst by using her head. Pat Mora's lyrical text is accompanied by whimsical illustrations by José Ortega. Let Me Read books use playful language, such as repetition and rhyme, to build interest and success. They are designed to develop positive attitudes toward reading, build on successful reading experiences, and create a positive, supportive role for parents. Suggestions are included for activities to help children relate to the written word such as "Find and learn the Spanish words." Three levels are available to provide gradual challenges to help young readers gain confidence and to become lifelong learners.

Agua Santa/Holy Water

Grades 11–Adult

- Poetry

Poet Pat Mora draws readers into the bountiful rivers of her poems, paying tribute to women who resist, create, nurture, and heal. The interior design of this affirming collection of poetry flows beautifully with waves of words and images, rich in history, mythology, and experience. As in her other collections, Mora draws inspiration from her Mexican American roots; here she contrasts cascading waters with the desert images of earlier works. Themes center around birth, death, adoption, racism, guilt, Frida Kahlo, Sor Juana, La Llorona, the Day of the Dead, Honduras, and more. One of the most powerful poems is "Let Us Hold Hands," calling on women of all backgrounds, past and present, to support each other, forming a ring around the world. The appended notes provide historical and cultural information about some of the poems.

The Bakery Lady/La señora de la panadería

Grades K–4

- Baking
- Bilingual
- Three Kings' Day

Mónica, who lives with her grandparents above their bakery, yearns to be a baker like her *abuela*. When she finds the doll hidden in the bread on the feast for the Three Kings, she rises to the challenge of baking the cookies for the next fiesta. In this colorful bilingual picture book, Pat

Mora weaves a playful tale rich with tradition and warm with the savory smells of the *panadería*.

A Birthday Basket for Tía

Grades Preschool–4

- Aunts
- Birthdays
- Cats
- Elders
- Gifts

With the help of her feline friend Chica, Cecilia selects a surprise gift for her great-aunt's ninetieth birthday. On the birthday morning, as her mother is preparing food for the surprise party, Cecilia, always accompanied by Chica, searches through the house for the perfect gift for her beloved Tía. She chooses objects that invoke special memories—a favorite book that her aunt reads to her; a bowl in which they mix cookie dough; a flowerpot in which they grow flowers for the kitchen window; a teacup in which Tía serves *hierbabuena* (hot mint tea) when Cecilia is sick; and a red ball that they throw back and forth—and lovingly places them in a basket. Later, Cecilia and Mamá fill a piñata with candy and decorate the living room with balloons, flowers, and tiny cakes. Soon the musicians, family, and friends arrive, and everybody shouts, "SURPRISE! *¡Feliz cumpleaños!* Happy birthday!" as Tía walks through the door. After Tía carefully inspects each object in the basket, the music begins. Now Tía has a surprise for Cecilia! She sets down her cane and invites her beloved niece to dance with her.

The pleasing cumulative text is accompanied by bright cut-paper collages that echo the excitement of the celebration and the closeness of the intergenerational bond. This book, along with *Pablo's Tree*, offers a refreshing approach to birthday celebrations in which gifts are much-loved items that have meaning for the characters; there is no need for expensive presents. Mora and Lang have collaborated beautifully to bring us a loving relationship between an ebullient young Mexican American girl and a stereotype-breaking elderly aunt, as well as a warm interspecies friendship between human and feline. In "Remembering Lobo," printed in *Napantla: Essays from the Land in the Middle*, Mora writes more about this aunt with admiration and affection. *A Birthday Basket for Tía* is an excellent read-aloud and read-alone book. Spanish edition: *Una canasta de cumpleaños para Tía*.

Borders

Southwest Book Award
Grades 11–Up

• Poetry

In a richly lyrical style, Pat Mora explores the complex borders that divide us. With a piercing look at the political, social, cultural, and emotional divisions that create painful chasms among people, she speaks with a spirited, inspiring voice. Her words about gender, prejudice, indifference, language, class, education, isolation, health, and anger are powerful and mesmerizing. As a poet and educator who lives between two cultures, two traditions, two languages, and two nations, Mora's poems call for validation and healing. Her fascination with the pleasure and power of words is evident here. When she speaks of "that familiar quite contrary pain" (39), and "Desert women know about survival. . . . Like cactus we've learned to . . . sprout deep roots" (80), readers learn something quite profound about tenacity, about hope. Her poems about immigration, being among the first of a people to go to college, bilingualism, cleaning women, maids, hysterectomies, addiction to approval, archaeology, healing, ancestors, thoughts of suicide, intimacy, love, disillusionment, cancer, and Tomás Rivera demonstrate the wide range of themes that she explores.

Chants

Southwest Book Award
El Paso Times Best Book of Poetry
Grades 11–Up

• Poetry

In her first book of desert incantations, Pat Mora speaks with muted, yet spirited, tones as she explores the themes of womanhood, political, gender, class, and age borders, loss, and healing. She celebrates the beauty and power of the desert, praising the magical presence of the teluric force. Two of Mora's poems have recently been adapted into books for children. "Mi Madre" grew into *The Desert Is My Mother*, and "Poinsettia" has been expanded into *The Gift of the Poinsettia/El regalo de la flor de Nochebuena*. Several poems feature old women: a grandmother who treasures her solitude; a beloved elderly aunt with whom Mora has switched roles; and a small, gray-haired woman who makes and sells crepe paper flowers to sell to bargain-hunting tourists. In "Bailando" we catch a glimpse of the dear aunt who might have provided the inspiration for another children's book, *A Birthday Basket for Tía*. Mora cries out against violence against women in several poems and speaks unflinchingly of fear, resentment, loneliness, and despair. Hers is a healing voice, one of promise and hope.

Communion

Grades 11–Up

- Poetry

Communion is Pat Mora's third collection of poetry. In this sensitive collection she adds a global perspective while building on her previous themes of political, gender, class, and age borders, loss, healing and womanhood. Nostalgia, literacy, tenacity, poverty, assimilation, violence, loneliness, language, aging, friendship, parenthood, and sisterhood are all here in this moving volume of poignant poems. Butterflies, snow geese, sandhill cranes, Canadian geese, sand, trees, dandelions, and wild grapes anchor these poems to Mother Earth. Mora explores the role that the past plays in our lives, and in two poems, she again exposes domestic violence against women. In a salute to unity among women, Mora writes: "Strong women, teach me courage to esteem" (90). Spanish words and phrases are translated into English at the bottom of each page.

Confetti: Poems for Children

Choices Award: Cooperative Children's Book Center
International Reading Association Notable Book for a Global Society
Grades K–4

- Poetry
- Southwest

In this imaginative and spirited collection of thirteen poems, poet Pat Mora and artist Enrique O. Sanchez celebrate the vivid landscape of the Southwest and the delightful connection that children have with the natural world—the sun, clouds, leaves, wind, and water. Appended is a glossary of Spanish words embedded in the poetry.

Delicious Hullabaloo/Pachanga deliciosa

Grades Preschool–3

- Bilingual
- Desert Animals
- Poetry

Lavender armadillos, lime lizards, and other animals of the desert playfully enjoy the sounds of a mariachi band while gleefully savoring a smorgasbord of tasty dishes. Pat Mora and Francisco X. Mora have teamed up again to create another delightful bilingual picture book.

The Desert Is My Mother/El desierto es mi madre

Skipping Stone Honor Award
Grades Preschool–3

- Bilingual
- Deserts
- Environment
- Poetry

Here the desert is lovingly portrayed as a place of great beauty and power rather than the barren, boring setting featured in many stories. Mora, an award-winning poet, and Lechon, a prizewinning painter, collaborated to present the desert as a provider of food, healing, comfort, music, spirit, and life. On each double-page spread, a young girl makes a request, and the desert responds. "I say heal me. She gives me chamomile, oregano, peppermint." The book ends with "The desert is my strong mother." The design of the cover and interior of the book is also very appealing. This beautiful celebration of the relationship between nature and humans is a significant contribution to literature for young readers. Books such as this one provide hope that young readers will develop a conservation ethic and learn to love and respect the earth. Superb for reading aloud, discussion, and art activities.

The Gift of the Poinsettia/El regalo de la flor de Nochebuena

Grades 2–5

- Bilingual
- Christmas

- Mexico
- Posadas

This beautifully illustrated, bilingual picture book is based on the Mexican tradition of *las posadas* in which villagers reenact Mary and Joseph's search for shelter for the nine nights before Christmas. The book begins, "Long ago, a boy named Carlos lived in the small Mexican town of San Bernardo." Carlos lives with his Aunt Nina and his canine companion, Chico; they are poor, but their house is full of love. Night after night, traveling from house to house, Carlos enjoys the festivities of *las posadas* but worries about finding a special gift for the baby Jesus. On Christmas Eve the children each will place a gift before the manger. Finally his aunt, sensing his concern, makes a suggestion; she reassures him that "Love makes small gifts special." On Christmas Eve, when Carlos presents his humble present, he realizes that love is the best gift of all. The authors not only tell the story of *las posadas* but lovingly weave in information about other Mexican traditions such as *papel picado*, piñatas, and *cascarones*. This exquisitely designed and illustrated book concludes with the music and text for the songs of *las posadas*.

House of Houses

Grades 12–Up

- Family Memoir
- History

A complex, psychologically rich family memoir told through the voices of ancestors, *House of Houses* is an innovative, powerful social and historical document. Using shades of magical realism, Pat Mora lovingly weaves recipes, prayers, jokes, and fragments of poems and songs into this vivid family portrait. Includes photographs and a genealogical chart.

A Library for Juana

Grades K–3

- Biography
- Poets

Juana Ramírez de Asbaje, a child prodigy born in the seventeenth century, became Sor Juana Inés de la Cruz, Mexico's most famous woman poet. Determined to learn to read at the age of three, Juana inspires us with her fervor for learning and her delight in languages. Spanish edition: *Una biblioteca para Juana.*

Listen to the Desert/Oye al desierto

Grades Preschool–3

- Animals
- Bilingual
- Deserts
- Environment
- Poetry
- Sounds

Pat Mora and Francisco X. Mora have teamed up to create an enchanting book that will help the reader and listener perceive the desert anew. This bilingual portrayal of animal sounds heard in the southwestern desert is an excellent choice for reading aloud and for dramatization. Listeners of all ages will love the predictable, repetitive text and enjoy joining in to repeat the sounds. The lines on each page, two in English and two in Spanish, provide an opportunity to compare and contrast the sounds of the two languages—they are different and yet alike. "Listen to the dove say coo, coo, coo. La paloma arrulla, currucú, currucú, currucú." We hear the owl, toad, snake, dove, coyote, fish, and mice as well as the rain and the wind. The watercolor illustrations feature a vast expanse of light blue sky with geometric shapes at the bottom of each page. The cheery animals face the text and seem to be reciting the poetry along with the reader. The desert will never quite be the same again after one enjoys this book.

Love to Mamá: A Tribute to Mothers

Grades 3–Adult

- Mothers
- Grandmothers
- Poetry

In this beautiful and celebratory collection, thirteen poets write with love, joy, and humor about the powerful bond between mothers, grandmothers, and children. Representing a wide spectrum of Latino/a voices, they write passionately about their Mexican American, Cuban, Puerto Rican, and Venezuelan backgrounds. Energetic mixed-media illustrations capture each poem's tone, theme, and setting. A glossary of Spanish terms and biographical information about the poets and the illustrator are appended.

My Own True Name: New and Selected Poems for Young Adults

Texas Library Association Reading List
Voice of Youth Advocates Poetry Pick
New York Library Books for the Teen Age
Grades 6–12

- Authorship
- Identity
- Poetry

In this powerful collection of sixty-two poems, Pat Mora passionately explores the origins of identity, celebrates her rich bilingual heritage, and invites young readers to "join the serious and sassy family of writers" (3). Dedicated to "young writers of all shapes, colors, and sizes," Mora introduces this anthology with a heartwarming section titled "Dear Fellow Writers," in which she shares information about her writing process and gives advice to young writers. Using the cactus as a symbol of survival, she divides the book into three sections: "Blooms," "Thorns," and "Roots." In addition to poems selected from earlier collections, she includes several new poems published here for the first time.

Nepantla: Essays from the Land in the Middle

Grades 12–Adult

- Autobiographical Essays
- Authorship

These twenty inspiring essays are so significant and powerful, they should be required reading for all educators and prospective educators. In her first collection of prose, Pat Mora writes with remarkable sensitivity and insight about many significant issues including race, class, age, and gender. Using an analytical and yet accessible style, she examines issues related to bilingualism, cultural awareness, ethnic loyalty, assimilation/acculturation, internalized oppression, shackling stereotypes, education, class privilege, children's literature, authorship, and much more. Nepantla means "place in the middle" in Nahuatl, one of Mexico's indigenous languages. Mora finds herself in the middle in a number of ways: she is in the middle of her life, she is between her daughter and her mother, and she is presently living in the middle of the United States. For years she worked in the middle land between the university and the community. From these unique perspectives, she is able to offer opinions, insights, concerns, and visions, all strengthened by her voice of poetic experience.

What Mora has to say is so important and expressed with such care and in such readable language, I found myself marking every other sentence to use for quotes. She explores issues of cultural conservation, beginning with the preservation of her own Mexican American culture. In her travel essays, she confirms the necessity of preserving the heritage of diverse ethnic groups. She chronicles her trips to Puerto Vallarta, Pakistan, the Dominican Republic, Guatemala, and Cuba and the ways in which they have given her a unique perspective on the United States from which she can better perceive its weaknesses and strengths.

Mora's views on the challenges and duties of the writer are illuminating. She believes that writers have a responsibility to struggle against injustice, to "bear witness." Her advice to a young Latina writer is thoughtful and inspiring, encouraging her to develop pride in being Mexican American and to discover what she has to say that no one else can say. Mora "believes in the power of the word, that language shapes as well as reflects reality, that it creates space for difference, that our varied national voices strengthen us, not only in English but in all the rich languages that are part of these United States" (180).

This collection of essays, which includes speeches, reminiscences, poetry, and lectures, provide validation and encouragement to others who are committed to social change. She affirms the need for, and the right of, Latinas and Latinos to be heard and to participate in the shaping of our country. She asks difficult and sometimes unwelcome questions that must be addressed. *Nepantla* is a significant contribution to the growing body of Chicano nonfiction as well as to American literature.

The Night the Moon Fell

Grades 1–5

- Folklore
- Mayas
- Milky Way
- Moon

In this beautifully retold Maya myth, the moon tumbles from the sky and falls to pieces at the bottom of the ocean. Calling upon her inner resources and enlisting the help of tiny fish, she struggles to heal herself. At last she rises into the sky, taking her new friends with her to create the Milky Way. Pat Mora has taken the traditional Mopan Maya (Belize) myth, in which the moon is a weaver and the fish are the Milky Way, and transformed it to present an indomitable moon who finds a way to save herself, making the archetypal journey from homeland to a strange new world and back. Exquisite illustrations add to the appeal of this unique story. Spanish edition: *La noche que se cayó la luna*.

Pablo's Tree

Grades Preschool–3

- Adoption
- Birthdays
- Grandfathers
- Trees
- Single Motherhood
- Traditions

Each year on his birthday, Pablo eagerly looks forward to seeing how his grandfather, Lito, has decorated the tree that he planted on the day that the boy was adopted. When Mamá first told her father that she planned to adopt a child, he lovingly selected a special tree for his new grandchild. On the day that Mamá brought the baby home, Lito planted the tree in the sun in his backyard. Each year since then, Pablo has spent the night after his birthday at his grandfather's house. Each year, Abuelito has decorated the tree in a different way as a surprise for Pablo. The two have established a loving tradition of sitting under the tree while they take turns telling the story of Pablo's arrival and the story of the tree.

Pat Mora has created a unique birthday story, special in many ways. Planting a tree is such a wonderful way to honor a loved one; this book is a step forward in nurturing a love of nature. Also refreshing is the lack of materialism—here is a child who looks forward to seeing a tree, not to how many toys he receives for his birthday! Both this birthday story and the earlier *A Birthday Basket for Tia* by the same author and illustrator are a welcome contrast to the usual birthday stories.

Single motherhood and adoption are a part *Pablo's Tree* but are not central issues. Mora sprinkles and defines Spanish phrases throughout the story. Lang's exuberant collages using bright cut paper with dyes, combined with the lively story, make this a great read-aloud as well as read-alone book.

The Race of Toad and Deer

Grades Preschool–2

- Folklore
- Guatemala

Pat Mora based this folktale on one that she heard from Don Fernando Tesucún, a mason of restoration at a Guatemalan archaeological site in Tikál. Similar to the tortoise-and-the-hare fable, this sly tale is about a race between Venado, an overconfident deer, and Sapo, a resourceful toad. Venado is swift, but Sapo is clever. Which one will win the race? A cast of enthusiastic animals turns out to watch the big event. The author has written a satisfying book about the small and courageous triumphing over the large and tyrannical. She has woven Spanish words and phrases such as *silencio, buenos días, adelante,* and *amigos* into the text. She has also created an authentic setting with animals and plants indigenous to the area. Readers will meet bush dogs, spider monkeys, javelinas, tapirs, iguanas, armadillos, and anteaters. First-time illustrator Maya Itzna Brooks provides playful paintings to accompany the text. Spanish edition: *La carrera del sapa y el venado.*

The Rainbow Tulip

Grades K–5

- May Day
- Individuality
- Newcomers
- Schools

In this eloquently written book based on an experience from her mother's childhood, Pat Mora tells of a Mexican American immigrant first-grader who experiences the difficulties and pleasures of being different. At home, where her loving family keeps a piece of Mexico, she is Estelita. At school, where she is a successful student, her Anglicized name is Stella. At first, she has mixed feelings about being different. But near the end of the school year, Estelita/Stella embraces all the parts of herself by choosing to be the only one to wear a tulip costume with all the colors of the rainbow to the May Day parade. Complemented by warm pastel paintings, this very special, tender story celebrates differences, mother–daughter relationships, and independence.

Tomás and the Library Lady

Grades K–5

- Farmworkers
- Libraries
- Tomás Rivera

Based on a childhood experience of writer Tomás Rivera (1935–1984), the son of migrant workers who became a chancellor of the University of California at Riverside, this inspiring book is a powerful tribute to librarians and storytellers. The story takes place during one summer in Tomás' childhood when he travels with his family from Texas to Iowa harvesting fruit and vegetables. Encouraged by his storytelling grandfather, Tomás searches for more stories at the public library, where his life is changed forever by the magic of books. Complemented by richly textured scratchboard illustrations, this deeply touching book radiates with hope and promise.

Uno, Dos, Tres/One, Two, Three

All Ages

- Bilingual
- Birthdays
- Counting Book

"Uno one/We'll buy Mamá a sun." So begins this exquisite counting book. Two girls go to a Mexican market to select presents for their mother's birthday. As they shop, the marketplace comes alive with music, dancing, singing, waterfalls, birds, and people. They carefully choose among the gorgeous items, counting as they go. They pick out ten presents, including a gaily decorated piñata horse, a dancing marionette, and a delicately painted wooden animal. This charming books ends when the girls surprise their mother by presenting the assortment of wrapped presents. "¡Feliz cumpleaños, Mamá!"

One of the many things that make this book so special is the refreshing images of the round characters. Fat oppressive sentiments have permeated every aspect of our lives, including children's literature. What a nice surprise to find full figures in this charming little picture book! Add to that the vibrant, colorful watercolors that provide just the right touch of whimsy and humor to a special day of shopping for a loved one. The trip through the market is filled with unique, inventive folk art, which is breathtaking. The textures of the rhythmic text correspond with the illustrations to inspire readers of all ages to learn to count in Spanish and English and to enjoy the pleasure of being bilingual. The resplendent book ends with a note from the author and a pronunciation guide.

Michael Nava

Photo: C. F. Berkstresser

Mexican American (1954–)
Birthday: September 16
Contact: Charlotte Sheedy Literary Agency
65 Bleecker Street, 12th Floor
New York, NY 10012
(212) 780-9800

"[I]f you are a member of an oppressed group in this country, then you have to really, really believe in principles like equal protection under the law. They're not intellectual abstractions to which you feel some sort of vague intellectual allegiance. They really have to exist, they really have to mean something, because they're your only protection in this society.

(*Bloomsbury Review*, 2)

I'm an outsider. . . . I'm no one's stereotype. . . . I think that the great mass of the American public still thinks that all homosexuals are white hairdressers, are promiscuous, are . . . well, fill in the blank. I'm here to say "Look at me: I'm Latino, I'm a lawyer . . . you can't make generalizations about my people, Latino or gay."

(*Bloomsbury Review*, 1)

Works by Michael Nava

For Young Adults

"Abuelo: My Grandfather, Raymond Acuña." In *A Member of the Family: Gay Men Write about Their Families*, edited by John Preston. Dutton, 1992.
Created Equal: Why Gay Rights Matter to America, written with Robert Dawidoff. St. Martin's Press, 1994.
"The Marriage of Michael and Bill." In *Friends and Lovers: Gay Men Write about the Families They Create*, edited by John Preston. Dutton, 1995.

For Adults

"Boys Like Us." In *Boys Like Us*, edited by Patrick Merla. Avon, 1996.
The Burning Plain. Putnam, 1997.
The Death of Friends. Putnam, 1996.
Finale: Short Stories of Mystery and Suspense (editor). Alyson Publications, 1989.
Goldenboy. Alyson Publications, 1988.
The Hidden Law. HarperCollins, 1992.
How Town. Harper and Row, 1990.
The Little Death. Alyson Publications, 1986.
Rag and Bone. Penguin Putnam, 2001.

Michael Nava is the highly acclaimed writer of an award-winning mystery series featuring a gay Latino lawyer. He is recognized as a first-rate novelist whose work is set apart by its insight, compassion, and sense of social justice. Nava attended Stanford Law School before becoming a Los Angeles city prosecutor in 1981. After several years, he opened a private law practice and later moved to a position in the California Appellate Court, where he helped a judge write opinions that were codified into law. Currently he lives in San Francisco, where he is a full-time writer.

Nava was born and raised in Sacramento, California, in a semirural barrio called Gardenland. Isolated from Sacramento proper, the poor neighborhood was "across the bridge instead of across the tracks." There were no sidewalks and no streetlights. Nava's great-grandparents came to the United States from Mexico during the Mexican revolution, starting as migrant workers and working their way to the Sacramento Valley, where they stayed. The second oldest of six children, Nava was an unhappy, moody child, "precocious at one moment and withdrawn the next" ("Abuelo," 16), turning to books for solace. "I knew that I was gay when I was 12, which was not a good thing to be in my family situation. I knew I had to leave Sacramento" (*Gay Community News, GCN*, 1). He was fourteen when he started writing poetry; since he couldn't talk to anyone about his feelings, he wrote about them. "I was a frenetic overachiever. . . . I focused in at an early age that education was going to be my way out of my family and the poverty-stricken community where I grew up" (*Bloomsbury Review*, 1). When he graduated from high school, he was the class valedictorian, captain of the debating team, and student body president. He earned a full academic scholarship to Colorado College and graduated cum laude with a major in history in 1876. Nava was awarded a Thomas J. Watson Fellowship and spent the following year in Buenos Aires, where he studied and translated the poetry of Ruben Dario.

After graduating from Stanford Law School in 1981, Nava embarked on a career as a prosecutor for the city of Los Angeles. He was intoxicated with the romance of being a trial lawyer and the feeling that he was doing something that had social utility. But after three years of toiling in grimy courtrooms and run-down prisons, he burned out. "The criminal justice system is a depressing place. It is a system of victims, no matter what side they're on. Terrible things happen to decent people, and there's nothing you can do about it" (*Los Angeles Times*, E1). He opened a private law practice in Los Angeles and later became a research attorney for the California Court of Appeals. There he researched legal issues and wrote opinions that were published and became a part of the body of California common law.

"When I was in college, I set out to be the great American poet" (*Bloomsbury Review*, 1). Some of his poetry was published in the early 1980s, but Nava decided to turn his attention to fiction. He started writing his first mystery, *A Little Death*, during his last year of law school. Rejected by mainstream publishers, it was published in 1986 by Alyson Publications, a small, gay-owned press in Boston. Publisher Sasha Alyson says, "It is rare for an unsolicited first book to be outstanding. . . . In a lot of mysteries, the mystery is good but the writing is so-so. Michael's work is different. He is a poet, and it shows" (*LA Times*, 2). Alyson also published his second mystery, the award-winning *Goldenboy*, and *Finale*, a collection of mysteries edited by Nava. Then in 1990, Nava made the leap from the small press to one of the largest commercial publishers in the United States, a move that has brought his work to the attention of a wider audience. The success of *How Town* firmly establishes Nava as one of the gay community's leading literary figures.

Because of his day job, Nava wrote at night and on weekends, generally writing three hours each evening and all day Saturday or Sunday. His work as a lawyer involves writing, and his fiction involves the law. His mystery series feature Henry Rios, a gay Latino lawyer who has much in common with his creator. But in a number of interviews, Nava makes it clear that Rios is not Nava: "[I]f you've spent much time with me you know we're not the same character" (*GCN*, 2). Nevertheless, they are similar in a number of ways: both are attorneys, gay, Latino, workaholics, and recovering alcoholics, and they both grew up poor in central California. They both live and work in Los Angeles and the San Francisco Bay Area. Unlike earlier generations of lesbian and gay writers, Nava never agonized over the sexual orientation of his protagonist. He knew that the best writers write from their own experience, and his experience is that of a gay Latino lawyer. He longs for the day when sexual orientation will be viewed as one of the many features of our nature. Given society's unrelenting hostility toward lesbians and gays, Nava is making an important contribution toward that awareness by creating a positive and affirming figure like Henry Rios.

Nava notes, "I try to depict the reality in which I live, which in California is multi-ethnic, multi-cultural, and certainly multi-sexual orientation. I live in a very rich world here, and I try to depict it with some veracity. This is one of my goals as a writer, to accurately paint a picture of my world" (*GCN*, 1). Nava has a worldview that stems from his experience of having grown up as an outsider. "I have spent my life being uncomfortable. As assimilated as I am, I have never for one day forgotten who I am and what I am: a homosexual Latino. Being uncomfortable makes you think, and mindless prejudice sparks anger. My fury has fueled all my accomplishments" (*LA Times*, E13). In accepting his gayness, he remembers saying to himself, "I am a homosexual, and I am still a good human being, notwithstanding what the Catholic Church, or my classmates, or my family members say. That act of compassion toward myself compels me to be compassionate toward others" (*LA Times*, E13).

In addition to his mystery series, Nava has cowritten a book calling for Americans to support the Bill of Rights and the Constitution of the United States and grant lesbian and gay people what should already be theirs: first-class citizenship. In *Created Equal: Why Gay Rights Matter to America*, the authors explain why anything less denies the guarantee of equality for all American citizens and widens the chasm between what our country promises and what it delivers.

Nava's gay-affirming voice addresses crucial social problems and issues. He unflinchingly tackles tough subjects such as child molestation and abuse, the psychology of addiction, political corruption, and the inequities in the criminal justice system. He has been praised for his insight into character and relationships, his skill with language, and his ability to create a suspenseful book. Although his mysteries are written for adults, some of his other work is appropriate for use with high school students. Given his interest in social and political issues and the paucity of good books for young readers about gay Latinos, perhaps Nava will choose the field of adolescent literature for some of his future writing projects.

More Information about Michael Nava

Journals and Newspapers

"Brains and Rage." *The Bloomsbury Review*. June 1991, 1–2.
"Gay Latino Lawyer Mystery Writer." *Gay Community News*. July 15–20, 1990, 1–4.
"Poetic Justice." *Los Angeles Times*. May 6, 1990, E1, E13.
"The Mysteries of Writer Michael Nava." *San Francisco Sentinel*. June 1990, n.p.
"Tough, Smart and Gay." *Los Angeles Times*. April 19, 1990, J1, J13.

Books

"Abuelo: My Grandfather, Raymond Acuña." In *A Member of the Family: Gay Men Write about Their Families*, edited by John Preston. Dutton, 1992.
Contemporary Authors. Volume 124, 323.
Contemporary Authors Online. Gale Group, 2002.
Contemporary Gay American Novelists, edited by Emmanuel S. Nelson. Greenwood, 1993.
Gay and Lesbian Characters and Themes in Mystery Novels by Anthony Slide, McFarland, 1993.
The Gay and Lesbian Literary Heritage, edited by Claude J. Summers. Henry Holt, 1995.
Lesbian and Gay Voices: An Annotated Bibliography and Guide to Literature for Children and Young Adults by Frances Ann Day. Greenwood, 2000.
"The Marriage of Michael and Bill." In *Friends and Lovers: Gay Men Write about the Families They Create*, edited by John Preston. Dutton, 1995.

Selected Works by Michael Nava

"Abuelo: My Grandfather, Raymond Acuña," in *A Member of the Family*

Grades 8–12

- Autobiographical Short Story
- Gay Issues
- Grandfathers

Michael Nava's poignant piece in *A Member of the Family* not only gives readers insight into his childhood but lends support to isolated gay teenagers and speaks to the desperation of anyone who feels confined in a family and society that do not value who they are. "Childhood had been a form of imprisonment for me," he writes (19). Neither paraphrase nor quote can convey the complexity of what Nava says in this revealing statement about a very painful time in his life. Nava writes about his grandfather, who was a Yaqui Indian, intelligent and solitary and the only person in Nava's family, besides Michael, who read for pleasure. "He represented a kind of masculinity from which I was not excluded by reason of my intelligence, or, later, my homosexuality. . . . Fat, myopic, and brainy, I escaped sissyhood only because of the aggressive gloominess I shared with my grandfather" (17). Nava's mother and grandmother loved the young boy and worried about his moodiness, but they did not know how to help him. He didn't know how to ask for support, because he didn't understand his own pain. He spent his childhood waiting for his life to begin, and when he left for college, he vowed never to return home again. When he did return later, his grandmother had died, and his grandfather had remarried. Nava observed the changes in his *abuelo* and later regretted that he hadn't talked with him about those years of estrangement. But Nava learned some important lessons from his grandfather. One of the most significant was that masculinity and self-denial are not the same thing. Nava writes with unflinching honesty about the isolation and unhappiness of his youth. His eloquent words will stimulate discussion and writing about family, culture, and society.

The twenty-four essays commissioned specifically for *A Member of the Family* feature some of the most talented gay male writers of our time. They turn their hearts and psyches inside out to show us the families who gave birth to them, raised them, rejected them, exiled them, and loved them. They write about the hurts that they received and sometimes gave, the letters that they left or sent, and unresolved conflicts and reconciliations. This is a powerful collection that exposes the pain and isolation that gay people often experience even within their own families. It is an excellent resource for educators, librarians, parents, and high school students.

Created Equal: Why Gay Rights Matter to America

Grades 10–Adult

- Civil Rights
- Lesbians and Gay Men

Michael Nava and Robert Dawidoff have written a compelling and galvanizing book calling for Americans to stand up for the Bill of Rights and the Constitution of the United States and give lesbian and gay people what should already be theirs: first-class citizenship. Anything less denies the guarantee of equality for all American citizens and widens the chasm between what our country promises and what it delivers. Everyone interested in justice, liberty, and the future of civil rights for all people in the United States will want to read this powerful book. Nava and Dawidoff answer crucial questions, debunk debilitating myths, define prejudice, and analyze the current campaign against lesbian and gay equality. Of necessity, their book is about what gays and lesbians do *not* want. The authors provide accurate information about the real lesbian and gay agenda, which is *not* to have special privileges but to have the ordinary rights that all Americans enjoy.

Why should heterosexual Americans care about the rights of lesbians and gay men? Because the movement for equality for gay and lesbian people is central to the continuing defense of individual liberty in America. What is at stake are the future of constitutional principle and the rights of free individuals in American society. The struggle is about privacy, civil equality, individuality, and the right of all citizens to be free. "The traditional American doctrine that governments are instituted for the purpose of protecting the fundamental rights of individuals, and the historical process by which these rights have been extended to groups who were enslaved, oppressed, and otherwise unacknowledged at the time of the founding, are the twin pillars of the gay rights movement—as they have been of every struggle to extend the promise of individual liberty to Americans" (8).

Nava and Dawidoff uncover the cruel lies and stereotypes that impede civil rights for lesbians and gay men. They examine the ways in which the antigay lobby exploits these stereotypes to justify the prejudices that support punitive laws and discriminatory practices. They discuss a number of court cases, analyze Colorado's Amendment 2, and expose tactics that the religious right employs in its ongoing war against lesbian and gay Americans. The authors document the ways in which the media perpetuate the invisibility of gays and lesbians and distort, sensationalize, and marginalize their efforts to gain equal rights. They list a number of lesbian and gay historical and cultural figures, arguing that if readers who are unsure of their stance on lesbian and gay rights make the effort to substitute for the unknown figure of the "homosexual" the faces of Eleanor Roosevelt, Langston Hughes, Tennessee Williams, Gertrude Stein, May Sarton, Leonard Bernstein, James Baldwin, or Lorraine Hansberry, they will be able to understand that what is at stake here are the lives of irreplaceable, valuable human beings.

Nava and Dawidoff point out that sexual orientation involves not only the body but the heart, mind, and soul. They cite the tragic statistic that one out of every three teen suicides is lesbian or gay. Isolated, devalued, and caricatured by the society in which they find themselves, they are often shunned, evicted, and disowned by their own families. The culture's bleak teachings about homosexuality lead to despair, shame, and feelings of worthlessness. The culture "makes it difficult for gays and lesbians to lead contented, happy lives, because it oppresses them and then it cites the resulting anxiety and unhappiness as proof that homosexuality is pathological and should continue to be repressed" (52).

What do lesbians and gay men want? Nava and Dawidoff's answer is simple: "What we seek is a space in which to construct our lives with the same opportunities that heterosexuals enjoy" (71). We do not want to be abused, discriminated against, or denied basic rights in our own country. We do not want to be subjected to vicious stereotypes that incite hostility and violence. "We want more than the absence of abuse. We want our rights as citizens; we want the chance to live our lives happily and morally" (135). The authors add that they think gay and lesbian people want other Americans to join with them in this cause. They have written this book with the hope that people will read it and see through the lies that are told about lesbians and gay men. The authors conclude, "We believe that you will join our cause because it is your cause, too, the cause of individual liberty and human equality" (167).

"The Marriage of Michael and Bill," in *Friends and Lovers: Gay Men Write about Their Families*

Grades 11–Adult

- Autobiographical Essays
- Gay Issues
- Nontraditional Families

Michael Nava's eloquent piece in this anthology not only lends insight into his childhood and young adulthood but provides hope to isolated gay teenagers whose relatives often deny their existence, disown and disinherit them, and throw them out of the house. Nava unflinchingly describes the despair of his early years when he blamed himself for his family's poverty and his stepfather's irresponsibility. When he realized that he was gay, it was "the final, crushing blow" (112). He shares the ways in which he tried to compensate by being a model child: smart, well behaved, and respectful of elders. After a suicide attempt when he was fourteen, he cut himself off from his feelings and became "driven to make up in outside achievement the inner deficiency I felt" (114). Years later at Stanford Law School, he met Bill, a fellow student, who would become his lover. After years of tortured boyhoods, the two set out to build a life together. Nava writes, "Bill was not the first family I had, but he was the first family I chose" (124).

Nava beautifully describes the ways in which love "softened the harshness with which I viewed myself and it opened up to me a possibility of happiness that I had never even considered" (112). His story will help educators, librarians, and parents comprehend the wounds inflicted on young gays and lesbians by a homophobic society. Growing up in a world that teaches them to hide their sexual orientation and to hate themselves has resulted in a national tragedy: lesbian and gay youth who take their own lives account for a disproportionate number of all teen suicides in the United States. Information such as that provided in Nava's writing is desperately needed to counteract the oppression experienced by lesbian and gay youth. Omission is one of the most painful and insidious forms of bias. The self-hatred and isolation imposed on many of our most talented young people can kill them as it almost did Michael Nava. It is the responsibility of educators, librarians, and parents to reach out to them and provide them with information and support. Even one positive comment from an adult can make a difference to an isolated youngster.

The Henry Rios Mystery Series: The Little Death, Goldenboy, How Town, The Hidden Law, Rag and Bone

Lambda Literary Award
Adults

- AIDS
- Gay Males
- Child Abuse
- Homophobia
- Mystery

Note: Michael Nava's mystery series is included as a resource for adults. His books are faithful to the conventions of the mystery genre, but they are set apart by their sensitivity, insight, and sense of social justice. Featuring Henry Rios, an ethical, compassionate, gay Chicano lawyer, the award-winning books in the series are well written, perceptive, and entertaining. However, they examine controversial issues such as sexual violence, child pornography, and pedophilia. The series provides important reading for adults who want to educate themselves about crucial issues facing their gay male students, colleagues, and community. In addition to being fascinating reading, the books in the series provide important insights into the ways in which homophobia damages the lives of some of our most talented young people.

It is important to remember that the issues that lesbians face are different from those faced by gay men. Lumping the issues faced by lesbians and gay men together leads to distortion, erasure, and marginalization and can be extremely harmful to both groups. For readers interested in additional information concerning lesbian issues, please see Gloria Anzaldúa's chapter.

The Little Death is the first novel in the Henry Rios mystery series for adults by Michael Nava. Henry Rios is a gay Chicano lawyer who practices law in a fictional college town near San Francisco. He graduated from law school ten years earlier, determined to be a good lawyer and an ethical person. At thirty-three, Henry is still a dedicated, but burned-out, public defender who has recently been demoted to handling arraignments after losing a major case. Increasingly disillusioned with the criminal justice system, he decides to quit his job and set up his own private practice. He meets and enters into a relationship with Hugh Paris, heir to a railroad fortune and a recovering heroin addict. Paris expresses fear for his own life, having recently become suspicious that his grandfather killed his grandmother and uncle. When his body is found in three feet of water in a creek near campus, the police call it an accident. Rios thinks it is murder and with a heavy heart sets out to prove his theory. As he takes on some of the most powerful people in the country, he finds himself in a tangled web of greed, corruption, and legal trickery. With unexpected twists and turns, Nava keeps the reader guessing up until the last pages of this engaging book.

Nava's first mystery has many interesting aspects, not the least of which is the introduction of a multidimensional gay Chicano lawyer/detective. Henry Rios is an intelligent, admirable character who charms the reader with a likable mixture of idealism and disillusionment. He sets out to change the world but after years of struggling with the numbing bureaucracy of his job and the hypocrisy of the criminal justice system, he reevaluates his mission in life. Grieving as he investigates the murder of his newfound lover, he thinks, "Surely we were never meant to live in the appalling circumstances in which we so often found ourselves, alone, fearful, mute" (57).

Goldenboy is the second book in the Henry Rios mystery series. Rios, who was a hard drinker in *The Little Death*, has fortunately three years later identified himself as an alcoholic, undergone treatment, and is now drinking tea and mineral water. The book opens with Rios reluctantly agreeing to join his friend Larry Ross in Los Angeles to work on a murder case. Ross and Rios had worked together several years earlier to knock a sodomy initiative off the California ballot with a lawsuit. Nava explains that sodomy is "a generic term for every sexual practice but the missionary position" (12). When Rios arrives in Los Angeles, he is saddened to discover that Ross has AIDS. As the book progresses and as his friend's health deteriorates, he tries to provide emotional support, but communication between the two is somewhat limited by years of socialization, resulting in difficulty expressing feelings.

The case involves Jim Pears, a gay teenager who was arrested for the murder of a coworker who threatened to reveal his sexual orientation to his conservative parents. Ross asks Rios to help "balance the accounts" by representing Pears, who is a victim of the same disease as his—bigotry. Nava does an excellent job of exposing the ways in which the media distort and sensationalize the case. He also portrays the abhorrent ways that homophobia has taught Pears to hate himself. Even compassionate Rios finds himself having difficulty dealing with Pears' self-loathing. Everyone, even Rios, thinks that Pears is guilty, and the district attorney seeks the death penalty. But as mystery lovers have learned to expect, there is much more to this case than is apparent at first. As the story unfolds, we meet Josh Mandel, a key witness who later falls in love with Rios.

This book is definitely for the mature reader with its sexual violence and somewhat explicit lovemaking scenes, but it provides information about the complexities of a number of important issues. The passages where Mandel, with Rios' help, comes out to his parents are written with sensitivity, insight, and humor. Nava's writing shows sensitivity to the rights of most groups; however, readers should be aware of a fat oppressive description of Blenheim in one of Rios' dreams. Otherwise, Nava's justified anger about prejudice comes through loud and clear. He has taken that anger and written an effective book about tough, timely subjects.

How Town is the third book in the Henry Rios mystery series. The plot revolves around the subjects of pedophilia and child abuse. Rios is adamant that he doesn't defend child molesters, so readers will be surprised to find him representing Paul Windsor, a wealthy, abominable pedophile accused of murdering a dealer in child pornography. Rios takes the case only after his estranged sister (a lesbian) appeals to him on behalf of her friend Sara Windsor, Paul's wife. As Rios unravels the tangled threads of the intricate crime, the reader is invited to examine a number of important issues including racism, homophobia, poverty, family secrets, alcoholism, and sexual violence against children. While entertaining the reader with a tale of suspense, Nava stretches the psychological and emotional boundaries of the genre, as a number of lesbian mystery writers have been doing for some time.

Reviews of *How Town* are filled with accolades, calling it one of the best gay-themed detective stories yet written. *How Town* has been praised for its strong structure; well-drawn characters; precise, elegant, and compelling prose; and uncluttered, but intriguing, dialogue.

The Hidden Law is the fourth book in the Henry Rios mystery series. Rios defends Michael Ruiz, a bitter, confused teenager who is accused of murdering state senator Agustin Peña, a suavely corrupt politician. Peña has just returned to public life after killing an elderly man while driving drunk and a stint in an alcohol rehabilitation center. As Rios investigates the case, he uncovers information about family violence, turf conflicts in a halfway house, political turpitude, and the losses incurred by upward mobility. The resolution of the case strikes a painful chord for Rios and helps him make an important decision about his career.

Rag and Bone is the last book in the celebrated Henry Rios mystery series. *Publishers Weekly* wrote, "The smoothly integrated plot strands conspire to test and push Rios into reassessing everything. . . . [His] humanity and decency shine through this satisfying novel." *Library Journal* added, "A super plot, memorable characters, and touching prose make this [book] essential for fans."

Luis J. Rodríguez

Chicano (1954–)
Birthday: July 9
Address: P.O. Box 328
San Fernando, CA 91341

I began a new season of life. Intellect and body fused, I now yearned to contribute fully, embodied with conscious energy, to live a deliberate existence dedicated to a future humanity which might in complete freedom achieve the realization of its creative impulses, the totality of its potential faculties, without injustice, coercion, hunger and exploitation.

(*Always Running*, 243–244)

Books by Luis J. Rodríguez

Always Running: La Vida Loca, Gang Days in L. A. Curbstone Press, 1993; Touchtone Books/Simon and Schuster, 1994; Libros en Espanol, Simon and Schuster, 1996.
America Is Her Name. Illustrated by Carlos Vázquez. Curbstone Press, 1997. Spanish edition: *La llaman América.*
The Concrete River. Curbstone Press, 1991.
Hearts and Hands: Creating Community in Violent Times. Seven Stories Press, 2001.
It Doesn't Have to Be This Way: A Barrio Story/No tiene que ser así: Una historia del barrio. Illustrated by Daniel Galvez. Children's Book Press, 1999.
Poems across the Pavement. Tía Chuchu Press, 1989, 1991.
The Republic of East L. A.: Stories. HarperCollins, 2002. Spanish edition: *La republica de East L. A.: Cuentos.*
Trochemoche. Curbstone Press, 1998.

Luis J. Rodríguez is an award-winning writer, journalist, and critic. His poetry and prose have been widely published in anthologies, magazines, textbooks, and newspapers. He helped start a number of prominent organizations, including Chicago's Guild Complex, one of the largest literary organizations in the Midwest, and its publishing wing, Tía Chucha Press. He is one of the founders of Youth Struggling for Survival, a Chicago-based, not-for-profit community group working with gang and nongang youth. Most recently, he helped start Rock a Mole (rhymes with guacamole) Productions, which produces music/arts festivals, compact discs (CDs), and film in Los Angeles. Rodríguez is also working with two partners to create Tía Chucha's Café Cultural—a bookstore, coffeehouse, performance space, art gallery, and computer center for the Northeast San Fernando Valley in California. He has conducted writing workshops in juvenile facilities, homeless shelters, prisons, and migrant camps as well as for gang members and Spanish-speaking children and their parents. He travels throughout the United States, Europe, and parts of Latin America, where he lectures, reads, and performs.

When Rodríguez was born, his family lived in the border town of Juárez, Mexico. But his mother made sure that he and his siblings were born on the El Paso side of the border, and the family soon moved to the Mexican section of Watts in Los Angeles. Describing himself as a quiet, withdrawn child, Rodríguez writes about the countless barriers set in their path. The Río Grande became a metaphor for their lives. "Our first exposure in America stays with me like a foul odor. It seemed a strange world, most of it spiteful to us, spitting and stepping on us, coughing us up, us immigrants, as if we were phlegm caught in the collective throats of this country" (*Always Running,* 19). The name-calling, the employment hurdles, the geographical boundaries that kept Mexicans on the east side of the city, the language restrictions, the school environment that failed to validate their culture, and the poverty all led Rodríguez to feel invisible, to feel that he didn't belong. He notes, "I . . . would learn to hide in imaginative worlds—in books; in TV shows, where I picked up much of my English" (*Always Running*, 14). He describes the humiliations at school, where speaking Spanish was considered a crime. He spent his first year building with blocks in the back of the classroom because his teachers didn't know what to do with a child who spoke only Spanish. There he suffered the indignity of not knowing how to ask to go to the bathroom and the danger of not understanding what to do during a fire drill. His older brother physically abused him, and they both suffered violence from other boys in the neighborhood. His anger and frustration festered, and when he was eleven, he joined his first club, which gradually became a gang. There were no sports groups, Boy Scouts, or camping groups available to him, and other clubs were popping up all around him, challenging any young male who wasn't part of a clique. His memoir, *Always Running*, is his chilling account of his seven years as an active gang member. By the time he was fifteen, his parents had kicked him out of the house, and he was living in the garage.

Somehow, amid the violence and drugs, Rodríguez became involved in a number of constructive projects. He joined a group that studied politics, philosophy, economics, and the dynamics of social revolution. At thirteen, he participated in his first conscious political act when he led a school walkout to demand quality and accountable education. He painted murals and wrote and acted in plays. Later, he became a mural project supervisor and painted several murals that are currently documented at the Social Public Research Center as part of the Smithsonian Institution's Chicano Mural Documentation Project. He was also a columnist for his school newspaper, a Student Council Speaker of the House, and president of the Chicano/a student group. He discovered the magic in books and read works such as *Down These Mean Streets* by Piri Thomas, which became his bible. At eighteen, he was an honorary winner in a literary contest and signed a book contract with a publisher in Berkeley.

When he was twenty, Rodríguez moved to south-central Los Angeles to distance himself from his gang. He worked as a blast furnace operator, carpenter, truck driver, steelworker, and chemical refinery mechanic and took night classes in creative writing and journalism. From 1980 to 1985, he worked as a journalist and organized Latino literary workshops. Then in 1985, he moved to Chicago to edit the *Peoples' Tribune*. He became involved with the burgeoning poetry scene, joining performance poets in theaters, clubs, and bars. His poetry books were published, winning awards for their literary excellence. Rodríguez founded his own press, Tía Chucha Press, named for his beloved aunt, "the most creative influence of my childhood" (*Always Running*, 59).

The recipient of numerous awards and honors, Rodríguez received a 1992 Lannan Fellowship for Poetry; 1992 and 1994 Illinois Arts Council

Fellowships; a City of Chicago Neighborhood Arts Program grant to do workshops in homeless shelters; and a 1990 Chicago Artists Abroad Grant to lecture and read in Paris. In 1993 he participated in a reading tour of Germany, Holland, and Austria with five other American poets. Rodríguez has taught poetry in elementary schools and prisons and to migrant workers and edited books of poetry and calendars by homeless people.

The publication of Rodríguez's autobiographical account of his days as a gang member in Los Angeles, *Always Running*, led to the next step in his career. As an expert on gangs, he travels the world on the lecture circuit, reading poetry and lecturing on the issues of youth, empowerment, and social justice. He has written a number of articles on this topic such as "Throwaway Kids: Turning Youth Gangs Around," printed in *The Nation*, in which he writes, "It's time the voices for viable and lasting solutions be heard. . . . First, that we realign societal resources in accordance with the following premises: that every child has value and every child can succeed. That schools teach by engaging the intelligence and creativity of all students. . . . And, that we root out the basis for the injustice and inequities that engender most of the violence we see today."

More Information about Luis J. Rodríguez

Books

Always Running: La Vida Loca, Gang Days in L. A. by Luis J. Rodríguez. Curbstone Press, 1993; Touchtone Books/Simon and Schuster, 1994; Libros en Espanol, Simon and Schuster, 1996.

Authors and Artists for Young Adults, Volume 40, 173–181.

Contemporary Authors, Volume 142, 372–374.

Contemporary Hispanic Americans: Luis Rodríguez by Michael Schwartz. Steck-Vaughnm 1998.

Dictionary of Literary Biography, Volume 209, 243–250.

Speaking of Poets II: More Interviews with Poets Who Write for Children and Young Adults, edited by Jeffrey S. Copeland and Vicky L. Copeland. National Council of Teachers of English, 1996.

Articles

"Gangs: The New Political Force in Los Angeles," by Luis J. Rodríguez. *Los Angeles Times*. September 13, 1992, n.p.

"Like Father, like Son" by Rosalind Cummings. *Reader: Chicago's Free Weekly*, June 30, 1995, 1, 13–18, 23.

"Throwaway Kids: Turning Youth Gangs Around" by Luis J. Rodríguez. *The Nation*, November 21, 1994, 605–609.

"Who We Are" by Luis J. Rodríguez. *Hungry Mind Review*. Fall 1994, 7–8.

Audiocassette

La Vida Loca: El testimonio de un pandillero en Los Angeles. AudioLibros del Mundo, 1998.

Videotapes

Luis J. Rodríguez. Lannan Literary Video #31. 1-800-869-7553.
The Choice of a Lifetime: Returning from the Brink of Suicide. New Day Films. 1-800-343-5540.

Selected Works by Luis J. Rodríguez

Always Running: La Vida Loca: Gang Days in L.A.

Carl Sandburg Literary Arts Award for Nonfiction
Chicago Sun-Times Book Award
New York Times Book Review Notable Book Award
New York Public Library Book for the Teen Age
Grades 9–Adult

- Gangs
- Memoir

Always Running is Luis J. Rodríguez's riveting account of his years growing up in poverty in East Los Angeles, his turning to gang life as a means of preservation, and his ultimate triumph against the odds. He started writing the book when he was sixteen but didn't complete it until his own son, Ramiro, joined a gang. He wrote it as a gift to his son, to provide support for him to find his way out of gang life. Hopefully, its message will reach other young people and help them understand the futility of gang warfare. Combining straightforward retrospection, philosophical commentary, and poetic insights, Rodríguez has created an unflinching book that will help readers understand why young people get involved in gangs. It provides insight into the roots of the problems while it describes the symptoms in raw detail. The author chronicles his experiences with racism in the schools, on the streets, in the police departments, and in the criminal justice system.

Rodríguez describes the uprootings, evictions, humiliations, and violence of his early years. He was a withdrawn, quiet child. "I was a broken boy, shy and fearful." His first encounter with gang members made a powerful impression on him. He realized that "[a]ll my school life until then had been poised against me: telling me what to be, what to say, how to say it" (42). He explains how the groups started as clubs and metamorphosed into gangs. Rodríguez was involved with gangs from age eleven to age eighteen. During this time, twenty-five of his friends died. Those years were filled with alcohol, drugs, sex, stealing, fighting, hijacking, shooting, and firebombing, as well as police harassment and brutality, jail cells, juvenile courts, and alternative schools. However, Rodríguez also became involved in painting murals, playing the saxophone, writing a book, student organizing, study groups, boxing, and writing plays, and he worked at various jobs, including mowing lawns, delivering papers, and washing cars. He would take one step forward just to end up taking one step back.

Always Running has some important messages for educators. Rodríguez's brother was put in a class for mentally disabled children because he couldn't speak English. Luis spent his first year of school building with blocks because the teachers didn't know what to do with him. The students weren't allowed to speak Spanish: if a Spanish word slipped out, even on the playground, they were sent to the office for detention or corporal punishment. Later, Rodríguez's high school "had two principal languages. Two skin tones and two cultures. It revolved around class differences. . . . The school separated these two groups by levels of education: The professional-class kids were provided with college-preparatory classes; the blue-collar students were pushed into industrial arts" (84).

How did Rodríguez find his way out of the world of gangs? How did he overcome all the problems that threatened to pull him into a bottomless chasm? How did he find the courage to stop running? These questions and more are answered in this anguished, lyrical memoir. Each of the ten chapters is prefaced with quotes such as "Go ahead and kill us, we're already dead" from a statement made by a young Latino participant in the 1992 Los Angeles Uprising (247). A glossary translates more than 200 Spanish words and phrases. Reviewers have praised the book as an absolutely unique work, richly literary and poetic, a work of enormous beauty, a forceful story of triumph, fierce and fearless, and an instant classic. *Always Running* has been compared with Piri Thomas' *Down These Mean Streets*, which Rodríguez discovered when he was in high school and which he says "became like a living Bible for me" (138). This award-winning book includes a Preface and Epilogue, which provide political and social analyses of the roots of violence. Gary Soto praised the book for the most part but felt that it was "flawed by occasional lapses into sociological diatribes" (*New York Times Book Review*, F. 14, 1993, p. 26). On the contrary, I found these so-called digressions to be exactly what distinguishes the book from those that are satisfied with merely describing the problem. Rodríguez, not content with presenting the "what," takes the next step of analyzing the "why." These insights are what saved his life and may very well save countless others as well.

América Is Her Name

Skipping Stones Award
Grades 1–5

- Immigrants
- Poets
- Writing

Nine-year-old América Soliz has recently moved with her family from their home in the mountains of Oaxaca to the Pilsen barrio in Chicago. As she faces daunting language, economic, and cultural barriers, she turns to writing to assuage the pain and isolation. Inspired by a poet who visited her school, América finds her voice and, with it, renewed hope for a bright future in her new country. With grace and passion this heartening book honors poetry: a refuge in times of suffering as well as times of joy. "There's poetry in everyone. When you use words to share feelings with somebody else, you are a poet, and poets belong to the world." Spanish edition: *La llaman América*.

The Concrete River

PEN Oakland/Josephine Miles Award for Literary Excellence
Grades 12–Adult

- Poetry

Dedicated to Nelson Peery, "who taught me the poetry of the fight, and the fight of the poetry," this collection of forty-three poems provides a tour of East Los Angeles with Rodríguez as the guide. With raw honesty and lyrical beauty, he describes the living conditions, the social realities, and the people who shaped his life. He paints vivid pictures of shattered glass, burned-out buildings, crumbling factory walls, and rusting cars. In "Watts Bleeds," he writes about the teachers who "threw me from classroom to classroom, not knowing where I could fit in" (13). He wasn't allowed to use the language that he knew and wasn't taught the language that was required. Rodríguez's poetry has been praised by reviewers for its poetic power, perceptive gaze, and passion and compassion. Through his poetry and prose, Rodríguez tells the truth about the lives of his people, many of whom have been heretofore ignored, silenced, and erased.

Hearts and Hands: Creating Community in Violent Times

Adults

- At-Risk Youth
- Building Community
- Gangs
- Violence

Empowered by his experiences as a peacemaker with gangs, Luis Rodríguez makes concrete suggestions for ways that we can create nonviolent opportunities to redirect youngsters toward productive, satisfying lives. Rodríguez, a powerful mentor, elder, and advocate for Latino youth, focuses on healing through building community. *Publishers Weekly* (November 5, 2001) wrote, "Never sentimentalizing or sensationalizing his materials, Rodríguez writes honestly and incisively from experience, knowledge and compassion."

It Doesn't Have to Be This Way: A Barrio Story/No tiene que ser así: Una historia del barrio

Américas Commended Book
Parents' Choice Award
Skipping Stones Award
Grades 2–7

- Bilingual
- Gangs

Ten-year-old Monchi tells the compelling tale of how gang membership first appealed to him and then why he finally rejected it. In the introduction, author Luis Rodríguez writes, "I know why kids join gangs: to belong, to be cared for, and to be embraced. I hope we can create a community that fulfills these longings, so young people won't have to sacrifice their lives to be loved and valued in this world" (3). This is an important book—one of the few that authentically address this issue for this age group.

Poems across the Pavement

San Francisco State University Poetry Center Book Award
Grades 12–Adult

- Poetry

This collection of nineteen poems by Luis J. Rodríguez embodies twenty years of revolutionary and literary endeavors. A former gang member and industrial worker, Rodríguez draws from his Los Angeles and Chicago experiences to weave an urban tapestry of voices, violations, and visions. His poetry speaks of class and race battles, industrial displacement, street turmoil, and police brutality. From a homeless shelter in Chicago, to a coastal town in Oaxaca, to an immigrant's trek across the border, to empowerment elections in Alabama, Rodríguez creates an alchemy of words, interlaced with anguish and hope. Throughout this collection, we hear the sounds of sweet music from a saxophone, the whisperings of people hungering for dignity, the humming of a soul lost to heroin, the blue chords of a guitar. What makes Rodríguez's poetry so powerful is its mixture of raw honesty and lyrical beauty, its passion about people, experiences, and conditions that are often distorted, ignored, and erased.

In one of the many powerful poems in the collection, "Piece of Piece," the poet urges his comrades to fight back by refusing to internalize the humiliating lies that society tells about them. Encouraging them to believe in themselves, to name themselves, to create their own codes, mantles, and morals, Rodríguez eloquently writes about the steady erosion of self-esteem, piece by piece, and the ways in which oppressed people can resist and regain their pride. In the last poem in the book, "The Calling," Rodríguez writes about that magic moment when, after sixteen years of captivity, invisibility, and directionlessness, his life was transformed and he was called to be a writer and "march with the soldiers of change." His words provide hope that, somehow, other oppressed people will find ways to escape the cruel imprisonment that society has imposed on them, join the movement for liberation, and find their voices.

Esmeralda Santiago

Photo: Rudi Weislein.
Courtesy of Perseus
Books

Puerto Rican American (1948–)
Birthday: May 17
Contact: Perseus Books
11 Cambridge Center
Cambridge, MA 02142

My characters will always be those people who can't speak for themselves. I was a child who could not find myself in the literature. There was no one telling my story. I don't want that to ever happen to any child or any woman. To really see yourself as nonexistent is the worst kind of insult that a person can have.

(*Latina Self-Portraits*, 133)

Books by Esmeralda Santiago

Almost a Woman. Perseus Books, 1998. Spanish edition: *Casi una mujer*.

América's Dream. HarperCollins, 1996. Spanish edition: *El sueno de America*.

Becoming American. Addison-Wesley Longman, 1998.

Las Christmas: Favorite Latino Authors Share Their Holiday Memories, coedited with Joie Davidow. Illustrated by José Ortega. Knopf, 1998. Spanish edition: *Escritos latinos recuerdan las tradiciones navidenas*.

Las Mamís: Famous Latino Authors Remember Their Mothers, coedited with Joie Davidow. Knopf, 2000. Spanish edition: *Escritores latinos recuerdan a sus madres*.

When I Was Puerto Rican. Vintage Books, 1994. Spanish edition: *Cuando era Puertorriqueña*.

Esmeralda Santiago, the highly acclaimed memoirist, novelist, journalist, and filmmaker, was born May 17, 1948, in Santurce, Puerto Rico. The oldest of eleven children, she reluctantly moved with her mother and siblings to New York City when she was thirteen. In her first memoir she recalls the day that she left her beloved homeland: "The Puerto Rican *jíbara* who longed for the green quiet of a tropical afternoon was to become a hybrid who would never forgive the uprooting" (*When I Was Puerto Rican*, 209).

Once in New York City, Santiago was determined to overcome the language barrier, cultural stereotypes, and limited class and gender expectations. She chronicles her teenage struggle for identity and independence in her second memoir, *Almost a Woman*. After graduating from New York City's prestigious High School of Performing Arts, she earned her B.A. at Harvard University and her M.F.A. at Sarah Lawrence College.

As a child, Santiago sought refuge in books during her parents' battles. "The school library became a refuge . . . and I sat for hours reading fairy tales, diving into them as into a warm pool that washed away the fear, the sadness, the horror of living in a home where there was no love" (*When I Was Puerto Rican*, 204). During her first year in New York City, she went to the library every day after school and checked out as many children's books as she was allowed. "I figured that if American children learned English through books, so could I, even if I was starting later" (*When I Was Puerto Rican*, 236). Now she is a passionate advocate for public libraries and often speaks at her local library in Westchester, New York.

Santiago wrote her first book when she was thirty-two. She notes, "I think I was driven to be a writer because I didn't exist in the literature [of the United States], and therefore didn't exist in the culture. . . . There were no books about Puerto Rican girls in Brooklyn" (*Latina Self-Portraits*, 129).

More Information about Esmeralda Santiago

Almost a Woman. Perseus Books, 1998.
Beacham's Guide to Literature for Young Adults.
Contemporary Authors. Volume 179, 390–391.
Contemporary Authors Online. Gale, 2000.
Latina Self-Portraits: Interviews with Contemporary Women Writers, edited by Bridget Kevane and Juanita Heredia. University of New Mexico Press, 2000.
Notable Hispanic American Women, Book 2. Gale Online, 1998.
When I Was Puerto Rican. Vintage Books, 1994.

Selected Works by Esmeralda Santiago

Almost a Woman

Grades 8–Up

- Immigrants
- Memoir
- Mothers and Daughters
- Puerto Rican Americans

In this lively sequel to her brilliant debut, *When I Was Puerto Rican*, Esmeralda Santiago continues her life story. Arriving in Brooklyn from Puerto Rico when she is thirteen, Santiago, the oldest of eleven children, meets the challenges facing young female immigrants head-on—language barriers, cultural stereotypes, gender restrictions, and limited expectations. From a series of tiny apartments occupied by her large extended family, she continues her search for identity and struggles for independence in an extraordinary journey that is both personal and universal. By day she perfects her roles as Cleopatra at New York City's Performing Arts High School and later, as a mermaid in Children's Theater International. At night she accompanies her mother and sisters to dances, but under such tight supervision that she has her first date at the age of twenty. How Santiago draws up a blueprint for her life while balancing her many roles—daughter of an overprotective mother and an absent father, role model for ten siblings, translator for her relatives, and aspiring actress/dancer—provides inspiration and hope. *Almost a Woman* is a vivid memoir distinguished by its passion, humor, and poignant detail. Spanish edition: *Casi una mujer*.

América's Dream

Grades 12–Up

- Domestic Workers
- Socioeconomic Class
- Violence against Women
- Vieques

Thirty-year-old América Gonzalez, a hotel housekeeper on an island off the coast of Puerto Rico, tries to cope with her alcoholic mother, resentful teenage daughter, and increasingly abusive boyfriend. When she is offered a job as a live-in housekeeper and nanny in Westchester, New York, she realizes that this is her chance to make a new life for herself. Once in New York, she begins the process of healing and adjusting to a new culture. But her newfound independence is overshadowed by the growing certainty that her possessive boyfriend will find her. In the hair-raising denouement, América finds the strength to defend herself and finally frees herself from her abuser. Her scars remind her that "she fought for her life . . . and she has a right to live that life as she chooses" (325). *América's Dream* has been praised for its immediate and tender prose; engrossing portrait of a tenacious protagonist; analysis of the vicious cycle of violence; and the articulation of the indignities of underpaid and undervalued domestic work. Spanish edition: *El sueno de America.*

Las Christmas: Favorite Latino Authors Share Their Holiday Memories

Grades 10–Up

- Christmas
- Poetry
- Music
- Recipes

Twenty-five celebrated Latino/a writers share Christmas memories that vividly capture the pride and pain, joy and heartbreak that so often accompany holidays. This book is richly illustrated and embellished with songs, poems, and recipes. Authors included are Julia Alvarez, Liz Balmaseda, Gioconda Belli, Denise Chávez, Sandra Cisneros, Judith Ortiz Cofer, Mandalit del Barco, Junot Díaz, Martín Espada, Francisco Goldman, Estela Herrera, Jaime Manrique, Victor Martínez, Aurora Levins Morales, Rosario Morales, Michael Nava, Gustavo Pérez Firmat, Luis J. Rodríguez, Esmeralda Santiago, Mayra Santos-Febres, Gary Soto, Ilan

Stavans, Ray Suárez, Piri Thomas, and Judy Vásquez. Spanish edition: *Escritos latinos recuerdan las tradiciones navidenas.*

Las Mamís: Famous Latino Authors Remember Their Mothers

Grades 10–Up

- Mother–Daughter Relationships
- Mother–Son Relationships

Fourteen Latino/a authors share memories of their mothers in poignant stories about mamís who, often pressed by conflicting cultural expectations, circumstances, and religions, nevertheless managed to leave enduing legacies for their children. Authors included are Marjorie Agosín, Alba Ambert, Liz Balmaseda, Gioconda Belli, Mandalit del Barco, Junot Díaz, María Amparo Escandón, Gustavo Pérez Firmat, Dagoberto Gilb, Francisco Goldman, Jaime Manrique, Esmeralda Santiago, Ilan Stavans, and Piri Thomas. Spanish edition: *Escritores latinos recuerdan a sus madres.*

When I Was Puerto Rican

Grades 8–Up

- Immigrants
- Memoir
- Puerto Rico
- Socioeconomic Class

In this highly acclaimed memoir, Esmeralda Santiago chronicles her bittersweet experiences growing up in Puerto Rico in the 1950s and the transition to New York City when she was thirteen. She writes movingly about a childhood punctuated by frequent moves from the country to the city and back again, each precipitated by the love-hate relationship between her parents; by the birth of a new sibling almost every other year; and by the expectations placed upon her as the eldest child. At once inspirational and heart-wrenching, this spirited memoir ends dramatically with Santiago's acceptance to New York City's High School of Performing Arts. *When I Was Puerto Rican* has been praised for its passionate, lyrical voice; its powerful story of true grit; and its evocative portrait of the Puerto Rican landscape. Glossary included. Spanish edition: *Cuandro era Puertoriquena.* Sequel: *Almost a Woman.*

Gary Soto

Chicano (1952–)
Birthday: April 12
Address: 43 The Crescent
Berkeley, CA 94708

I'm a fan of Old Yeller, but wouldn't it be wonderful to discover in books the names of our dogs—Humo, Pecas, Tigre, Macho, and Princesa.

(Personal Communication)

Books by Gary Soto

Baseball in April: And Other Stories. Harcourt Brace, 1990. Spanish edition: *Beisbol en abril: y otros historias.*

Big Bushy Mustache. Illustrated by Joe Cepeda. Knopf, 1998.

Body Parts in Rebellion: Hanging Out with Fernie and Me. Illustrated by Regan Dunnick. Penguin Putnam, 2002.

Boys at Work. Illustrated by Robert Casilla. Delacorte, 1995.

Buried Onions. Harcourt Brace, 1997.

California Childhood: Recollections and Stories of the Golden State (editor). Creative Arts Books, 1988.

Canto Familiar. Illustrated by Annika Nelson. Harcourt Brace Children's Books, 1995.

The Cat's Meow. Illustrated by Joe Cepeda. Scholastic, 1995. Spanish edition: *El maullido de la gata.*

Chato and the Party Animals. Illustrated by Susan Guevara. Putnam, 2000.

Chato's Kitchen. Illustrated by Susan Guevara. Putnam, 1995. Spanish edition: *Chato y su cena.*

Crazy Weekend. Scholastic, 1994.

The Effects of Knut Hamsun on a Fresno Boy: Recollections and Short Essays. Persea, 1983, 1988, 2000.

Everyday Seductions (editor). Ploughshares, 1995.

Father Is a Pillow Tied to a Broom. Slow Loris, 1980.

Fearless Fernie: Hanging Out with Fernie and Me. Putnam, 2002.

A Fire in My Hands: A Book of Poems. Scholastic, 1990.

If the Shoe Fits. Illustrated by Terry Widener. Putnam, 2002.

I Thought I'd Take My Rat to School: Poems for September to June. Written with Karla Kuskin. Little, Brown, 1993.

Jesse. Harcourt Brace, 1994.

Jessie De La Cruz: A Profile of a United Farm Worker. Persea Books, 2000.

Junior College. Chronicle Books, 1997.

Lesser Evils: Ten Quartets. Arte Público Press, 1988.

Living Up the Street: Narrative Recollections. Dell, 1992.

Local News. Harcourt Brace, 1993.

The Mustache. Putnam, 1995.

A Natural Man. Chronicle Books, 1999.

Nerdlandia: A Play. Penguin Putnam, 1999.

Neighborhood Odes. Illustrated by David Diaz. Harcourt Brace, 1992.

New and Selected Poems. Chronicle, 1995.

Nickel and Dime. University of New Mexico Press, 2000.

Novio Boy: A Play. Harcourt Brace, 1997.

Off and Running. Illustrated by Eric Velaquez. Delacorte, 1996.

The Old Man and His Door. Illustrated by Joe Cepeda. Putnam, 1996. Spanish edition: *El viejo y su puerta.*

Pacific Crossing. Harcourt Brace, 1992. Spanish edition: *Cruzando el pacífico.*

Petty Crimes. Harcourt Brace, 1998.

Pieces of the Heart: New Chicano Fiction (editor). Chronicle, 1993.

Poetry Lover. University of New Mexico Press, 2001.

The Pool Party. Illustrated by Robert Casilla. Delacorte, 1993.

The Skirt. Illustrated by Eric Velasquez. Delacorte, 1992.
Small Faces. Dell, 1993.
Snapshots from the Wedding. Illustrated by Stephanie Garcia. Putnam, 1997.
A Summer Life. University Press of New England, 1990.
Summer on Wheels. Scholastic, 1995.
Taking Sides. Harcourt Brace, 1991. Spanish edition: *Tomando partido*.
Too Many Tamales. Illustrated by Ed Martinez. Putnam, 1993. Spanish edition: *¡Qué montón de tamales!*

Films by Gary Soto

These films are available directly from Gary Soto. Call (510) 845-4718 to order or for more information.
The Bike. Rudy's odyssey around the neighborhood on his new bicycle. VHS,11 minutes.
Novio Boy. Rudy's first date. VHS, 30 minutes.
The Pool Party. 1993 Andrew Carnegie Medal winner. VHS, 28 minutes. For more information, see the review for the book.

Gary Soto, recognized as one of America's best Chicano writers, was a senior lecturer at the University of California in Berkeley, California, for many years. A celebrated poet, he also creates short stories, picture books, novels, and films. He is one of the few Mexican American authors who write for adults, young adults, and children. He celebrates and remains true to his heritage in his writing; the universality of his vision and his skill with the use of words have established him as a major contemporary writer. His writing springs from his Chicano heritage and working-class background; his probing, yet lyrical, poetry and prose provide inspiration for all his readers, especially those who seldom read about themselves in books.

A third-generation Mexican American, Soto was born and raised in the San Joaquin Valley in Fresno, California. Like many Latinos in the area, his parents and grandparents worked in the fields hoeing cotton and picking grapes or worked in the packinghouses, factories, or warehouses. In addition, his mother candled eggs for a major supermarket. When Gary was only five years old, tragedy struck his family: his father, aged twenty-seven, was killed in a factory accident. Soto has written about this trauma repeatedly; almost every collection of poetry or prose refers to it in some way. In *Lesser Evils*, he writes that his mother never talked about his father's death; his name was never mentioned in their house. They saw his grave only in photographs: "a quiet settled on us like dust. . . . We lived poor years because he died. We suffered quietly and hurt even today" (83).

Soto's mother remarried two years later; his stepfather was an alcoholic white man who worked loading boxes onto a conveyor belt at a warehouse. Soto describes him as "a tired man when he came into my life. . . . He hurt from the house payments, the asking wife, the five hungry kids to clothe" (*Small Faces*, 17–18). Soto and his siblings were home alone much of the time while their parents were at work. In "Being Mean," he writes, "We were terrible kids, I think. My brother, sister, and I felt a general meanness begin to surface from our tiny souls." (*Living Up the Street*, 1). Living in the middle of industrial Fresno, once rated the worst city in the United States by the Rand-McNally Report, surrounded by factories, warehouses, and junkyards, Soto remembers the summers when he was four and five. He writes that there was much to do: "Wrestle, eat raw bacon, jump from the couch, sword fight with rolled-up newspapers, steal from neighbors, kick chickens, throw rocks at passing cars" (*Living Up the Street*, 2). They also drank Kool-Aid, fought, set fires, swiped apricots and peaches from the trees in neighbor's yards, and watched television, where Soto learned about "the comfortable lives of white kids. There were no beatings, no rifts in the family. They wore bright clothes. . . . They hopped into bed with kisses and woke to glasses of fresh orange juice" (*Living Up the Street*, 30).

Soto attended parochial school until he was in the fifth grade; at St. John's Catholic School, nine-year-old Gary, nicknamed Blackie, was seated among the "stupids" (*Living Up the Street*, 28). When asked what he wanted to do when he grew up, Soto's responses ranged from priest to hobo and, later in sixth grade, paleontologist. He decided to attend summer school one year; there he took a special interest in history and earned his first A. He became a school cadet in junior high; when he was sixteen and couldn't find a summer job, he worked as a volunteer recreational assistant for the city parks department. During his younger years, he tried various schemes to earn money, doing yard work and running errands. When he was old enough, he started working in the fields, hoeing cotton and picking grapes to earn money to buy his school clothes. Peer pressure from his classmates, whom he describes as "clothes conscious and small time social climbers" (*Living Up the Street*, 107), pushed him to endure the backbreaking, mind-numbing work in the fields. In one strikingly poignant piece, Soto described a jacket, the color of day-old guacamole, that he was forced to wear for several years; this hated jacket symbolized all the hurts and embarrassments that he suffered during his childhood (*Small Faces*, 37–41).

Soto was often told by those around him that he "would never do anything, be anyone. They said I would work like a donkey" (*Living Up the Street*, 110). When he was seventeen, he ran away from home for the summer to work in a tire factory in Glendale, California. He had a 1.6 average at Roosevelt High School. But he was afraid that he would have to spend his life working in the fields, so he decided to go to a community college and later to Fresno State University. It was there that he discovered poetry. At first he majored in geography, but when he stumbled across an anthology of contemporary poetry in the library, his life changed forever. "I was really little more than a boy when I first scribbled out a few sad lines of poetry. . . . Having come from a family with no books . . . I began writing my first poems in 1973" (*New and Selected Poems*, 1–2). Suffering through college poverty, he worked at all kinds of odd jobs, including washing cars, picking grapes, digging weeds, mowing lawns, and chopping beets and cotton. He was inspired by César Chavez and the United Farm Workers and was "given over to the destiny of poverty, unmanageable and angry in my ragged Levis, . . . given myself over to the alchemy of poetry" (*New and Selected Poems*, 1–2). "When I first studied poetry, I was single-minded. I woke to poetry and went to bed with poetry" (*A Fire in My Hands*, 5). From the poetry that he was reading, he learned that he was not alone in his alienation; he discovered the power of the written word to capture his experience and share it with others.

With strict discipline, Soto developed his gift for writing. He graduated from Fresno State University magna cum laude in 1974 and married Carolyn Sadako Oda in 1975. In 1976 he earned an M.F.A. in creative writing from the University of California at Irvine, spending that year as a visiting writer at San Diego State University. In 1977 he started teaching at the University of California at Berkeley, where he was until recently a senior lecturer in the English Department. His poetry appears frequently in literary magazines, and he has received fellowships from the Guggenheim Foundation, the National Endowment for the Arts, and the California Arts Council. The recipient of many honors and awards, Gary Soto has written numerous books; over forty of these books of poetry, prose, and children's stories are currently in print.

When asked about his writing process, Soto reveals that he works on one book at a time because he is afraid of getting scattered if he tackles too many projects. He writes in the mornings because his mind is clear, and he can concentrate then. He works in his garage, which he has turned into a study. He feels that "[i]t is a brave act to keep the rush of words going. It . . . is utter loneliness and uncertainty" (*Pieces of the Heart*, vii–x).

Although Gary Soto is best known for his poetry, he also writes in a number of other genres. Most of his work is unflinchingly personal; the majority of it springs from his memories of a childhood spent in the barrio. When asked how he remembers the details of his childhood so precisely, Soto answered, "For a long time I never left my childhood. I was always thinking about it . . . my father was killed in an industrial accident . . . I kept going over those events in my mind until I was into my 30s—thinking that if we'd done this instead of that, everything would have been different" (*NEA Today*, 9). Reflecting on his early years, he does not think that he came from a culturally rich family in the educational or academic sense of the word. "We had our own culture which was more like the culture of poverty, as I like to describe it" (*Dictionary of Literary Biog-*

raphy, 246). He notes that "I don't think I had any literary aspirations when I was a kid. In fact we were pretty much an illiterate family. We didn't have books and no one encouraged us to read" (*Something about the Author*, 211). This was before the belief in ethnic pride gained momentum; Soto remembers feeling "that being poor and Mexican was wrong" (*Lesser Evils*, 84). Assimilation was the rule of the time and as a result, Soto did not become fluent in Spanish. In all his writing, he never mentions a teacher who took a special interest in him when he was a child or encouraged him to pursue his dreams.

But Soto believes that "[l]iterature can make a difference to the marginal kid" (*NEA Today*, 9). He read *To Sir with Love* in high school and felt that it was written for him. This sensitivity to young people's concerns and the ability to portray the world as it is perceived by youngsters enable Soto to write books that appeal to young readers of all backgrounds. As can be expected, his books for children and young adults are more playful and humorous than his writing for high school students and adults. Though entertaining and often tinged with humor, these works often have an angst at their core, reflecting his concern with social issues such as poverty, violence, and racism. Soto asserts, "I write because there is pain in my life, our family, and those living in the San Joaquin Valley. . . . I write because those I live and work with can't write" (*Contemporary Literary Criticism*, 275). He speaks for those who have been relegated to the fringes of society, who do not have a voice to express the pain, humiliation, and disillusionment of their lives. He is able to incorporate information about significant issues into his stories and poems in such as way as to leave the reader with hope and renewed determination to continue the important work that needs to be done.

The critical reception to Gary Soto's writing has been overwhelmingly positive. Time and again, reviewers praise his ability to tell a story, to transcend the boundaries of ethnicity and age, and to transport his readers beyond the present time, place, and perspective. His work has filled a gap in literature for children and young adults; hopefully, his books are reaching young people who may feel doomed, as Soto once did to a future in the fields or factory. Eloquently speaking to the aspirations and dilemmas in young people's lives, his voice helps to encourage them to strive to fulfill their dreams. Hopefully, his work will inspire young Chicanos and Chicanas to become writers themselves.

More Information about Gary Soto

www.garysoto.com

Books

Authors and Artists for Young Adults, Volume 10, 176–182.
Contemporary Authors, Volume 119, 352.

Contemporary Authors, Volume 125, 424–427.
Contemporary Authors Online. The Gale Group, 2001.
Contemporary Literary Criticism, Volume 32, 401–405.
Contemporary Literary Criticism, Volume 80, 275–303.
Dictionary of Literary Biography, Volume 82, 246–252.
Hispanic Literature Criticism. Gale, 1994.
Nea Today, November 1992, 9.
Something about the Author, Volume 80, 209–215.
Ten Terrific Authors for Teens by Christine M. Hill. Enslow, 2000.

Videotape

Gary Soto. Lannan Foundation, 1995.

Selected Works by Gary Soto

Baseball in April

American Library Association Best Book for Young Adults

Booklist Editor's Choice

Horn Book Fanfare Selection

California Library Association's John and Patricie Beatty Award

Parenting Magazine Reading Magic Award

Grades 5–9

- Short Stories

This award-winning collection of eleven short stories depicts the everyday experiences of young Latino/a people growing up in Fresno, California. The main characters ride bicycles, try out for Little League, study karate, play with Barbie dolls, participate in the school talent show, compete in a marbles tournament, and try to earn money to buy a guitar. Soto writes the stories of the kids we usually don't read about: the ones who do not make it into Little League, who do not excel at karate, and who ride old bicycles that break down. These refreshing stories show what young people do when they are not chosen to play on Little League teams: they find a way to play baseball anyway. In "The No-Guitar Blues," Fausto earns a twenty-dollar reward for finding a lost dog but ends up putting the money in the collection plate at church instead of buying a long-yearned-for guitar. In "Mother and Daughter," Yollie and her mother dye an old dress for her to wear to the eighth grade fall dance. We meet a highly gifted young woman in "The Marble Champ"; Lupe Medrano, already accomplished in piano, spelling, reading, science, and chess, decides to try her hand at marbles. This story is a lesson in determination, as Lupe overcomes her image as a brain who is no good in sports. Soto's stories, moving yet humorous, present themes of friendship, family relationships, independence, success, and learning to cope with failure. He captures a certain vitality of language: "his teeth were crooked, like a pile of wrecked cars" (2); "Great rosebushes of red bloomed on Victor's cheeks" (72); and "his mind had melted into a puddle of misfiring cells" (89). Soto's characters shake hands *raza*-style, eat sunflower seeds and *nopales*, pick grapes in order to buy school clothes, and suffer the universal emotions of embarrassment, nervousness, joy, and pride. Glossary included. Spanish edition: *Beisbol en abril: Y otros historias.*

Big Bushy Mustache

Grades K–3

- Costumes
- Fathers and Sons

Ricky is proud of his costume for the Cinco de Mayo play—a big bushy mustache just like his father's—but runs into problems when he sneaks the prop out of school and loses it on the way home. After several frustrating attempts to create a replacement, Ricky is delighted when his father shaves off his own mustache and gives it to him to wear in the play. *BookList* wrote, "Cepeda's vibrantly colored and wonderfully sympathetic illustrations . . . expand the heart and humor implicit in the text."

Boys at Work

Grades 3–6

- Friendship
- Moneymaking Projects

When ten-year-old Rudy Herrera accidentally breaks an older boy's Discman, he and his friend Alex Garcia join forces to earn money to buy a new one—and hopefully save their necks. *School Library Journal* wrote, "With its universal growing up themes of bully-fear, friendship, and family relationships, *Boy at Work* is a reader-friendly addition."

Buried Onions

Grades 8–Up

- Barrio Life
- Friendship
- Violence

Nineteen-year-old Eddie is trying to make a life in Fresno, California, but like many other Mexican Americans, he's not finding it easy. His father, his best friend, and now his cousin are all dead—victims of the violence that Eddie is desperately trying to avoid. His aunt and some of his friends are urging him to avenge his cousin's murder, but Eddie just wants to find a way out. "I felt like crying. I sat on the steps for a few moments. My eyes were raw, my soul was trampled by bad luck and bad luck's brother, hard times" (108). He finally leaves town to join the navy, but it isn't clear what he decides to do in the ambiguous final scene. *Horn Book* described *Buried Onions* as one of the most somber books of 1997. *BookList* wrote, "The 'buried onions,' which Eddie imagines as the underground source for the world's tears, pervade the tone and plot, but the unvarnished depiction of depressed and depressing barrio life is as important as the positive images of Latinos that Soto has created in his other works." Note: Most of the female characters in this book are one-dimensional. Glossary included.

Canto Familiar

Hungry Mind Review Children's Book of Distinction

Grades 3–6

• Poetry

This companion volume to *Neighborhood Odes* includes twenty-five poems about the pleasures and woes that Mexican American children experience growing up. The cantos (songs) sing the praises of familiar activities such as picnics, soccer, gathering *nopales*, dancing *folklórico*, and eating watermelon. Children wear their shoes on the wrong feet and put their coats on backward just for fun. They gaily toss *bebé* into the air on an old hand-me-down serape. They create drums out of oatmeal boxes and guitars out of shoe boxes. They savor *menudo, chicharrones*, sunflower seeds, and snow cones. They roll out tortillas into the shapes of faraway lands. They do the dishes, iron, take math tests, lose eyeglasses, and accidently lock handcuffs on their wrists. Teachers will especially enjoy "My Teacher in the Market." Many of us can remember jumping from bed on a cold morning and running to warm ourselves by the furnace. As in all of Soto's books, feline companions have a featured place in this volume: we meet Hambre, who loves tortillas; Pleitos, who wrestles socks and bullies yarn; Slinky, who tips over garbage cans; and the good-luck kitten, who gets stranded on the roof. These poems sing about an ironing board that squeaks with pain, a face as shiny as a moon over a hill, the animals of hunger inside a growling stomach, and the big hand on a clock washing its face over and over. Soto has done it again—found an exuberant way to celebrate the ordinary events of life. No glossary is provided for the Spanish terms, which can be understood through the context of the poetry. This is illustrator Annika Nelson's first children's book; eleven of her prints grace the pages of this jaunty volume, one of Soto's most lighthearted works.

The Cat's Meow

Grades 2–5

- Cats
- Language
- Humor

Eight-year-old Graciela can't believe her ears when her feline friend, Pip, looking at her empty food bowl, says, "*Quiero más*, Graciela" (I want more). But when Graciela tries to get her to say something else, she clams up and runs across the street. Graciela tries to discuss this strange development with her good-natured and absentminded parents, but they are too distracted with their daily events and, both having hearing losses, misunderstand her. This pattern continues until Graciela finally convinces Pip to explain how she learned to talk. It seems that once when the humans were out of town on vacation, Pip made friends with a kindly neighbor, Sr. Medina, who taught her to speak Spanish. After hearing this story, Graciela is anxious to meet Sr. Medina. As the story unfolds, she also meets a tarantula, a snake, some mice, a nosy neighbor, several news reporters, and a police officer. She even receives a Spanish dictionary in the mail. But why did Pip and Sr. Medina disappear? And who is this new cat who knows how to speak French?

This is one of Gary Soto's most humorous books. Revised from an earlier version published by Strawberry Hill Press in 1987, this story is illustrated with whimsical black-and-white drawings. Spanish words are translated at the bottom of each page; non-Spanish-speaking students may pick up a few words or develop an interest in learning a second language. Animal lovers will be relieved with the way that the story ends. Soto dedicated this book to his daughter's feline friend, Pip, who once said, "Mama." Spanish edition: *El maullido de la gata*.

Chato and the Party Animals

Pura Belpré Illustrator Award
Grades K–Adult

- Birthdays

- Cats
- Friendship
- Humor

Chato, the coolest cat in *el barrio*, decides to throw a surprise *pachanga* for his best buddy, Novio Boy, who was raised in the pound and has never had a birthday party. Chato invites all their friends and cooks up a storm but forgets the most important detail—inviting the birthday cat. Happily, Novio Boy appears at the last minute, and the party is a wild success. *BookList* wrote, "Soto's story, both edgy and warm, spills over with feline wordplay kids will love . . . which Guevara expands on in her glorious, detailed paintings. Startlingly expressive animals, symbols of Latino culture, and winged-cat angels form dynamic, wild compositions." Glossary included.

Chato's Kitchen

Pura Belpré Award for Illustration
Tomás Rivera Mexican American Children's Book Award
Parents' Choice Honor Award
Parenting Magazine Reading Magic Award
Grades K–Adult

- Cats
- Mice
- Food
- Humor

Chato, the coolest, low-riding cat in East Los Angeles, can't believe his luck. The new neighbors busily moving in next door are no other than the plumpest, juiciest little *ratoncitos* (mice) that he has ever seen. Ever the quick thinker, he extends a neighborly invitation to the tasty, or lovely family for a surprise dinner at his house. The *ratoncitos* RSVP in the affirmative, if they can bring a friend. The roguish cat gleefully agrees, figuring six mice are better than five. Whistling "La Bamba," he starts to prepare the feast; before long his best friend, Novio Boy, a cat with the loveliest growl in the barrio, drops by. Soon the feline duo is whisker-deep in food-fixing: fajitas, *carne asada, chiles rellenos*, salsa, enchiladas, and a sweet, smooth flan. Meanwhile the mice family, although busy settling into their new home, remember to prepare a special dish—quesadillas—to take to their evening engagement. Soon their friend, Chorizo (sausage), arrives, and they all descend upon Chato's door at the appointed hour. Chato and Novio Boy are all set for the main course to walk through the door, but they haven't prepared themselves for Chorizo, who turns out to be a cool, road-scraping dachshund. Foiled, the two would-be villains resign themselves to a meal sans mouse. With this minor change in the menu, the dinner party assembles at the table and proceeds to enjoy the meal.

This tale is rendered hilarious by Soto's scintillating wit and Guevara's bold, innovative illustrations. Each page, with the savory seasoning of Spanish words and the feast of salty paintings, captures the flavor of life in *el barrio*. Spanish edition: *Chato y su cena*. Related article: "Chato's Kitchen," by Gary Soto. *Book Links*, January 1996, 54–55.

Crazy Weekend

Grades 5–9

- Humor
- Photography
- Robbers

Seventh graders Hector Beltran and Mando Tafolla spend a zany weekend in Fresno visiting Hector's uncle, Julio Silva. When Hector's mother first suggested that he needed to get out of East Los Angeles and see some of the world, he had visions of Paris or Madrid. But now here they are in Uncle Julio's messy apartment sleeping on a lumpy couch and eating cold cereal. When Julio, a photographer, takes them on an aerial photo shoot of a local farm, the boys find themselves in the back of a rickety, rusted-out old airplane. While flying, they spot a broken-down armored truck and two suspicious men; Uncle Julio quickly snaps some pictures of the robbers. The next morning they read about a robbery in the newspaper, and Uncle Julio takes his photographs to the paper. Hector and Mando are interviewed for the Today's Youth section, and the article is mistakenly printed in the next paper. The two robbers, Freddie Bork and Huey "Crybaby" Walker, see the article and decide that they have to teach the boys a lesson. But the bumbling villains are not prepared for the scared, but quick-witted, boys. The resulting comedy of errors is hilarious.

This is an action-packed, humorous adventure story. With the lively sprinkling of Spanish words and phrases translated in a glossary at the end of the book, Soto throws in some interesting information about photography and journalism as well. His characters are likable and well-drawn; even minor characters such as Mrs. Inouye, whose farm is photographed, are portrayed with complexity. After reading this crime-doesn't-pay thriller/comedy, readers will want to check out the further adventures of Hector and Mando in the sequel, *Summer on Wheels*.

The Effects of Knut Hamsun on a Fresno Boy: Recollections and Short Essays

Grades 11–Adult

• Autobiographical Essays

Set mostly in the author's hometown, Fresno, California, the forty-eight pieces in this volume bring together all of the contents of the previously published *Small Faces* and a good portion of *Lesser Evils*, both books long out of print, as well as five recent essays. In the title piece, Soto fashions himself to be Fresno's own Kunt Hamsun, the Norwegian writer of the 1920s who walked around his town observing the ordinary with amazement. Also included are the much-lauded recollections "The Jacket" and "Like Mexicans." Written from the heart and enlivened by imaginative spirit and gentle humor, these wry and deceptively simple stories surprise, refresh, and enlighten.

A Fire in My Hands: A Book of Poems

Grades 7–12

• Poetry

This collection of twenty-three poems originally intended for adults celebrates small, significant moments in the poet's life. In the foreword, Gary Soto notes that he thinks of his poems as a "working life, by which I mean that my poems are about common, everyday things." His unusual poems celebrate ordinary topics such as baseball, earning money, music, dancing, hitchhiking, oranges, and feeding birds. Each poem is prefaced by a short introduction in which the poet explains its origin. Arranged in roughly chronological order beginning in childhood and moving through adolescence and young adulthood, the poems provide a glimpse into the way that the poet's mind works. The informal free verse utilizes consciously plain language; the skilled use of words and images will stay with readers of all ages.

In the foreword, Soto shares that at first he was scared to write poetry, in part because his poetry teacher, to whom the book is dedicated, was a stern man who could see the errors in his poems. There is a message here for teachers and for young writers who are seeking to express themselves through language. The friendly four-page "Questions and Answers about Poetry" section at the end of the book provides gentle encouragement for poetry enthusiasts and struggling writers of all ages.

If the Shoe Fits

Grades K–3

- Clothes
- Peer Pressure
- Poverty
- Uncles

Rigo doesn't like wearing his brothers' tattered hand-me-downs, so he is delighted when his mother gives him a brand-new pair of loafers for his ninth birthday. But after being teased by neighborhood bullies about the style of the shoes, he puts them away for so long that he outgrows them. This touching story ends with Rigo giving the shoes to his uncle to wear to his new job as a waiter. Adapted from a story with the same title in *Petty Crimes*.

Jesse

Grades 9–Up

- Art
- College
- Farm Labor
- United Farm Workers
- Vietnam War

Loosely autobiographical, this tenderly written, contemplative novel is one of Gary Soto's most poignant books. Set in Fresno, California, in the late 1960s and using a first-person narrative, the book chronicles seventeen-year-old Jesse's painful search for a way out of a lifetime of poverty and backbreaking labor in the fields. He and his older brother, Abel, know that the way to get ahead is to work hard and get an education. Jesse leaves home and quits high school during his senior year to join Abel in community college. Sharing a run-down apartment, they supplement their meager Social Security payments by spending the weekends working in the fields and scrounging junk to sell. (Their father was killed in an factory accident when they were "small, twigs of flesh" [5].) Introspective Jesse, plagued by self-doubts, searches for meaning in his dubious classes, often succumbing to pressure from his politicized friends to join the protests led by César Chávez and Dolores Huerta. His art classes provide the most comfort; he enters his drawing, titled "*¡Huelga!*," of the United Farm Workers strike in an art exhibit at the college after working and reworking it "until I thought I had finally got their sadness right" (122). After months of work and study, the brothers attempt to hitchhike to the beach during spring break; however, they spend two forlorn days camping beside the highway waiting for a ride. When passing teenagers throw eggs at them, they trudge off in different directions to cry; eventually, they get back home and spend the remainder of their vacation chopping cotton. Soto eloquently describes the pain and isolation: "I felt bad then, a bruise growing inside me" (48); "A lump of sorrow formed in my throat, and when I swallowed, some of the sorrow dripped into my stomach" (61); and "Something dropped like a rock inside me" (126). However, Jesse is young, and, somehow, hope survives. He considers majoring in Spanish to keep the language alive. Jesse finds pleasure in the small things in life: a field trip to the country with his biology class, inner-tubing on the Piedra River, memories of elementary school, and riding in the back of a truck with the wind in his face. All the while, the Vietnam War and the threat of being drafted cast a cloud over their lives. The story ends when Abel is drafted and leaves for Vietnam, and Jesse is left alone to ponder his future. He fears that he will never escape the "fields running for miles with cantaloupes like heads, all faceless in the merciless sun" (166). Yet the reader is left with the feeling that, somehow, Jesse will find a way to follow his dreams.

Jessie De La Cruz: A Profile of a United Farm Worker

Grades 6–Up

- Biography
- Farmworkers
- History
- Labor Leaders
- United Farm Workers

This is the inspiring biography of Jessie De La Cruz, a migrant farmworker and United Farm Worker organizer. For nearly half a century, starting when she was five years old, she worked in the fields in the San Joaquin Valley in California. Based on personal interviews, this story of her life is told within the context of the era—from the Great Depression to the social movements of the 1960s until today. *BookList* wrote, "From the Depression to the grape boycott to the farmworkers' fight to own some of the land they worked, this is stirring American history." Black-and-white photographs are included. Appended is the text of Jessie De La Cruz's congressional testimony given on July 17, 1975, titled "Will the Family Farm Survive in America?"

Junior College

Grades 10–Up

• Poetry

In his fifteenth book of poetry, Gary Soto offers poignant recollections from his childhood, adolescence, and early college days. In pieces that are at once humorous and tender, Soto demonstrates a rare understanding of how the ordinary and the transcendent meet in the fleeting pleasures and pain of everyday life.

Lesser Evils: Ten Quartets

Grades 11–Adult

• Autobiographical Essays

Forty autobiographical essays, arranged in groups of four by theme, capture significant details of Gary Soto's life and the people around him. He writes, often philosophically, about parenthood, teaching, writing, animal companions, marriage, friends, and responsibility. Always a keen observer, Soto shows a humorous and mellow side in many of these essays. He often reflects on the passage of time, commenting in one piece that his life is half over; like one of the characters in his movie review, he is always thinking about the world and his impermanence. "I'm between two points, the first days and the last days, and I'm wondering what I should do about this" (7). He notes that when he was young, he thought that he could help the world, but recently he is not so sure. He feels a duty to explain this unjust world to his daughter. "I think she has to know about difficult lives . . . there's a chance she'll grow up unappreciative" (31–32). For animal lovers, his passages about his feline and canine friends are very touching. Soto's use of language is a delight: in describing an aging sweater, he notes that "a herd of fuzz balls has multiplied around the armpits" (57); he observes a group of ants "mill(ing) around like nervous shoppers" (137); and he reminisces about climbing a mountain when he was a child: "I was happy. All the badness in my life was momentarily gone, flooded with sunlight, and I believed I could lie down in the grass *forever*" (87). This collection of essays is out of print, but many of the pieces have been reprinted in *The Effects of Knut Hamsun on a Fresno Boy*.

Living Up the Street: Narrative Recollections

American Book Award from the Before Columbus Foundation
Grades 10–Adult

• Autobiographical Short Stories

Gary Soto offers twenty-one narrative recollections of his life growing up in Fresno, California; he dedicates this book to the people who lived these stories: his brother, Rick, his sister, Debra, and Little John and Scott. These autobiographical short stories cover over twenty years of Soto's life, beginning when he was five years old and proceeding roughly chronologically until shortly after his first book was published in 1977. The book opens with a description of the street where Soto's family lived in 1957; Braly Street was in the middle of industrial Fresno, surrounded by factories and a junkyard. In the second vignette, Soto shares more details about his father's accidental death and his reactions than he does in any other work; he refers to this tragedy in a number of other poems and stories. He writes about summers spent drinking Kool-Aid, fighting with his siblings and neighbor kids, participating in the local city parks recreational activities, and watching television, where he learned about the "comfortable lives of white kids" (30).

Soto writes with amazing detail about the traumas and triumphs of his early years. He generously shares information about his mistakes and embarrassments as well as his successes. This collection will help readers gain insight into his other works. His prose often reads like poetry: "We walked without saying too much because talking ruined the joy of noiseless minds" (77); his early poems "limped like old dogs in the hallway" (128; and waiting for a poem to surface, he is "eager to push words from one side of the page to the next" (145). This book includes three school photographs of Soto and his classmates in 1st grade, 5th grade, and 6th grade.

Local News

Grades 4–7

• Short Stories

In this companion book to *Baseball in April*, Gary Soto again touches a universal chord. In his second volume of short stories, as in his poems, the author uses his ability to perceive and share the common events that make life interesting. Readers are introduced to Araceli, whose adventurous spirit leads her to take a long-awaited, but disappointing, nickel-a-pound airplane ride to benefit Children's Hospital. We meet Blanca Mendoza, whose determination to stay up until midnight on New Year's Eve results in her being accidentally locked out of the house in the cold. Elizabeth and Leonard Aguirre's experiences going door-to-door selling candy and coloring books of superheroes whom no one has ever heard of bring back memories of selling greeting cards in the 1950s. Other stories feature a school play, radio program requests for "Oldies but Goodies," racquetball games, and a mean, older brother who plays dirty tricks on his little brother.

The small touches make these stories even more special: the hot coffee over soggy cornflakes; the dark paneled walls hung with pictures of happy and sad clowns and the Kennedys; the Sears catalog game, in which the children take turns choosing the toys that they like; and the tennis shoes lined with plastic sandwich bags to keep one's feet dry. Readers searching for positive portrayals of fat people will be disappointed in "Nickel-a-Pound Plane Ride" but may find "El Radio" somewhat more encouraging. The peppering of Spanish words and phrases adds to the vitality of the vignettes. A glossary is included.

A Natural Man

Grades 12–Up

- Poetry

In a departure from the poet's earlier work, the gritty landscape of these new poems is populated by big talkers, wanna-be mariachis, lazy souls, and teenage werewolves looking for their first date. With a dizzying mixture of comedy and heartbreak, this collection documents the poet's ongoing struggle to make sense of a disorienting world. *School Library Journal* wrote, "Soto's poetry is not for the naive or faint of heart; it is replete with grizzly images and crude and lewd anecdotal details. There is, however, much that is beautiful in the language of this book."

Neighborhood Odes

Grades 4–7

- Poetry

Twenty-one poems full of laughter, love, joy, regret, and humor celebrate everyday things such as lawn sprinklers on a hot day, a day in the country, feline and canine friends, and eating warm tortillas with butter.

Soto shows us that there is poetry in the common, ordinary events of our lives. The Spanish words in the text can be understood by non-Spanish readers through the context of the poems; a glossary is available so one can confirm the meanings. These poems are written with such humor and perceptivity that they will appeal even to youngsters who are reluctant poets. Soto's sensitivity is apparent in poems such as "Ode to Mi Gato," in which he expresses his love for the white cat that he had found abandoned as a kitten. Librarians will enjoy "Ode to My Library," in which the poet confides that he devoured thirty books in a summer read-a-thon, researched the Incas, and helped paint a mural about the Aztecs. This is Caldecott Award-winning illustrator David Diaz's first children's book; his playful black-and white cut paper illustrations accompany ten of the poems.

New and Selected Poems

Grades 10–Adult

• Poetry

Selected poems from six of Soto's previous books, some of which are out of print, and twenty-three new poems make up this brilliant collection. The poems are organized into chapters, titled from the previous books: "The Elements of San Joaquin," "The Tale of Sunlight," "Where Sparrow Work Hard," "Black Hair," "Who Will Know Us?" and "Home Course in Religion." In the preface, "Sizing Up the Sparrows," Soto chronicles his early development as a poet, beginning when he "was really little more than a boy when I first scribbled out a few sad lines of poetry" (1).

Soto draws upon his experiences growing up in Fresno, California, to present a multifaceted collage of vividly drawn characters living amid urban violence, racism, backbreaking labor, and disillusionment; with a vision that transcends the ordinary, he chronicles the small joys and large angers of their lives. The opening poem, dedicated to César Chávez, focuses on the elements of field, wind, stars, and sun. Soto's poems are about alienation, struggle, and the universal themes of birth and death, but they also confirm the power of the human spirit to survive and soar. He has a special gift for speaking eloquently and unflinchingly of the struggles of his life: the accidental death of his father when he was five years old, the poverty and economic hardships that he grew up with in California's central valley, and the racial prejudice against his people. His poetry calls into question the social and political order of America, asking profound questions that need to be addressed. Soto has the rare ability to write about the harsh realities of life and, at the same time, evoke feelings of hope.

Nickel and Dime

Grades 12–Up

- Friendship
- Homelessness

A trio of brutally honest interconnected stories follows the declining fortunes of three Mexican American men in Oakland, California, during the 1990s. Roberto Silva, a thirty-three-year-old bank security guard, is downsized out of his job and soon finds himself living on the street. Roberto's campadre, fifty-nine-year-old Gus Hernandez, eventually retires from his job and takes him in. Silver Mendez, a thirty-eight-year-old poet devoted to the Chicano movement in the late 1960s and 1970s, who has "bottomed out in life" (87), is the protagonist in Soto's later book, *Poetry Lover. Library Journal* wrote, "Soto's low-key literary style again serves him well in this story of three anti-heroes." *BookList* added, "Soto's narrative voice avoids any overt endorsement of [the] poetics of suffering, but the novel's underlying plot and focal alignment . . . inscribe such a poetics nonetheless."

Novio Boy: A Play

Grades 6–10

- Dating
- Drama
- Humor
- Plays

In this lighthearted play, ninth-grader Rudy (from *The Pool Party* and *Boys at Work*) anxiously prepares for, and then goes out on, his first date with Patricia, a high school junior. His friends and relatives all have plenty of advice, but Rudy doesn't expect to see them at the restaurant on the big day. This seven-scene play includes performance notes, a descriptive character list, extensive scene notes, and a glossary.

Off and Running

Grades 4–7

- Leadership
- Schools

Fifth grader Miata Ramirez (protagonist of *The Skirt*) is running for class president, and her best friend, Ana Avila, is her running mate. Their opponents are popular Rudy Herrera (who appears in several other books) and his friend Alex Garcia. This lighthearted book ends with Miata and Ana winning the close race and following through on their campaign promises to clean up the school grounds, plant flowers and trees, and involve the parents. One of the most inspiring chapters features Doña Carmen Elena Vasquez, who was once the mayor of her town in Mexico. She graciously responds when Miata asks her for advice about how to be a good leader and later donates dozens of plants, supervises the planting, and serves Mexican hot chocolate to the parents and students.

The Old Man and His Door

Grades K–3

- Humor
- Listening Skills

This is an amusing story about an old man who doesn't listen carefully and ends up taking *la puerta* (the door) to a party instead of *el puerco* (the pig). Proving that sometimes mistakes have a way of turning out for the best, the author follows a strand of funny mishaps to a happy conclusion. Bold illustrations add to the enjoyment of this warmhearted tale. Glossary included.

Pacific Crossing

Grades 6–10

- Exchange Programs
- Japan
- Martial Arts
- Travel

In this sequel to *Taking Sides*, fourteen-year-old Lincoln Mendoza and his *carnal*, Tony Contreras, participate in a six-week summer exchange program to Japan. From their Noe Valley school in San Francisco, the two almost-eighth graders are selected for the cross-cultural experience because of their interest in the Japanese martial art of *shorinji kempo*. After the nine-hour flight to Tokyo, they travel to Atami, a town of 20,000 people, where they meet their host families. They encounter new experiences, meet interesting people, and discover a Japan much different from the one that they expected. When they prepare a feast of frijoles, salsa, and tortillas for their host families, they realize that cooking Mexican food is not as easy as they had assumed. They learn to enjoy the public baths and attend a sumo wrestling match, Lincoln tolerates an ear cleaning, and they spend interminable hot hours tending the egg-plants in the family gardens. On a camping trip, Lincoln, unlicensed and nervous, drives his host family's father to a hospital after a deadly spider bite. Lincoln spends many arduous, satisfying hours practicing *shorinji kempo*; in his final test, he passes to *nikkyu* rank, two steps from black belt. He establishes a special friendship with fourteen-year-old Mitsuo Ono, his new Japanese brother; the two look forward to the day that Mitsuo can visit Lincoln in San Francisco; this reunion has interesting potential as a sequel.

With humor and sensitivity, this book challenges numerous misconceptions that each boy has about the other's culture and language and brings to life the truism that people are more the same than different. The reader, along with the characters, learns much about both cultures and about the potential that people have to grow and change as a result of multicultural experiences. Soto includes numerous terms in Spanish and Japanese that non-Spanish and non-Japanese speakers will enjoy trying to translate from the context; glossaries are available for confirming the meanings. Followers of Lincoln's problems adjusting to his move to suburbia in *Taking Sides* will be interested in the fact that the family decided to move back to San Francisco, this time settling in the Noe Valley near the Mission District, where Linc had spent his first twelve years. Spanish edition: *Cruzando el pacífico.*

Petty Crimes

Grades 5–10

- Short Stories

This collection of ten realistic short stories about Mexican American teens dealing with tough issues is punctuated by conflict, sadness, and flashes of affectionate humor. From Alma, who tries to cope with her mother's death by buying back her clothes from thrift stores, to Manuel, who resents wearing his brothers' hand-me-downs, to Norma, who is beaten up by classmates, Soto's characters are portrayed with unflinching clarity. These gritty stories about poverty, shoplifting, bullies, death, scams, shame, and violence are leavened by loyalty to friends, growing independence, and family love. *School Library Journal* wrote, "Rich in simile and metaphor and sprinkled with Spanish words and phrases, these simply told memorable stories . . . resonate with realism because they deal with concerns most young people have."

Poetry Lover

Grades 12–Up

- Poets

Silver Mendez, a thirty-nine-year-old unemployed poet (introduced in *Nickel and Dime*), receives an invitation to participate in a conference in Spain on Chicano literature. All he needs is money for a plane ticket, a passport, and a place to stay. Twenty years ago he was the youthful author of two published books of poetry, but his career has been going steadily downhill ever since. Now without a job, a home, or even a typewriter, he has his work cut out for him. How the bumblling poet overcomes these and other obstacles has been described as hilarious, ironic, and life-affirming. Even while we laugh at his misadventures, we cheer him on as he lurches toward a new life with an old love.

The Pool Party

Grades 3–5

- Parties
- Socioeconomic Class

Ten-year-old Rudy Herrera is surprised and excited when he receives an invitation to a pool party from Tiffany Perez, the richest and most popular girl in school. He has spent most of the summer helping his father with his gardening jobs. Now his thoughts turn to finding just the right inner tube to take to the party. His family has plenty of advice: his older sister tries to improve his manners, and his father teaches him how to make small talk. Gently reassuring his son that Tiffany will like him because he is real, Father adds, "Listen, they may be rich folks, but don't worry. Just go and have fun" (80). After a narrow escape involving a stolen car and a trial ride down the river on the inner tube, Rudy is ready to make a big splash at the party. The partygoers snicker at first ("Tiffany invited *him* to the party?"), but their snobbishness soon turns to curiosity as they compare their fancy pool toys with Rudy's huge, decorated inner tube. By the time Rudy leaves the party, his eyes are red from the chlorine and the tube is nearly flat because everyone has used it.

Gary Soto gives young readers a light, funny story with likable characters. The contrasts between Rudy's and Tiffany's lives are evident. While Rudy's family eats frijoles, *papas*, and Kool-Aid and snacks on corn nuts and root beer, Tiffany serves brie, carrot sticks, ambrosia, and miniature cobs of corn at her party. When Rudy tells Tiffany about his adventures on Francher's Creek, she responds that her parents usually take her to Hawaii. When the harpist who is providing music for the party finishes playing, Rudy is puzzled that she cannot play his requests for "'96 Tears" or "Woolly Bully." But Rudy, undaunted, follows his father's advice and has fun.

Within this story are the stories told by Rudy's grandfather, "El Shorty," who lives with the family and helps with the gardening jobs. These are the stories about the poor days in California, just after he arrived from Mexico with the dream of a home with an orange tree in the backyard. He tells of hitchhiking to California and, after his shoes were stolen, using cardboard to jump from place to place. Rudy and his family usually ignore these stories. Rudy sometimes "wondered if his Grandfather was right in the head" (7). Grandfather spends his spare time "taping a splintered shovel back to life" (7) and digging a swimming pool in their backyard. Perhaps when Rudy is older, he will want to know more about those difficult years and listen more patiently to what his grandfather is trying to say. Sequel: *Boys at Work*. Film: *The Pool Party*.

The Skirt

Grades 3–5

- Dance
- *Folklorico*
- Lost and Found

Fourth grader Miata Ramirez has lost something again—this time she left her treasured *folklorico* skirt on the school bus. This is the skirt that belonged to her mother when she was a child in Hermosillo, Mexico. Now Miata needs all her wits to retrieve the precious skirt before her upcoming dance group performance, for which she has practiced three long months. Rallying all her courage and enlisting the help of her best friend, Ana, she slips into the bus yard and rescues the skirt. However, an unexpected twist near the end of the book finds Mama giving her daughter a new skirt. With characteristic ingenuity, Miata, feeling sorry for the old skirt, finds the perfect solution—she wears the old skirt under the new one.

Set in the San Joaquin Valley in California, where the Ramirez family moved to escape the pollution and long commute in Los Angeles (and where Gary Soto grew up), this lightly suspenseful story weaves information about Latino culture and Spanish words into the text. Taking a situation that many young readers can identify with—that of losing something and trying to explain it to parents—the author brings us an engaging female protagonist and a good read-aloud story that invites discussion and writing extensions.

Small Faces

Grades 10–Adult

• Autobiographical Short Stories

The thirty-one prose reminiscences that make up this moving collection were written in 1983 and 1984. Gary Soto is always observing and thinking about the world and weighing his place in it. Describing himself as mercurial, fickle, and capricious, he confides that he and his wife are constantly moving. In the first ten years of marriage, they "lived in twenty different places, two states, two countries, eight cities and five counties" (27). He muses that maybe this moving around is due to his migrant genes; perhaps he is destined to continually break camp and hit the road for another field. Somedays he wants money and nice things, and other days he thinks about the richness that a poor life can bring (16). He finds himself looking forward to the future and yet mourning for the past. This is the past about which he often writes, "the same past that won't lie down and die for good" (48). He is haunted by the specter of poverty: a jacket the color of day-old guacamole that he had to wear in fifth and sixth grades symbolizes the many embarrassments and hurts that he suffered as a child and adolescent. "I blame that jacket for those bad years" (40), during which he lost confidence and his grades dropped. He recounts his childhood fear, which recurs periodically, that he would have no choice but to follow in his family's footsteps as a field or factory laborer. "Now I am living this other life that seems like a dream. How did I get here?" (58). The book ends with Soto's wondering if we can really make a difference. "We can say things but solve nothing. Today I've listened to a line in my head over and over: 'the past seems horrible to me, the present gray and desolate, and the future utterly appalling'" (137). This book of highly poetic prose is out of print, but all of the contents have been reprinted in *The Effects of Knut Hamsun on a Fresno Boy*.

Snapshots from the Wedding

Grades K–3

• Weddings

Maya, the flower girl, describes an elegant wedding through snapshots of the day's events, beginning with the procession to the altar and ending when she falls asleep after the dance. The three-dimensional illustrations were created from clay, wood, fabric, acrylic paint, and found objects.

A Summer Life

Grades 10–Adult

- Autobiographical Short Stories

A Summer Life consists of three parts, each made up of thirteen short stories and essays about growing up in the industrial section of Fresno, California. Soto reminisces about the years when he was around four or five years old in Part 1; Part 2 is about his life between the ages of six through twelve; and Part 3 covers his years from thirteen through seventeen. Writing in the first person with vivid language and rich imagery, he captures the innocence, humor, loneliness, and energy of a Latino childhood spent in a working-class neighborhood surrounded by factories, diesel trucks, and junkyards during the 1950s and 1960s. The first story, "The Buddha," features a ceramic statue of Buddha that Soto's Uncle Shorty brought back from the Korean War. Five-year-old Soto carries the statue with him as he plays in the neighborhood. The Buddha, half hidden in the weeds, watches as the young boy runs under a slowly moving diesel truck and skids in the dust on the other side. As Soto grows older, he starts developing a sensitivity toward animals, which is evident in many of his books. In "The Chicks," he tries unsuccessfully to protect three baby chicks from the neighbor's cat. Later, his loneliness in temporarily eased by the company of a stray dog in "The Stray." He confides that it was scary at home with an alcoholic stepfather who pressured him to keep his hair short, unlike the Beatles, who were popular at the time.

The stories in *A Summer Life* are excellent models for young writers. Soto's example of writing about everyday events and experiences will inspire others who may at first think that they have nothing about which to write. Most of the stories have a happy, carefree tone in spite of the dangers that the unsupervised children playing on busy streets face while their parents try to eke out a living working in the factories.

Soto's stories defy labels. They have the smell of crushed chinaberries in the warm summer air and the joy of wearing cutoffs and a peach-stained T-shirt on a hot day. Soto has adapted two of the stories, "The Bike" and "The Inner Tube," into films and "The Inner Tube" was rewritten for another book, *The Pool Party*.

Summer on Wheels

Grades 5–9

- Bicycling
- Travel
- Vacations

In this sequel to *Crazy Weekend*, thirteen-year-old Hector Beltran Molina and his amigo, Mando Tafolla, end the summer by hitting the road on an exciting bicycle trip from East Los Angeles to the Santa Monica beach. They have barely left home when Hector finds himself in the starring role in a television commercial. Before long, they are singing backup for a recording that Uncle Ricardo is making. Next, when they attend a baseball game, Hector is the one-millionth fan to enter the stadium. Staying with relatives in East Los Angeles, Maywood, Culver City, Beverly Hills, West Los Angeles, and Santa Monica, the two happy-go-lucky boys find new adventures at each stop—painting a "Reading Is Power" mural on a library, pretending to be wax figures at the Hollywood Wax Museum, teaching a cousin how to ride a bicycle, and finally surfing the waves at the beach. They also renew connections with relatives and meet new friends along the way. When they return home, Hector's enthusiasm influences his parents to put old disagreements aside and invite everyone to a family reunion. Hector and Mando even paint a mural of their trip on the family garage.

Taking Sides

Grades 6–10

- Basketball
- Moving
- Single-parent Family
- Socioeconomic Class

Fourteen-year-old Lincoln Mendoza faces some tough questions when he and his mother move from the Mission District of San Francisco, an urban barrio, to Sycamore, a suburban town with tree-lined streets. He often wonders if their new location is really an improvement. At first he liked the peacefulness of the new neighborhood, but he soon starts missing his old school and its mural of brown, yellow, and black kids. "There are no brown people here," he muses as he compares the pluses and minuses of each location. He notices that he and his mother have started using English, even at home, and that his Spanish is getting worse and worse. On the other hand, he and his new friend, Monica, bemoan the fact that their parents often reminisce about their hard work in the fields, saying that the kids are spoiled. Linc is tired of "nine years of hauling bologna sandwiches to school" as well as the pollution, graffiti, and noise of the old neighborhood.

One of Linc's biggest challenges is coming to terms with his divided loyalties to the two basketball teams. A racist coach, an injured knee, a disagreement with his old friend, Tony, his mother's Anglo boyfriend, and the burglary attempt on the Mendozas' new house add to the confusion. Near the end of the book during the big game between his two schools, Linc realizes that "he was a Franklin boy beneath a Columbus uniform. He was brown, not white; poor, not rich; city, not suburbia" (127).

Besides providing an interesting look at class and race issues, the book also lightly addresses gender issues. Linc is surprised and then pleased to learn that Monica is also a basketball player and interested in math. His father, who left the family when Linc was seven, sends Linc birthday cards with one-dollar bills while his mother provides daily support, continuity, and love. Linc notices that his new basketball buddy's mother, not his father, brings in the big bucks.

One of the many noteworthy touches in the story is the relationship between Linc and his canine companion, Flaco, who also has an injured leg. Another is the integration of Spanish terms and phrases into the text (a glossary is available). Readers will want to read the sequel, *Pacific Crossing*, to find out what new adventures await Lincoln and his family and friends. Spanish edition: *Tomando partido*.

Too Many Tamales

Grades K–3

- Christmas
- Food
- Keepsakes
- Lost and Found

Maria happily helps her parents make tamales for a Christmas family gathering. When her mother leaves her diamond ring on the kitchen counter while she leaves the room to answer the telephone, Maria cannot resist trying it on. Hours later, while playing with her cousins, Maria remembers the ring. Assuming that it fell into the *masa* (cornmeal dough) while she was kneading it, she desperately enlists the help of her cousins. Together they eat every one of the twenty-four tamales, all the while waiting to bite down on something hard. Corn husks littering the floor, stomachs stretched till they hurt, the only clue that they discover is cousin Danny's confession that he thinks he swallowed something hard. Finally, a guilt-ridden Maria decides that she must confess to her mother. Just as the words start to form, she spies the ring sitting safely on her mother's finger. The story ends on a happy note with the family good-naturedly gathering in the kitchen to cook up another batch of tamales.

Everyone who has ever lost something, especially if it belonged to someone else, will identify with this story. During the course of producing the rich oil paintings with their delightful facial expressions, illustrator Ed Martinez and his wife cooked and ate more tamales than they ever dreamed possible. This book, a refreshing change from the usual Anglo holiday story, is an excellent choice for creative dramatics. Spanish edition: *¡Qué montón de tamales!*

Who Will Know Us?

Grades 10–Adult

- Poetry

In the poem from which the title of the book was taken, dedicated to Jaroslav Seifert, Gary Soto asks, "Who will know us when we breathe through the grass?" (19). A number of the poems in this volume are about death: the untimely death of his father; the death of Moses, his friend's gallant collie dog; and the death of Sadao Oda, who had thinned grapes and hoed beets, for whom Soto writes an elegy. He writes about his seventy-year-old grandfather, who wants to die. Soto's poems are about the emotions that we all experience: shame, grief, worry, loneliness, melancholia, guilt, boredom, and uncertainty, but he has a way of writing about these feelings that gives us hope that we can move on to happiness, joy, and tranquillity. His use of language is always fresh, often surprising. The fear of returning to the poverty of his childhood still haunts him: in "Worry at the End of the Month" (52–53), he sees his perfect life overturning, and he prepares to say good-bye to his fancy clothes and weekend trips. Other poems are about trying to fly when he was a child, worrying about disease, a stray dog eating in an alley, playing chess with his daughter, visiting a sugar plant, masturbation, the joys of swimming, and traveling by train. In poem after poem, Soto remains faithful to the common things in life.

Jan Romero Stevens

Latina (1953–2000)

Writing within a particular cultural setting validates the importance of that culture, its customs and language for those children who are a part of it. Just as importantly it brings understanding and appreciation to those children who are not familiar with it. Through my writing, my goal is to foster pride in our cultures, recognizing the differences between us but celebrating the equality of us all in God's world.

(Personal Communication)

Books by Jan Romero Stevens

Carlos and the Carnival/Carlos y la feria. Illustrated by Jeanne Arnold. Northland Publishing, 1999.

Carlos and the Cornfield/Carlos y la milpa de maíz. Illustrated by Jeanne Arnold. Northland Publishing, 1995.

Carlos and the Skunk/Carlos y el zorrillo. Illustrated by Jeanne Arnold. Northland Publishing, 1997.

Carlos and the Squash Plant/Carlos y la planta de calabaza. Illustrated by Jeanne Arnold. Northland Publishing, 1993.

Carlos Digs to China/Carlos excava hasta la China. Illustrated by Jeanne Arnold. Northland Publishing, 2001.

Twelve Lizards Leaping: A New Twelve Days of Christmas. Illustrated by Christine Mau. Northland Publishing, 1999.

Jan Romero Stevens, a journalist and writer from Flagstaff, Arizona, often spoke to students about her writing and conducted workshops for adults. Her engaging bilingual books for children identified her as an important writer in the field of children's literature. She was the recipient of several awards, including the 1998 Children's Author Award given by the Arizona Library Association and the 1998 Copper Quill Award from the Flagstaff Public Library. After battling breast cancer for six years, Romero Stevens died on February 23, 2000. A portion of the proceeds from her last book is being donated to the American Cancer Society's Tell-a-Friend Project in Flagstaff, Arizona.

Born in Las Vegas, New Mexico, Romero Stevens lived in New Mexico and Arizona all her life. She was a writer and columnist for Flagstaff's *Arizona Daily Star* (ADS) for fifteen years. Romero Stevens life as a writer was often tied to her role as a mother. Carlos, the hero of five of her books, is a composite of her two sons. "I didn't want him to be a real modern-day boy. I wanted him from a time when family was important and things were safe, because that's the way I think things should be" (*ADS*, 5C). The plots for her books were taken from her personal experiences. She based her first book on her childhood memories of her mother's warning her that if she didn't wash her ears, a potato plant would sprout in them. She repeated the warning to her own children and later used it as the basis for *Carlos and the Squash Plant*. This bilingual book was met with such enthusiasm that she was inspired to continue writing about Carlos and his adventures. The second book, *Carlos and the Cornfield*, was based on her younger son's penchant for planting too many seeds in each hole in the family garden.

Schools and libraries frequently invited Romero Stevens to speak with young readers. After she read from her books, she talked with the students about the writing process. She showed them revised copies of her own writing, pointing out all the words that were crossed out and all the revisions that were made. Encouraging them to relax and enjoy writing, she reassured them that everyone makes mistakes on the first draft and that numerous revisions are common even for the most accomplished writers. She also talked about the differences between newspaper writing and fiction writing.

In her workshops for adults, Romero Stevens explored writing and publishing literature for children. She encouraged participants to submit a work in progress to be critiqued in class. She also consulted with individuals, sharing her experiences and insights into the world of writing for youngsters. She believed that the most important requirement for becoming a successful writer for young readers is that we love children and enjoy writing for them, in addition to being familiar with the body of children's literature.

Romero Stevens was entranced by the culture, history, food, and people of the Southwest. She explored her Latina heritage by studying Spanish with her children and by writing bilingual books. She wrote her books to help her children develop connections with their Latino culture. "We live in such a diverse society, I wanted them to appreciate their own heritage and also learn to appreciate other cultures" (*Mountain Campus News*, 2, 6).

More Information about Jan Romero Stevens

Arizona Daily Star. October 26, 1995, 1C, 5C.
Mountain Campus News. Northern Arizona University, October 15, 1993, 2, 6.
Sierra Vista Herald. March 15, 1994, 1A, 3A.

Selected Works by Jan Romereo Stevens

Carlos and the Carnival/Carlos y la feria

Grades K–3

- Bilingual
- Carnivals
- Money
- Recipes

This fourth book in the Carlos series finds the youngster heading off to the county fair with his hard-earned money burning a hole in his pocket. Even though his father warns him that a fool and his money are soon parted, Carlos, as usual, is too stubborn to listen. Sure enough, he discovers that his pockets are empty long before he is ready to go home. Complete with an important life lesson and a recipe for *sopapillas*, this endearing book is richly satisfying.

Carlos and the Cornfield/Carlos y la milpa de maíz

Grades K–3

- Bilingual
- Gardening
- New Mexico
- Recipes

In this engaging story, Carlos finds out what his father means when he says, "You reap what you sow." The book begins with Carlos admiring a beautiful red pocket knife in Señor Lopez's store. In order to earn the money to buy it, he agrees to plant the sweet corn in the family garden. Papá explains that the seeds must be planted in a very special way, exactly three kernels in each hole. As Carlos works, he decides that it won't hurt to take a few shortcuts. All goes well at first, and he rushes off to buy the knife. But when the corn sprouts, he has an uneasy feeling. Instead of confessing to his parents, he sets out to correct his mistakes, with humorous results. The book ends with a mouthwatering recipe for cornmeal pancakes *(panqués de maíz).*

Carlos and the Skunk/Carlos y el zorrillo

Grades K–3

- Bilingual
- Skunks
- Recipes

In this third book in the Carlos series, the youngster decides to show off for his friend, Gloria, by catching a skunk. But his idea about how to do that backfires, and he soon finds himself taking a bath in tomato sauce. This funny book ends with a recipe for fresh tomato salsa.

Carlos and the Squash Plant/Carlos y la planta de calabaza

Western Books Exhibition Award of Merit
Grades K–3

- Bilingual
- Gardening
- New Mexico
- Recipes

This lively tale features Carlos, a boy with a yen for gardening. He lives on a farm in the fertile Española Valley in northern New Mexico, where he helps his parents tend a large garden plot. As he works, the rich brown soil ends up between his toes, under his fingernails, and inside his ears. His mother warns him that if he doesn't wash his ears, a squash will grow in them. But Carlos doesn't believe her, and, besides, he hates washing his ears. As the story sprouts, Carlos finds himself with a problem that he didn't anticipate. What is that itchy feeling in his ear? Why is he wearing that wide-brimmed hat? And why does he go right to bed after dinner each evening? This humorous book ends with a recipe for *calabacitas*, a spicy dish that features the tasty vegetables from Carlos' garden.

Carlos Digs to China/Carlos excava hasta la China

Grades K–3

- Bilingual
- Excavations
- Recipes

Carlos is back, and this time he is determined to dig a hole straight through the earth to China so he can eat Chinese food all the time. When his neighbor, Señor Griego, cautions him that the grass is always greener on the other side of the fence, Carlos just keeps digging. As the hole gets deeper and deeper, a crowd gathers to watch. Finally Carlos breaks through and, much to his dismay, finds himself in Señor Griego's backyard. This humorous story ends with Carlos in Señor Griego's kitchen eating three bowls of *arroz con dulce*. A recipe for the sweet rice dessert is appended.

Twelve Lizards Leaping: A New Twelve Days of Christmas

Grades K–4

- Christmas
- Music

This version of the familiar Christmas song features such gifts as a quail in a paloverde tree, two prickly pears, six piñatas swaying, and ten tamales steaming. The exuberant book opens with the musical score and lyrics and is illustrated with richly textured paintings.

Leyla Torres

Colombian (1960–)
Birthday: October 28
Contact: Publicity Department
Farrar, Straus, and Giroux
19 Union Square West
New York, NY 10003
(212) 741-6900

Do not be afraid of taking a risk, even if you fail. Without failing you won't get the chance to succeed. Failure is something you can only avoid by saying nothing, doing nothing, and being nothing.

(Personal Communication)

Books by Leyla Torres

Written and Illustrated

Liliana's Grandmothers. Farrar, Straus, and Giroux, 1998. Spanish edition: *Las abuelas de Liliana*.

Saturday Sancocho. Farrar, Straus, and Giroux, 1995. Spanish edition: *El sancocho del sábado*.

Subway Sparrow. Farrar, Straus, and Giroux, 1993. Spanish edition: *Gorrion del metro*.

Illustrated

Two Days in May by Harriet P. Taylor. Farrar, Straus, and Giroux, 1999.

Leyla Torres is an artist, writer, teacher, and storyteller. Her beautifully illustrated picture books feature people of different ages, different cultural backgrounds, and/or different languages, working together to solve a problem.

Torres was born in Bogotá, Colombia, the oldest of four children. Her interest in art began early in life with the strong support of her mother. After earning a bachelor of fine arts and education at the Universidad de la Sabana in Bogotá in 1982, she began her career as a painter and illustrator. She worked with *Los Matachos*, a talented group of puppeteers, designing puppets, developing scripts, and illustrating promotional materials. These experiences sparked Torres' interest in the art of storytelling.

Torres taught watercolor techniques at the Universidad de la Sabana in Bogotá for several years. During this time, she was commissioned to create a mural for Gustavo Restrepo High School in Bogotá, where she also taught art classes.

In 1985, Torres traveled to the United States with the desire to stay for one year. She writes, "During that time I saw new possibilities to further my career and I decided to stay" (Personal Communication). For the next three years, she studied printmaking at the Art Students League of New York. Since then, her art has been shown in various solo and group exhibits both in the United States and in Colombia.

Torres has worked as a Spanish-language instructor and provided individual and group language instruction for children and adults. As a freelance interpreter and translator, she has facilitated pediatric basic life support workshops for Spanish-speaking audiences. She was a guest author at the Miami Book Fair International's tenth anniversary celebration in 1993 and a featured author at the International Reading Association annual convention in New Orleans in 1996.

One of Torres' dreams was to write and illustrate books for children. Not sure how to go about achieving this dream, she kept it to herself until she discovered the children's room at the New York Public Library. "The desire to do my own book blossomed and each author was like a teacher to me. I positively sensed that with hard work and perserverance I could write and illustrate my own books" (www.leylatorres.com).

Leyla Torres currently lives in Brooklyn, where she divides her time between painting, writing, and teaching the Spanish language and literature. She goes back to Colombia periodically, where most of her family lives. Despite the stresses of living in a large foreign city, New York has provided her with an opportunity to reaffirm and expand her identity as an artist and writer.

More Information about Leyla Torres

www.leylatorres.com

Selected Works by Leyla Torres

Liliana's Grandmothers

Américas Commended List

Grades Preschool–3

- Differences
- Grandmothers

Mima and Mama Gabina are Liliana's beloved grandmothers. Mima lives down the street in Liliana's New England town, and Mama Gabina lives far away in a country in South America. Both grandmothers love to tell stories, but otherwise they are very different: their houses, their interests, their food—even their languages are different. Liliana enjoys two very different ways of life when she visits them. Gentle watercolors illustrate this thoughtful celebration of differences. In one of the pictures, the book Mima is reading to Liliana is *Subway Sparrow*, also written by Leyla Torres. Spanish edition: *Las abuelas de Liliana*.

Saturday Sancocho

Grades K–3

- Bartering
- Culinary Arts
- Grandmothers
- Ingenuity

Leyla Torres has set her second book in her native Colombia. Every Saturday, Maria Lili looks forward to making *sancocho* with her grandparents, Mama Ana and Papa Angelino. But one Saturday morning they discover that all they have is a dozen eggs, and there is no money to buy the ingredients for their special dish. Maria Lili is disappointed, but Mama Ana is undaunted. As the day progresses, Maria Lili learns an important lesson about solving problems. Detailed, double-page watercolors enhance the mystery and provide a glimpse into Colombian culture. The engaging scenes at the outdoor market are abundant with green plaintains, thick cassava, fresh corn, tender carrots, onions, cilantro, and other tantalizing vegetables and fruits. Each person is portrayed as an individual with unique features; their subtle facial expressions and body language add to the humor of the story. As Mama Ana deftly bargains and as Maria Lili assists, their playful canine companion finds plenty of mischief to keep herself occupied. When they return home with their mission accomplished, Maria Lili savors each spoonful of their culinary treat. This creative variation on the cumulative story ends with a recipe for the popular South American stew along with a reminder to have an adult help in the kitchen. Spanish edition: *El san cocho del sábado.*

Subway Sparrow

Parents' Choice Award

Bank Street School Book of the Year

Grades Preschool–3

- Birds
- Cooperation
- Kindness to Animals
- Subways

This is the engaging story of a sparrow trapped on a subway car in New York City along with four humans who speak three different languages. They work together to rescue the bird before the train reaches the next platform and a waiting crowd of people. Leyla Torres' first book will capture the hearts of readers of all ages. She skillfully combines her warm, appealing plot with detailed, vivid watercolors. Her use of unusual angles and perspectives extends and enriches the simple text. The inclusion of stark subway advertising and announcements contrasts with the human concern for the vulnerable sparrow. *Subway Sparrow* paints an optimistic urban scene, showing how four caring strangers working together can achieve a common goal in spite of the language, age, and cultural barriers that divide them. It is significant that Torres has chosen a young girl to lead them to break out of the anonymity induced by public transportation in a large city. This heartwarming book will encourage readers to reevalute their image of New York City as a cold, impersonal place. In addition, this may be the first time some youngsters have been given information about the importance of respecting all creatures, no matter how small and ordinary. Spanish edition: *Gorrion del metro.*

Two Days in May

Américas Commended List

Grades Preschool–3

- Cooperation
- Deer
- Wildlife Rescue

Based on a real incident that occurred in Chicago in 1996, this is a heartwarming story about a multiracial group of neighbors who work together to help five deer who wander into the city in search of food. When the neighbors learn that the animal control policy is to exterminate the deer, they stage a peaceful protest until a wildlife rescue organization arrives to relocate the animals. This very special book incorporates information about habitat loss, overpopulation, and, of course, kindness to animals. Leyla Torres' delicate watercolors beautifully capture the gradually strengthening bonds among the neighbors as they work together to save the deer.

Gloria Velásquez

Chicana (1949–)
Birthday: December 21
Address: California Polytechnic State University
Modern Languages and Literatures Department
San Luis Obispo, CA 93407

Educate, raza,
young Chicanitas
women warriors of Aztlán.

(Personal Communication)

I want to inspire people to believe you can dream and be anything you want to be. Never forget your community.

(*La Voz Hispana de Colorado,* May 31, 1995, 10)

Books by Gloria Velásquez

Ankiza. Arte Público Press, 2000.
I Used to Be a Superwoman. Santa Monica College Press, 1994; Arte Público Press, 1997.
Juanita Fights the School Board. Arte Público Press, 1994.
Maya's Divided World. Arte Público Press, 1995.
Rina's Family Secret. Arte Público Press, 1998.
Tommy Stands Alone. Arte Público Press, 1995.

Gloria Velásquez, an award-winning writer of poetry and fiction, graduated from Stanford University in California in 1985 with a Ph.D. in Latin American and Chicano literatures. Her short stories and poetry have been widely published in journals and anthologies. She has been a guest author at various universities in Europe, including France and Germany, where her fiction has been studied. She was the first Chicana writer to read her poetry and fiction at the University of Río Piedras in San Juan, Puerto Rico. She is currently a professor in the Modern Languages and Literatures Department at California Polytechnic State University in San Luis Obispo, California.

Born in the small town of Loveland, Colorado, Velásquez grew up in Colorado and Texas. Her parents were migrant workers, traveling between Colorado and Texas, working in the fields until they settled as factory and hospital workers in Johnstown, Colorado, in 1963. Velásquez often writes about the experiences of growing up within the migrant cycle of backbreaking, low-paying work and constant change. She recalls that some of the restaurants in Loveland had signs that read NO MEXICANS ALLOWED. Childhood memories of work thinning sugar beets, prejudice toward Latinos, and Eurocentric schools appear in a number of her poems. Her teachers and school counselors didn't recognize her strengths. "There wasn't a high school English teacher available to listen to a girl's poem of anguish written in 1968, upon the death of a brother in Vietnam. Pain was doubled, as their mother tried in vain to borrow funds to speed to his side" (*Denver Post*, August 1995, 18). Velásquez adds, "No one ever told me I was smart—that I was going to be a well-known Latina author. In spite of that, I created my own vision" (*La Voz Hispana de Colorado*, May 31, 1995, 3).

After graduating from Roosevelt High School in Johnstown, Colorado, Veláquez attended college classes at night while she worked as a secretary in a local factory. She also worked as a teacher's aide at local primary and secondary schools until she received a full-time fellowship to study at the University of Northern Colorado in Greeley. She earned her B.A. in 1978, with a double major in Spanish and Chicano studies.

In the late 1970s, Velásquez participated in "Canto al Pueblo" (Song of the People) festivals in Albuquerque, Milwaukee, and Corpus Christi,

Texas. Her experiences at these festivals had a profound impact on her thinking and writing and inspired her to pursue graduate studies in Latin American literature at Stanford University. Because of her academic achievement, she received a full scholarship. During her second year there, she won a literary prize in poetry from the Department of French and Italian. Her interest in women in Chicana literature from the early 1900s to the 1970s led to her doctoral dissertation on "Cultural Ambivalence in Early Chicana Prose Fiction." Subsequently, she received her Ph.D. in Latin American and Chicano literatures from Stanford in 1985.

Growing up in the 1960s, Velásquez's role models were people like Delores Huerta and César Chávez, cofounders of the United Farm Workers, and Maya Angelou, African American poet and writer. Velásquez emphasizes the significance of having Latina/o role models, and after all her achievements, she has never forgotten her roots. She is proud of her heritage and wants to encourage all Chicano/as to be proud of who they are. "I came from the barrio and I will never change. . . . It's important to make an effort to not distance yourself from the culture. I haven't changed in twenty years—I'm still a grass roots person" (*La Voz Hispana de Colorado*, May 31, 1995, 10). She feels that it is crucial to feature people of color in literature for young readers. Her Roosevelt High School series (named after her high school in Johnstown, Colorado) is about the pressures faced by young Chicana/os growing up in a society that does not value their heritage. The series has unlimited potential, and Velásquez has a number of significant topics planned for future installments.

In 1989, Velásquez was the first Chicana to be inducted into the Hall of Fame at the University of Northern Colorado, where she was honored for her achievements in creative writing. Almost thirty years after her own graduation, Velásquez became the first Chicana to be invited to give the commencement address to graduating seniors at Roosevelt High School. Stanford University recently honored Velásquez with "The Gloria Velásquez Paper," archiving her life as a writer and humanitarian.

In addition to her Roosevelt High School series, Velásquez is writing an autobiographical novel, *Toy Soldiers and Dolls*, which deals with the Vietnam War. (Her older brother, John, was killed in the war in 1968.) She also discusses her work on talk shows, speaks at conferences, schools, and bookstores, and travels throughout the United States performing songs and poetry from her *Superwoman Chicana* compact disc (CD).

Gloria Velásquez tackles a number of significant issues in her writing. She uses irony, satire, humor, and symbolism in her poetry to challenge the marginalization and erasure of Chicana/o history, the roles of women, the plight of the farmworker, and the problems of poverty, ageism, and alcoholism. She writes about educational achievement, male dominance, incest, the desertion of single mothers, and much more.

In her compelling books for young adults, Velásquez incorporates important issues such as racism in schools, divorce, domestic violence, and the harassment and degradation of gay students into stories that are very readable, interesting, and well written. Each of the books in the series, while featuring the same group of high school students, focuses on one member of the group and the problems that she or he is facing. Velásquez's Roosevelt High School Series is particularly noteworthy because the cast of characters is multiracial, a rarity in young adult fiction; she shows African Americans, Puerto Ricans, and Chicano/as developing strong friendships and supporting each other in signficant ways. Velásquez is adept at capturing teenage emotions and thought as well as the nuances of Latina/o culture. She hopes to inspire teamwork and a better understanding of diverse cultures. She notes, "I want to inspire social change and get people to care about human dignity. I want to educate our youth. I want to politicize them" (*Rocky Mountain News*, July 25, 1994).

More Information about Gloria Velásquez

Contemporary Authors Online, 2001.
Denver Post, August 16, 1995, 18.
Dictionary of Literary Biography, Volume 122, 302–305.
La Voz Hispana De Colorado, May 31, 1995, 3, 10.
Rocky Mountain News, July 25, 1994, and May 29, 1995, n.p.
Something about the Author. Volume 113, 210–212.
Who's Who among Hispanic Americans, 856.

Selected Works by Gloria Velásquez

I Used to Be a Superwoman

Grades 12–Adult

- Poetry
- Bilingual

In this rich collection of bilingual poetry, Gloria Velásquez conveys a strong personal and political message that her voice as well as the Chicana/o voice will not be silenced. She takes us back to her childhood and then to Stanford, contrasting her early life with the present. From thinning sugar beets and picking potatoes, to days locked up in a cold city, "surrounded by mediocrity," Veláquez searches for a better world among the limited choices. She contrasts a past of sugar factories, run-down shacks, baskets of food from the Salvation Army, scrubbing floors, picking strawberries, playing marbles, and borrowed houses with a present of useless theories, bourgeois words, cement walls, unfulfilled dreams, and "academic pimps." Drawing inspiration from Frida Kahlo, Crazy Horse, and other sung and unsung kin, she cries out for the freedom to run free like the wind on the mountaintops. "Wonderful Youth" is a poem that should be required reading for all teachers: it provides an excellent definition of "Eurocentric Curriculum." In several poems, she challenges the traditional role of the selfless woman who thinks only of her family. Velásquez eloquently expresses the universal needs to be valued and acknowledged and to make a difference in "Self-Portrait 1991": "Will I die in obscurity? . . . Will society yearn for my lonely words?" (103). In "Letter to a Patroncito," Velásquez refers to a school board meeting that undoubtedly led her to write *Juanita Fights the School Board*, her first book in the Roosevelt High School series.

Velasquez's poems are about prejudice, poverty, survival, disillusionment, loneliness, solitude, violence, war, death, grieving, self-doubts, and despair. But they also ring with a hunger for social justice, a pride in her people, a search for human dignity, a hope for social equality, and a determination that the children of the sun will survive.

Juanita Fights the School Board

Grades 7–11

- Discrimination
- Schools

Juanita Fights the School Board is the first book in Gloria Velásquez's Roosevelt High School series. Fifteen-year-old Juanita "Johnny" Chávez is expelled from high school after a fight with a white classmate. The school district doesn't ask for Juanita's side of the story and doesn't punish Sheena Martin, the young woman who started the fight and who has been taunting Juanita with racial slurs since school started. At first Juanita is devastated; her dreams of graduating from high school and continuing her education to become a Spanish teacher are shattered. But with the support of a counselor, a lawyer, and her family and friends, she sets about fighting for her rights.

Juanita lives with her parents and five siblings in the barrio. She is one of a handful of students of color in a predominantly white high school. Her father, who is very strict and sometimes abusive, works in the fields, and her mother works hard to take care of the family, also working in the fields from time to time. They do not speak English, so their children often translate for them.

Narration in the book alternates between Juanita and her counselor, Ms. Martínez, opening two perspectives on the story. Juanita's chapters show how prejudice impacts self-esteem. She suffers through the long weeks at home, helping with the housework and younger children, all the while longing to return to school. Her best friend, Maya, keeps her informed about the social events at school, and a home tutor keeps her up-to-date in her studies. Martínez's chapters reveal that she endured similar humiliations when she was a child. The author skillfully juxtaposes the two viewpoints, one before and one after assimilation into the dominant culture of the United States. Velásquez fully develops Sandra Martínez's character, demonstrating the complexities faced by a Latina who struggled to escape her family and class background to find herself still searching for validation. Juanita and the discrimination case provide the bridge that Sandy needs, and she finds herself feeling rejuvenated by the experience. She muses, "She reminded me so much of myself at that age, young, scared and angry. Angry at the whole world and not able to express it" (53).

This is an engrossing, accessible novel that deals with a number of significant issues. Injustice, class differences, upward mobility, peer pressure, tradition and change, ageism, friendship, biculturalism, gender roles, institutionalized racism, assimilation, language differences, teenage emotions, intergenerational conflicts, civil rights, peaceful resistance, and the collision of cultures are just a few of the issues that Velásquez skillfully weaves into this interesting, timely story. However, several unchallenged, fat-oppressive remarks made by the students are especially hurtful in a book that is about justice and fairness. Glossary included.

Maya's Divided World

Grades 7–11

- Divorce
- Mother–Daughter Relationship

Maya's Divided World is the second book in Gloria Velásquez's Roosevelt High School series. Readers will recognize Maya as Juanita's best friend, who stood by her when she was expelled from school in *Juanita Fights the School Board*. Maya Gonzales is the only child in a middle-class family. Her mother, Sonia, has a Ph.D. from Stanford and is a college professor, and her father, Armando, is an engineer. Life seems perfect for Maya with her gorgeous house, her position on the tennis team, and her success in school. But all this changes the summer before her junior year in high school. When she accompanies her mother on a trip to Santa Fe to visit relatives, Maya overhears her mother telling her grandmother that she is getting a divorce. Later, when school starts, Maya is ashamed to tell her friends about the divorce. When she tries to call her father, he is too busy to talk or to plan a time for them to get together. Becoming increasingly confused and disillusioned, Maya finds that tennis, school, and even her friends have lost their meaning. She starts hanging out with the heavy-metal crowd, sneaking out at night to spend time with them. Finally, when she is arrested for shoplifting, her mother consults Sandra

Martínez, the psychologist who helped Juanita with her battle against the school board. Sonia and Sandy are the only Chicana professionals in Laguna and have developed a friendship over the years. But Maya refuses to see a "shrink" and ends up running away from home. She turns to her old friend, Juanita, who convinces her to see Ms. Martínez. This is the turning point in the story, after which Maya gradually starts the long, difficult process of healing.

Gloria Velásquez has written another interesting, accessible novel, again tackling a number of important issues. She challenges the societal expectation that women, particularly Latinas, will put men first and give up their own dreams. She unobtrusively weaves information into the story about peer pressure, parental responsibility, class differences, tradition and change, friendship, possessive relationships, assertiveness, and the importance of communication. Glossary included.

Rina's Family Secret

Grades 7–11

- Alcoholism
- Family Violence
- Puerto Rican Americans

This fourth installment in the Roosevelt High School series features Rina Morales, a Puerto Rican American teenager who describes her family's life with her abusive stepfather. She tries to hide her problems from her friends while attempting to cope with her fear and shame through alcohol and directionless rage. But with the support of her friend Tommy (featured in *Tommy Stands Alone*), she finds the courage to ask for help. *Rina's Family Secret* has been praised for its believable portrait of teen culture, strong Latino/a role models, and realistic portrayal of emotions. *School Library Journal* wrote, "Velásquez accurately portrays the destructive cycle of domestic violence as well as the potential roles of counseling and social services in solving what may seem like insurmountable problems." Glossary included.

Tommy Stands Alone

Grades 7–11

- Gay Males
- Homophobia
- Suicide (Attempted)

Tommy Stands Alone is the third book in Gloria Velásquez's Roosevelt High School series. Readers will recognize Tommy as a friend of Juanita's and Maya's from the first two books in the series. Tomás Montoya is a quiet, light-skinned, green-eyed Chicano living with his working-class family in the same barrio in Laguna, California, where Juanita and several of their friends live. Although Tommy enjoys art class, he is becoming increasingly more uncomfortable at school and with his friends' expectations that he date. But he finds himself going along with them to keep from being noticed. Trying to maintain his cool, he even goes so far as to laugh at their homophobic jokes. One day Rudy reads a note that Tommy accidentally drops, and Tyrone asks him in front of all their friends, "Are you a faggot or what, Tommy?" Angry and confused, Tommy runs away and tries to commit suicide. Luckily he calls Maya, who calls 911, and his life is saved, but his problems are far from over. Maya finally convinces him to see Ms. Martínez, the psychologist who helped both Maya and Juanita in Velásquez's earlier books. Ms. Martínez not only works with Tommy but also counsels his mother, who has convinced herself that it was an accident and told her husband that Tommy has pneumonia. When his father learns the truth, he kicks his son out of the house. As the story unfolds, Tommy struggles through the long, painful coming-out process that reveals not only his inner resources but who his real supporters are.

Passages narrated by Tommy are juxtaposed with those narrated by Ms. Martínez, who has just learned that her gay brother-in-law is HIV positive. She also has painful memories of her brother's suicide years before and of her parents' subsequent denial. As she works with Tommy, she too learns from the process. The double narration works well again as it did in the first two books in the series, opening windows on important issues from two perspectives.

Gloria Velásquez's third installment in the series is especially important because, until recently, there were very few good young adult books about homosexuality. Homophobia oppresses at least one-tenth of our population; education should be a vehicle for counteracting *all* forms of oppression and for providing accurate, honest information about sexuality as well as other relevant topics. Our society is still appallingly misinformed about homosexuality; well-written books such as *Tommy Stands Alone* are desperately needed to support lesbian and gay youth in the process of coming to terms with their sexuality and to educate their heterosexual student peers. Velásquez does a superb job of portraying Maya as an incredibly strong friend to the suffering Tommy. She valiantly goes against the pressure from the group to stand alone with Tommy, leading the way for others to change their homophobic attitudes and behaviors. Hopefully, her example will provide a model for readers in similar situations.

Many adult lesbians and gays report searching in vain for information when they were younger; omission is one of the most insidious and painful forms of bias. As Velásquez demonstrates in this book, growing up in a society that teaches them to hide their sexual orientation and to hate themselves has resulted in a national tragedy: lesbian and gay youth who take their own lives account for a disproportionate number of teen suicides in the United States. Literature is one way to counteract the homophobia that is injuring and killing many of our most creative young people. The harassment, isolation, and self-hatred that our society imposes on lesbian and gay teenagers can kill them as it almost did Tommy. As educators, writers, and librarians, it is our responsibility to reach out to them. It is crucial that we stop students who are harassing other students and let them know that bigotry of every kind will not be tolerated. Even one positive comment from a teacher can mean a great deal to an isolated student. Teachers and writers who are providing support for lesbian and gay youth are not recruiting or advocating. We are saving lives!

Victor Villaseñor

Chicano (1940–)
Birthday: May 11
Contact: Margaret McBride Agency
7744 Fay Avenue, Ste. 201
La Jolla, CA 92037

I grew up in a house where there were no books. When I started school, I spoke more Spanish than English. I was a D-student and every year of school made me feel more stupid and confused. . . . In my junior year of high school, I told my parents I had to quit school or go crazy.

(*The Hispanic Literary Companion*, 364)

Books by Victor Villaseñor

Jury: The People vs. Juan Corona. Little, Brown, 1977; Dell, 1997.
Living Miracles. Doubleday, 1998.
Macho! Bantam, 1973; Arte Público Press, 1991; Dell, 1997.
Rain of Gold. Arte Público Press, 1991; Dell, 1992; Turtleback Books, 1994. Spanish edition: *Lluvia de oro*.
Thirteen Senses: A Memoir. HarperCollins, 2000, 2001. Spanish edition: *Trece sentidos: Una memoria*.
Walking Stars: Stories of Magic and Power. Arte Público Press, 1994; Dell, 1998.
Wild Steps of Heaven. Delacorte, 1996; Dell, 1997.

Victor Edmundo Villaseñor is the noted author of a number of books, including the highly acclaimed family memoir *Rain of Gold*. His works have brought to millions of readers the family stories of economic, social, and political struggles of Mexican immigrants. He has also written several screenplays, including the award-winning *The Ballad of Gregorio Cortez*.

Born on May 11, 1940, in Carlsbad, California, to Mexican immigrant parents, Villaseñor grew up on a ranch in Oceanside with three sisters and one brother. School was difficult for him not only because he spoke mostly Spanish but because, unknown to his family, he had a learning disability: dyslexia. He eventually dropped out of school and became a laborer. However, his love of language combined with his family tradition of storytelling and his discovery of the richness of his Mexican heritage inspired his interest in writing. He decided that by writing good books, he could reach out and touch people and influence the world.

"I got a dictionary and a high school grammar book and I built a desk and I began to read books eight months out of the year. I'd go to bookstores and buy ten books at a time, read them and dissect them and then reassemble them. Then for four months of the year I'd support myself in construction" (*The Hispanic Literary Companion*, 365). After hundreds of rejections, his first book was published in 1973, and his writing career was launched.

Villaseñor lives on the family ranch in Oceanside, California. He starts his writing day long before dawn, inspired by his grandmother's words, "[T]here are no strangers, once we get to know each other's stories" (*Thirteen Senses*, xiv). He travels around the United States sharing his passion for life and his vision for world harmony. His topics of family, pride, and global peace are told through personal stories filled with humor and emotion.

More Information about Victor Villaseñor

Dictionary of Literary Biography, Volume 209, 291–294.
The Hispanic Literary Companion, edited by Nicolás Kanellos. Visible Ink, 1997.
Rain of Gold. Arte Público Press, 1991; Dell, 1992; Turtleback Books, 1994. Spanish edition: *Lluvia de oro*.

Thirteen Senses: A Memoir. HarperCollins, 2000, 2001. Spanish edition: *Los trece sentidos.*
Walking Stars: Stories of Magic and Power. Arte Público Press, 1994; Dell, 1998.
Wild Steps of Heaven. Delacorte, 1996; Dell, 1997.

Selected Works by Victor Viallaseñor

Rain of Gold

Grades 12–Adult

- Family Memoir
- Social History

Magnificent in scope, this treasure focuses on three generations of Victor Villaseñor's family, their cultural and spiritual roots in Mexico, their immigration to California, and their overcoming poverty, prejudice, and economic exploitation. The author spent twelve years interviewing, researching, and writing this powerful saga. It has been described as warmhearted, fast-paced, moving, dramatic, and passionate. *Publishers Weekly* wrote, "Villaseñor is a born storyteller, and this Latino Roots . . . is a gripping, inspirational epic full of wild adventure, bootlegging, young love, miracles, tragedies, murder and triumph over cultural barriers." Black-and-white family photographs are included. Spanish edition: *Lluvia de oro.*

Thirteen Senses: A Memoir

Grades 12–Adult

- Family Memoir
- Social History

Continuing the family saga begun in the widely acclaimed best-seller *Rain of Gold*, the author follows the lives of his parents, Lupe and Salvador Villaseñor, who were brought to the United States from Mexico as children by their courageous mothers. This is the powerful story of their passionate and turbulent early married life in southern California when they coped with the economic and social effects of the Great Depression. *BookList* wrote, "There are elements of magic realism here. . . . and powerful descriptions of discrimination between the races and among the Mexican American community. An enchanting, larger-than-life tale of how extraordinary ordinary people can be." Black-and-white family photographs are included. Spanish edition: *Trece sentidos: Una memoria.*

Walking Stars: Stories of Magic and Power

Américas Young Adult Literature Award
Grades 6–12

- Autobiographical Short Stories
- Family History

We are all "walking stars" if only we believe in ourselves and recognize the brilliance and power that we each have as human beings. Villaseñor presents inspirational stories from his own family history, stories of his parents facing the ridicule of other children; developing the confidence to encounter the unknown; escaping from persecution by soldiers during the Mexican revolution; and enduring hunger, thirst, and stress. In the preface, Villaseñor describes his first day of school, when he knew very little English, and his teacher yelled at him, "No Spanish!" She punished the students if they spoke one word of Spanish and hit them on the head if they continued. Villaseñor writes, "I didn't become a writer because I did well in school and got A's. No, I became a writer because I had so much confusion and anguish inside of me" (10). His exquisite stories, written from the heart, speak of pain and confusion and self-hatred, and "then finally, that great 'real' magic of life that's sitting there, within each of us, waiting to erupt and help us overcome against all odds" (11). After each story, the author provides brief notes in which he interprets the story and explains the effect that it had on his life.

Wild Steps of Heaven

Grades 12–Adult

- Family Memoir
- Social History

In this second volume of Victor Villaseñor's family trilogy, the author offers a powerful portrait of his father's family in the highlands of the western Mexican state of Jalisco in the early twentieth century. In the preface, Villaseñor writes that "my father's story [was] filled with love and fire, rage and hate, and the yet the profound understanding that everything is all right, if only we have enough faith. . . . [It] was the story of all Mexico, and the story of Mexico was the story of the last five hundred years of European dominance all over our globe" (1–3). *Wild Steps of Heaven* has been described as profound, funny, accessible, old-fashioned, and affectionate. *Publishers Weekly* wrote, "Drawing on his father's stories and those of other members of his extended family, the author reconstructs their loves, lusts, madness, deaths, births, hunger, massacres, joy, and heroism in a folkloric tale reminiscent of the magical realism of Gabriel Garcia Marquez."

Appendixes

1: Awards

Américas Award for Children's and Young Adult Literature

The Center for Latin American and Caribbean Studies
University of Wisconsin-Milwaukee
P.O. Box 413
Milwaukee, WI 53201
(414) 229-5986
www.uwm.edu/Dept/CLACS/outreach_americas.html

Pura Belpré Award

REFORMA: National Association to Promote Library and Information Services to Latinos and the Spanish-Speaking
P.O. Box 832
Anaheim, CA 92815-0832
www.ala.org

Tomás Rivera Mexican American Children's Book Award

SWT School of Education
2001 Education Building
601 University
San Marcos, TX 78666
www.education.swt.edu/Rivera

2: Calendar

Note: The events on this calendar include those that are unique to Latino/a cultures. For books about these and other holidays, please see the Topic Index.

January 6	Epiphany: *El día de los tres reyes* (Three Kings' Day)
February 2	Candelaria
March 31	César Chávez Day
April 30	*Dia de los Niños/Dia de los Libros* (Day of the Children/Day of the Books) www.patmora.com
May 5	Cinco de mayo (The Fifth of May)
September 15–October 15	Hispanic Heritage Month: www.macontel.com/special/latino
September 16	*El dia de independencia* (Mexican Independence Day)
November 1 and 2	*Los días de muertos* (Days of the Dead)
December 12	*El día de la Virgen Guadalupe*
December 16–24	*Las posadas* (The Inns)
December 31	*El día de gracias*
Resources	*Piñatas & Smiling Skeletons: Celebrating Mexican Festivals* by Zoe Harris and Suzanne Williams, illustrated by Yolanda Garfias Woo. Pacific View Press, 1998.
	Fiestas: A Year of Latin American Songs of Celebration, selected, arranged, and translated by José-Luis Orozco. (Songbook and audio recording.) Arcoiris, 2002.

3: Optional Activities

Note: These activities may be used with any of the author units. Of course, the major goal will be to enjoy fine literature; however, teachers, librarians, and parents might choose to extend the literary experience by selecting some of these activities. Many adults will invite individual youngsters or groups of youngsters to choose among the activities and to create some of their own.

1. Setting the Stage: Set up an author center or author corner. Include a photograph of the author, a display of her or his books, posters, realia, maps, book jackets, a bulletin board, and so on. Add student work as it is completed. Youngsters enjoy being involved in the planning of these author units. They might write to the publisher requesting materials such as posters featuring the author's

books. Encourage them to take leadership roles in setting up the centers, creating the bulletin boards, and planning the activities.

2. Complete Works: Provide an overview of the complete works of the author. As you read a book, discuss it within the context of the complete collection.

3. Authors as Individual People and as Writers: Study the author's life. What experiences shaped their lives and thinking and led them to share their joys, struggles, defeats, and triumphs with their readers? What role does their cultural heritage play in their writing? Personal connections establish strong and long-lasting ties with the author. Even adults get excited when they have the same birthday or grew up in the same area as an author. Personalize the author units by focusing on the author's motivation for writing as a career and for writing each book. Why did the author write this particular book? Why did she or he choose this writing style? These words? How did the author's writing style or genre change from one book to the next?

4. Literature Logs/Response Journals/Writer's Notebooks: Young readers may respond in writing to the selection read each day or week. These journals may be ongoing all year or semester-long, or shorter journals may be kept for each author or book. Encourage a wide variety of responses such as poems, letters, thoughts, feelings, illustrations. Youngsters may choose to share these journals with partners, small groups, or the large group. These logs or journals may also be used for self-evaluation and/or teacher assessment.

5. Point of View: Compare the points of view in books with similar themes. Discuss or rewrite the story from the points of view of selected characters. Perhaps each youngster or group of youngsters could choose a character and present the book(s) from a variety of points of view.

6. Quotes: Select or encourage youngsters to select quotes from the books for discussion and/or written response. Use a quote from a book for the caption of a bulletin board or in a newsletter, essay, or story.

7. Predictions: Predict what will happen in the book, on the next page, in the next chapter, and/or in a sequel. These predictions may be written in the literature logs and/or discussed.

8. Dedication Page: Discuss and/or respond in writing to the dedication page. What additional information does it give us about the author? Encourage youngsters to create a dedication page for the next book that they write.

9. Character Letters: Adults and youngsters might write a letter from one of the characters in the book to the class introducing, motivating, summarizing, embellishing, and so on. Or one character could write to another character (within books or from book to book). For an engaging example of this idea, read *Dear Peter Rabbit* by Alma Flor Ada.

10. Letters: Some youngsters might be interested in writing letters to the authors. Addresses for most of the authors are included in the author units. Some authors are too busy to respond to each letter individually but might write a note to a class, school, or library.

11. Author Visits: Invite the author to visit your class or school. Contact the publisher to arrange the visit. A resource that is helpful in planning and implementing an author visit is *Inviting Children's Authors and Illustrators: A How-to-*

Do-It Manual for School and Public Libraries written by Kathy East and published by Neal-Schuman Publishers. This practical manual includes steps including how, why, when, where, and who. Sample letters, advertising, bookmarks, budget forms, checklists, timelines, and photographs of some of the authors are included.

12. Conference Calls: Arrange to make a conference call from your class to the author. Youngsters will enjoy reading the author's books and preparing questions in advance. This call might be taped and listened to again later.

13. Interviews: Role-play an imaginary interview with an author or character from a book. Or pretend that one character is interviewing another character.

14. Recipes: Write individual or class recipes based on the book's message such as "A Recipe for Friendship" or "A Recipe for Combating Prejudice." Display on the bulletin board featuring the author.

15. Travel: Plan an imaginary or real trip to the places featured in the book. Write for travel brochures, study maps to plot your route, develop a budget, plan an itinerary.

16. Newsletters: Include items from author units in your class, school, or library newsletter. Youngsters enjoy interviewing authors and writing about these intriguing discussions.

17. Drama: Youngsters love to create and perform in plays, puppet shows, pantomime, readers theater, skits, dance, and so on based on a book or a collection of books.

18. Book Talks: Invite youngsters to prepare short book talks to introduce and inspire others to read the books that they recommend. These may be done a few at a time whenever you have a few minutes or during an assigned time. Students may also do extra book talks for extra credit.

19. Book Reports: Use some of the ideas in this section to make book reports more interesting.

20. Book Boxes: Combine art and book reports. Students cover a box with paper and then decorate it with words, drawings, cutouts, and so on that represent the book. The book boxes may hold items or tasks related to the book. These items may be used to dramatize the book, or other students might write questions or comments about the book and put them in the boxes. Arrange for a book box exhibit with boxes created by several individuals or groups displayed.

21. Author Boxes: Do the same as in #20 but with the focus on the author.

22. Book Buttons: Youngsters love designing buttons. These might be centered around themes from the books that they have read. If you don't have a button maker, students may cut out a circle on construction paper and another on tagboard. Decorate with book title, author, illustrator, and pictures. Glue the construction paper to the cardboard. Tape a safety pin on the back. Wear these buttons during book talks, book reports, books fairs, and so on.

23. Book Ribbons: Young readers design ribbons to advertise their favorite books. Display on bulletin boards, around the room, halls, or library to encourage others to read the books.

24. Character Board: For each character in a book or series of books, make a five-to-seven-inch-high paper figure. Place these figures on a chart or mural depicting the roles played in the book. Print their names above each. Below each write some of their personality traits.

25. Character Growth: To demonstrate the growth and changes in a character within a book or within a series, a student role-plays the character at each stage of her or his development. (Example: In Nicholasa Mohr's books, in what ways does the protagonist change from the beginning of the first book *Felita*, to the end of the second book, *Going Home*?)

26. Character Cutouts: Enlarge pictures of characters onto a large piece of paper. Cut out and use to start a bulletin board. Youngsters might then add words describing the characters printed on colorful strips of paper and other creative illustrations depicting the setting of the story.

27. Art: Study the art techniques used in the book. Research. Then experiment with those techniques. Add the resulting creative efforts to the author center.

28. Bookmarks: Design bookmarks to go with selected books.

29. Collage: Create individual or group collages portraying aspects from a book, a collection of books, and/or the author's life.

30. Book Hunt: Hide a book and create a coded message to help others find the book. Perhaps one youngster or group of youngsters could be in charge of this activity each day or week.

31. Timeline: Make a timeline for the events in a book, a series of books, or the author's life.

32. Sequence Cards: (Created by youngsters and/or adults.) On each of four or five cards cut in a shape that symbolizes the story, write a word or sentence or draw a picture showing something that happened in the book. Youngsters may work individually or in groups to put the cards in order. Add these to the author center.

33. Class Booklet: Collect all the work done by the youngsters related to a book or author into a class booklet. Display.

34. Board Games: Youngsters might choose to create board games based on the events in a book. These may be used in a variety of ways, including during free time and indoor recesses.

35. Birthdays: On an author's birthday, declare that day "___Day." For example, January 19 is Pat Mora Day. Have a readathon featuring the author's books. Youngsters might design cards and/or write letters to the authors. People of all ages are interested in which authors have birthdays on the same day as theirs or someone in their family.

36. Dioramas: Youngsters might create dioramas based on the author's life, a book, or a series of books.

37. Pop-up Books: This is an optional activity for talented or older youngsters. Create a pop-up book based on the book being read.

38. Mapping and Webbing: At first, make the character maps or semantic maps together as a group. Gradually, youngsters will be ready to create their

own or to work together in groups. These might be displayed at the author center or added to the class booklet.

39. Cartooning: Create cartoons based on the events in a book or as a sequel to a book.

40. Advice Box: Youngsters write letters from or to the characters in the books asking for advice. Periodically, the teacher or students read these letters to the class, and they respond in writing, with discussion, or by role-playing. A fun example would be to write letters to Pip, the cat, in Gary Soto's book *The Cat's Meow*, asking advice on everything from the best ways to learn a new language to how to communicate with another species.

41. Mobiles: Design a mobile to introduce, promote, or represent a book or author.

42. Recommendations: Write a letter to the school media director recommending a book or series of books for purchase.

43. Book Jackets: Youngsters might choose to design new book jackets for the books.

44. Diary: Youngsters might pretend that they are one of the characters in a book. They prepare a diary that the character might have kept during the beginning, middle, and end and/or the most significant parts of the story. This activity enables them to "walk a mile in the shoes of the character" and to better understand the complexities and commonalities of the human experience.

45. Survey: Some youngsters might be interested in checking the public and/or school library to see which of the books by selected authors are included. Make a checklist or graph. They might want to check how many books about an ethnic group are included. Discuss the results and discuss ways to respond.

46. Place Mats: Pretend that an author or several authors are coming for lunch. Design place mats to honor your guests. Use fabric, yarn, and so on. This would make a great culminating activity at the end of the year or semester to review all the authors studied. This idea was inspired by *The Dinner Party* by Judy Chicago, which features a place setting for each of thirty-nine women from history.

47. Author Quilt or Mural: Quilts and murals make good culminating activities. A quilt might feature one square per author.

48. Author or Character Party: At the end of the semester or year, youngsters might dress as their favorite character or author. They give a short talk from the point of view of the author or character, using the voice, gestures, and props that they think appropriate, avoiding stereotypes or caricatures. These talks could be videotaped. Later, they could watch the video and serve refreshments provided by the youngsters, inspired by the books represented. The video could also be used to introduce the author units to another group or shown at community events such as Parents' Night.

49. Riddles: Youngsters enjoy creating riddles based on the books or author studies. This activity is excellent for review. For example: "I'm thinking of a book about a girl who writes an essay that helps her teacher understand how she feels about her name." Answer: *My Name Is María Isabel* by Alma Flor Ada.

50. Review Bulletin Board: Invite youngsters to create and display cutouts of all the characters from all the books read during the semester or year.

51. Book Jamboree: Invite youngsters to sit in a circle. Place all the books from a unit in the middle of the circle. Children select books for a final short browse, and then they each share one or two comments about the book. This is an excellent review activity.

52. Book Fair: This schoolwide or library event is similar to the familiar science fair. Once a year, all the projects created by the youngsters are displayed. Parents, community members, and other youngsters will enjoy viewing the wide variety of projects.

53. Assessment: Youngsters might write tasks or questions that could be included in an evaluation instrument. Encourage high-level questions that inspire critical thinking rather than recall of details. Example: Why was María Isabel's name so important to her?

54. Assessment: (Pre and Post) Invite individuals (any age) to make a list of all the authors that they can think of. Evaluate together as a group or individually. Did they include authors from diverse groups? Which groups were included? Excluded? Why? What recommendations do the members of the group have for improving this situation?

55. Assessment: Library Checkout: Are books available that represent diverse groups? Are youngsters requesting and checking out these books? What recommendations do youngsters have for books to be purchased?

4: Resources

Catalogs

Arte Público Press, University of Houston, 452 Cullen Performance Hall, Houston, TX 77204-2004. (800) 633-ARTE, www.arte.uh.edu
Bilingual Educational Services, 2514 South Grand Avenue, Los Angeles, CA 90007-9979. (800) 448-6032.
Bilingual Review Press, Hispanic Research Center, Arizona State University, P.O. Box 872702, Tempe, AZ 85287, (602) 965-3867.
Children's Book Press, 2211 Mission Street, San Francisco, CA 94110, (415) 821-3080. www.cbookpress.org
Curbstone Press, 321 Jackson Street, Willimantic, CT 06226-1738. www.curbstone.org
Del Sol Books, 29257 Bassett Road, Westlake, OH 44145. (888) 335-7651.
Lectorum Publications, 205 Chubb Avenue, Lyndhurst, NJ 07071-3520. (800) 345-5946. www.lectorum.com
Teaching for Change, Network of Educators on the Americas, P.O. Box 73038, Washington, DC 20056-3038. (800) 763-9131. www.teachingforchange.org

Organizations and Centers

Barahona Center for the Study of Books in Spanish for Children and Adolescents
CSU San Marcos
San Marcos, CA 92096-0001
(760) 750-4070
www.csusm.edu/csb/

California Association for Bilingual Education
16033 East San Bernardino Road
Covina, CA 91722-3900
(626) 814-4441
www.bilingualeducation.org

Center for Multicultural Literature for Children and Young Adults
School of Education
2130 Fulton Street
San Francisco, CA 94117-1080
(415) 422-6878
www.soe.usfca.edu/childlit

National Association for Bilingual Education
1220 L Street, N. W. #605
Washington, DC 20005-4018
(202) 898-1829
www.nabe.org/

Resource Center of the Américas
317 17th Avenue SE
Minneapolis, MN 55415
(612) 627-9445

Title Index

Topic Index

About the Author

FRANCES ANN DAY teaches children's literature at Sonoma State University and conducts workshops nationwide. She is the author of *Multicultural Voices in Contemporary Literature* (1994, 1999) and *Lesbian and Gay Voices: An Annotated Bibliography and Guide to Literature for Children and Young Adults* (2000). Both books won Skipping Stones Awards, which honor social justice and multicultural understanding. *Gay and Lesbian Voices* was also an ALA finalist for a Gay, Lesbian, Bisexual, and Transgendered Book Award.